LEARN TO DANCE THE

SOULSALSA

Also by Leon@rd.Sweet

- *11 Genetic Gateways to Spiritual Awakening*
- *AquaChurch*
- *Communication and Change in American Religious History*
- *A Cup of Coffee at the SoulCafe*
- *FaithQuakes*
- *Health and Medicine in the Evangelical Tradition*
- *The Jesus Prescription for a Healthy Life*
- *Quantum Spirituality: A Postmodern Apologetic*
- *SoulSalsa*
- *SoulSalsa* audio
- *SoulTsunami*
- *SoulTsunami* audio
- *Strong in the Broken Places: A Theological Reverie on the Ministry of George Everett Ross*

Learn about these books at http://www.leonardsweet.com

Leon@rd.Sweet

Learn to Dance the
SoulSalsa

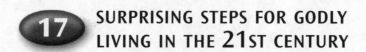

17 SURPRISING STEPS FOR GODLY
LIVING IN THE **21**ST CENTURY

ZondervanPublishingHouse
Grand Rapids, Michigan

A Division of HarperCollinsPublishers

SoulSalsa
Copyright © 2000 by Leonard I. Sweet

Requests for information should be addressed to:

■ ZondervanPublishingHouse
Grand Rapids, Michigan 49530

Library of Congress Cataloging-in-Publication Data

Sweet, Leonard I.
    SoulSalsa : 17 surprising steps for godly living in the 21st century / Leonard Sweet.
       p. cm.
    Includes bibliographical references.
    ISBN: 0-310-23014-4 (hardcover)
    1. Spiritual life—Baptists. I. Title.
  BV4501.2 .S8785 2000
  248.4—dc21
                                     00-020787
                                         CIP

This edition printed on acid-free paper.

All Scripture quotations, unless otherwise indicated, are taken from the *Holy Bible: New International Version®*. NIV®. Copyright © 1973, 1978, 1984 by International Bible Society. Used by permission of Zondervan Publishing House. All rights reserved.

Interior design by Sherri Hoffman

Printed in the United States of America

00 01 02 03 04 05 06 /❖ DC/ 10 9 8 7 6 5 4 3 2 1

If God held all truth in [the] right hand, and in [the] left hand held the lifelong pursuit of it, [God] would choose the left hand.

—Søren Kierkegaard (1813–55),
Concluding Unscientific Postscript,
quoting Gotthold Lessing

For my salsa
Soren Coventry Sweet
who teaches me every day this:
truth is not a possession you wield
but a life you yield.

This learn'd I, watching where she danced,
Native to melody and light,
And now and then toward me glanced,
Pleased, as I hoped, to please my sight.

—Coventry Patmore (1823–1918),
"The Dance," *Poems of Coventry Patmore*

CONTENTS

Introduction

Faith in God is dangerous thinking.

Even more, faith in God is dangerous living.

This book is a *lifeware design package* for

work,

play,

love

—and everything else.

You probably already have a college degree. This book enrolls you in a lifestyle seminary where you can get a life degree in artful, soulful living. *SoulSalsa* hopes to make you an artist in being.

Lifeware design requires patience. A New World visitor, admiring the lawns of an English country estate, asked the gardener, "How do you make these beautiful British lawns?" The answer: "Oh, you just roll them for two hundred years." Don't expect quick returns on long-term, lifestyle investments. We who are Jesus' followers have time on our side. We must be willing to wait it out.

Lifeware design takes practice (spiritual practice, or what I call "faith practice"). You practice the Christian life. Faith takes practice. A practice-oriented spirituality delights as well as bedevils everyday life as relentlessly as tenor saxophonist/Methodist John Coltrane practiced scales and chord patterns.

Lifeware design involves training. It's not enough to try to do better; we must *train* to do better. Jesus said, "Everyone who is fully trained will be like his teacher" (Luke 6:40). Paul said, "Train yourself to be godly" (1 Timothy 4:7). There is no try. Only do.

Lifeware design involves downloading. Biblical truth is not some boxed concepts or bound doctrines but a way of living, an active being, a free moving in the world. Truth as faithfulness is only true when it becomes something that is downloaded and enacted in one's life.

A professor is said to have responded to a proposal with the words "That's all right in practice, but will it work in theory?" A lot of Jesus "professors" are more worried about theories of faith than practices of faith.

Book after book, writer after writer, calls for Christians to develop a biblical worldview. Few are the books that lift up a biblical "worldlife." Modern Christians prefer to talk about how to think Christianly than how to live Christianly, and thus they expose their rationalist fallacy: if only we can get our thinking right, all else will fall into place. Even those who wrote the most about "practice" in the 1970s and 1980s seemed seduced by this modern delusion that right thinking leads to right living.

The truth is much more complex and interlinked: right thinking follows and informs and only sometimes precedes right living. Or as Anglican bishop Rowan Williams puts it, "Orthodoxy is common life before it is common doctrine." It is the practice of spiritual values that brings one into the presence of God and truth. A soulful ritual is something that is performed; it is never fully comprehended. Soulful practices represent not just the "doing" of theology but the mysterious dance of theology itself. In fact, in ancient Greece the single word *mousike* (music—literally, "the art of the Muses") referred to words, music, and dance equally.

When I got real with life, I got a life designer. My soul carries the label "Designed by Jesus." My life designer and soul couturier is not Calvin Klein of Hollywood or Donna Karan of New York or Thierry Hermès of Paris but Jesus of Nazareth.

I do the Savior no favor by calling him "friend." Jesus is the Master, Mentor, and Maestro of my life. Friendship with Jesus is a lot less rigorous than discipleship with Jesus. To be a disciple of someone is to follow in the steps and spirit of that master artisan. Jesus has too many friends, too many "believers." Jesus does not have enough disciples, not enough "behavers."

Your life is not your own; it belongs to God. To "be yourself" is not to just be anything you want to be. To "be yourself" is to be and do what God wants you to be and do, knowing that God created you for a mission and knows you and your mission better than you do. Biblical faith is a mission faith—a pilgrimage faith, not a preservation faith. To be yourself is not to be "with it" but to be with God. That's why the ultimate in being "with it" is to be yourself . . . with God.

I have a lecture that has two beginnings, one optimistic ("It's a whole new world out there!") and one pesimistic ("The world has come to an end"). In our lifetime, one way of living in the world has ended (modern) and a new way has begun (postmodern). Individuals and churches can *never* be the same again. You can try to block from your lives, you can try to block from your church these changes. But these changes won't go away. Chances are, your church will go away. But they won't.

If George Barna's research is to be believed, over half of all unchurched people say they want to find a closer, personal relationship with God. They just don't know how to find it. Barna's conclusion: "These are not people who are anti-religion. These are people who

preach the Gospel at all times. If necessary, use words.

—St. Francis of Assisi

believe for the most part in some kind of god or deity. They simply haven't been able to figure out, 'How do I make it real . . . in my life.'"

These Boots Are Made for Walking

SoulSalsa is dedicated to helping people redesign a biblical spirituality for this new world, a theology with legs. The question that every page seeks to answer is this:

How can one live a biblical faith that emerges from everyday living?

To build a relationship with God requires the same kind of activity that building a relationship with your kids, your spouse, your friends involves: daily rituals, presence, a commitment to certain behaviors, and so on. My favorite book title of the 1990s was *Jesus with Dirty Feet*. How does biblical faith become a sandals spirituality that hits the pavement and is in touch with postmodern culture but true to itself?

I'm not the first to say it: The highest art form is the art of living. How do disciples of Jesus make living into an art form? Books on the soul have become an unstanchable tide. But the rediscovery and rehabilitation of the concept of the soul is taking place largely *outside* of Christianity. Why are people reading Larry Dossey, Deepak Chopra, and Marianne Williamson instead of Jesus and Paul, Matthew, Mark, Luke, and John?

Most soulware merely plays about the surface. Jesus' soulware dives into the depths. Jesus makes us get rid of life as agenda and take up life as adventure. Where modern believers said, "Jesus is the answer," postmodern pilgrims say, "Jesus is the problem" (the best "problem" one could ever have).

If the question of the modern world was "Why do I live?" the question of the postmodern era is "How should I live?" This book tries to answer that question: "How do I do it?" It is the third and last volume in a trilogy that began with *SoulTsunami*, which laid the theoretical framework for understanding the postmodern waterfront. It was followed by *AquaChurch*, which was written to help churches sail these new seas and avoid shipwrecks now that the tidal wave has hit.

SoulSalsa is written as an exercise in sandals spirituality, a faith that tracks. It's a guidebook for individuals and communities who want to add traction and depth to an everyday spirituality through the integration of ritual, ceremony, and art. Its silhouette of changes to live by is dedicated to all who are struggling to be faithful to the gospel while making the transition from modern to postmodern.

The organization of the book is inspired by science fiction writer Robert A. Heinlein's famous twenty-one requirements for membership in the human race—or, in my preferred way of phrasing it, how not to become a hive insect. According to Heinlein, a human being should be

Either what we do every day is important, or nothing is. In a sense, we can live our entire life every day.
—RUNNING GURU
GEORGE SHEEHAN

Introduction

11

able to change a diaper, plan an invasion, butcher a hog, conn a ship, design a building, write a sonnet, balance accounts, build a wall, set a bone, comfort the dying, take orders, give orders, cooperate, act alone, solve equations, analyze a new problem, pitch manure, program a computer, cook a tasty meal, fight efficiently, die gallantly.

Specialization is for insects.

Moderns liked to draw up lists of *principles* for which they were willing to *die*. Postmoderns draw up lists of *practices* we are willing to *live by*. Here's my list of seventeen lifestyle requirements for membership in the postmodern body of Christ—or, in my preferred way of phrasing it, how not to become a pew-sitting toad:

Disciples of Jesus ought to be able to:

mezuzah their universe
make a moment
think Methuselah
bounce their last check
never graduate
do dirt and do the dishes
cycle to church
brush their tongue
cheer rivals from the bench
give history a shove
kill two birds with one stone
build a compost heap
declare a sabbatical
play at life
make love like Tobias and Sarah
not fall out of the family bed
dance the salsa

Pew-sitting is for toads.

Given an array of surpassing possibilities, the soul is searching for new ways of being in this postmodern world. Each one of these arts of living godly identifies a trajectory for one's life that comes from within the soul, not from without. Soul-design issues are a top theological imperative. Our choices in life and our design for life tell us more about our souls than do our abilities. How you live is a measure of your soul.

The construction of your soul is like that of a cathedral. It is the result of thousands of little decisions, countless carvings, and innumerable everyday rituals guided by centuries of tradition and the gathered wisdom of the saints on how to get to know Jesus and the promises of God. But every cathedral has its own singular character. The art of living soulfully is different for everyone. There is no one soul size; they come in all shapes and sizes. What makes one soul sing may singe another. That's why *SoulSalsa* entails an ergonomic spirituality that tailors spiritual practices to diverse soul sizes and lifestyles.

To a larger degree than I feel comfortable with, this book gives a street address—mine—to the story of a biblical postmodern spirituality. So let me say it here: in my attempt to live a life of superlatives, not merely positives, I blow it more often than I make it. It is not just some people who have "character flaws"; all character is flawed. All of us tend to lose our way. All my life I will struggle with unworthy, unsanctified thoughts, unholy behavior, and a splintery self.

For someone whose heart has been "strangely warmed," as John Wesley said of his own heart, I suffer from far too much unholy heartburn. I've yelled at the kids more than my share; I've forgotten to let the dog in; I don't always pay my bills by the due date. And that's just the beginning. No matter how hard I try, I know what that nineteenth-century politician felt like after he was introduced in this fashion: "Soldier, statesman, patriot, but still a disappointment to his mother." Without mentors and masked angels who routinely apply swift kicks to my soul's backside, my mother would have been still more disappointed.

The Doubter's Companion (1994) defines "ethics" ironically as "a matter of daily practical concern described glowingly in universal terms by those who intend to ignore them." I don't intend to ignore them, but too often I trespass on them. William Wordsworth wrote some of the greatest poetry ever penned, but he also shows up in the collection of *Very Bad Poetry*. I show up at my worst when I'm trying to be at my best. I'm especially bad when I'm traveling. In airports and on planes, I'm the most unfriendly person you've met in a long time. On the road is where I write my books, but this takes bubble-wrapping my body, mind, and spirit from external bumps and relational diversions. When I hear the Tony Campolos of the world tell seatmate stories that end with the person sitting at the righthand of Jesus, I slink down in my seat and feel ashamed. I've never led a person sitting next to me to Christ.

Dances with Cows More Than Wolves

I am also at my worst in writing a book on soul dancing when I myself can't dance. Because I was born with "Baptist feet," even my ballet-dancer wife has given up hope of moving me beyond an errant waltz or elephantine square dance.

All the same, I will dance, if asked. I can hope. And my hope is built on nothing less than a dancing God. Even if I can't dance with my feet, my "heart [can] dance at the sound of His Name!" (Charles Wesley). My soul can learn the dance steps of the Lord of the Dance—proving

It is more difficult to write a book than to spend a day well.

—ANCIENT
POLISH ADAGE

my not total unfitness for writing this book. Plato said that humans should spend their lives "singing, sacrificing, dancing." In Hasidic communities the people literally dance their way out of the synagogue. And at their homes, around the table, on the Sabbath, they dance again.

Jesus came to make all of life a dance. It was his musical metaphor for the life of faith (Matthew 11:17), one of the greatest metaphors ever offered to express life itself. In fact, the Aramaic word for "rejoice" is the same as the word for "dance," leading one to wonder whether Jesus was actually telling people to experience the joy of living or to get into the dance of life. The gospel of Jesus can be expressed in one sentence: There is some music you face; there is other music you dance to. In the energy and movement and teachings of Jesus, I have found the music to dance my way through life.

The difference between the best and worst in me is as tissue-thin as the difference between the words *amorous* and *amorphous*. That's why I recite more times a day than I care to admit this signature song of the St. Louis Jesuits. It's a mantra I've more than memorized; it's carved on my soul's character:

> We hold a treasure
> Not made of gold
> In earthen vessels
> Wealth untold.

This book is about teaching the treasure in these earthen vessels to dance the salsa. Why salsa? First, it is one of the first global rhythms. In fact, most dance classes in USAmerica, and 80 percent of all dance clases in Britain, include the transnational sounds and rhythms of the salsa. Although New York City was "the cauldron where salsa was cooked," the ingredients originally came from Cuba and other Caribbean countries. Second, salsa is theology in motion. You can't define the salsa, only dance the salsa. And you can't dance the salsa until its Pan-Afro-Latin-American rhythms have made its way through each and every one of the senses—as all participants (singers, musicians, dancers) converge into one kinesthetic sound and at the same time diverge into parallel dimensions of kinesthetic light. I came, I saw, I salsa'd.

SoulSalsa is not a timeless edifice. Like any cathedral worth its candles, the guidance it offers will be renovated, reroofed, altered, and added to many times during its lifetime. I offer it here as a part of the "long trip, first step" methodology of any voyage into the unknown.

Shall we dance?

They profess to know God, but they deny him by their actions.

—PAUL (TITUS 1:16 NRSV)

SoulSalsa

1. Saints, it is said, are sinners who go on trying. True or false?

2. Close your eyes and picture in your mind an image of the cruci-fixion that you've seen in a painting or a movie. Then read the following quote by Maria Teresa Porcile:

   > How can we defend our poor privacy while the Lord of Glory is exposed naked on the cross for all the world to see? Allowing ourselves to be seen in our search for God is to show ourselves as beggars of the cross and the glory. It is, perhaps, the true marrow of Christian identity.

   How might striving to live soulfully expose parts of you to the world that you'd rather keep hidden? What good might come out of it anyway?

3. In Turin on 3 January 1889 (before his descent into madness), Friedrich Nietzsche referred to Jesus on the cross as "the last Christian." Nietzsche argued that Jesus' followers, on the basis of their actions, did not believe in him. Do you agree?

4. New Zealand theologian/novelist Michael Riddell has written powerfully about the decline of Christianity in the West. Here are some of his reasons. With which ones do you agree?

   a. "To them [postmoderns], the contemporary Christian church is a relic of a bygone era; a monument to religious sentiment in the past, but irrelevant to the vital pilgrimage they are embarked upon. Those expressions of spirituality which are demonstrated by the church are regarded as shallow and repressive. Christian people seem to them to be materialistic and emotionally stunted. They further appear dogmatic, rigid, and unwilling to experiment spiritually or to learn from experience."

   b. In contrast, alternative spiritualities appear to explorers "open, exciting, inspiring, adventurous, and enriching. There is a sense that the participants are spiritually alive, and that their explorations of the spiritual realm are the most impor-tant thing in life for them."

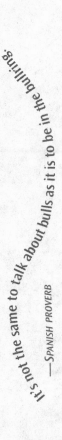

It's not the same to talk about bulls as it is to be in the bullring.

—Spanish Proverb

c. "Christianity in the West is seen as a legitimate religious option for those who are into it, but having no bearing on the broad movement of culture or human evolution."

d. "Most damning of all, Christians are regarded as dull people who are lacking in spiritual depth."

5. Lifestyle maven Martha Stewart has been billed as a great life designer. Spend a few minutes browsing around her Web site at http://www.marthastewart.com/ to see how many aspects of a life her work touches. Why do you think people in our world today are looking to life stylists like Martha and her competitors? What would it mean if Jesus were your life stylist par excellence?

6. The Disney corporation states that "at every daily activity and holiday, Disney is there with whatever the consumer is doing right now." And when you think about their theme parks, toys, cruise ships, movies, and TV channel, you realize the claim is not too strong.

    Besides Disney, what other secular organization has a powerful lifestyle platform? What is your church doing to be present and relevant in people's lives?

7. Barry Baker, president and chief operating officer of USA Networks, reflected on his past this way: "I wasn't a human being. I was a human doing." Why do people get in such a situation? What does it take to turn them back into human beings?

1

Mezuzah Your Universe

The origins of the Christian church lie in Jewish discipleship, which is rich and full of home rituals. On the right side of every Jewish doorpost is nailed a small piece of parchment rolled and inserted into a wood, metal, stone, or ceramic case called a *mezuzah.* On the front of the parchment are lettered the twenty-two lines of the Shema (Deuteronomy 6:4–9 and 11:13–21). The Hebrew word *Shaddai* is inscribed on the back in such a way that it can be seen from the outside.

The mezuzah was a ritual code that said to everyone entering and leaving that home, "As for me and my house, we shall serve the Lord." A postmodern mezuzah is a ritual that helps us grow our own souls by modulating the mundane into the eternal. A mezuzah connects us to our Creator, Redeemer, and Sanctifier.

"These Things Shall Be a Sign Unto You"

The Christian faith is a sign language.

Postmodern disciples read the signs of the divine and make sign language about the divine. The true language of biblical faith is not phonetic but ideographic. It is not formed with our mouths so much as with our bodies and lives.

Our biggest signs have been handed down to us in the Last Supper and the Last Sacrifice—the meal and the cross. A disciple of Jesus Christ is someone who eats a common meal and who baptismally lifts a rugged cross.

But there are sacraments and there are "sacramentals" (a phrase coined by medieval theologian Peter Lombard). In sacraments, sanctifying grace is conveyed *"ex opere operato,"* by the act itself. Sacramentals are rites that reveal the "signs of the Trinity" (Augustine), which are everywhere in creation when viewed through the eyes of faith.

Sacramentals communicate grace. Sacraments convey grace. The challenge of discipleship is to make one's own life a sacramental, a sign of love and grace, a sacred gesture inserted in a world flaunting other gestures.

Faith's signage must sacramentalize our spaces, places, and faces. To mezuzah our universe is to create sacred space and sacred rituals wherever we go. The space from which we speak and live is more than a contrivance. Space shapes who we are. Space carves the soul. In liturgics, there is a saying: "The building always wins." The cathedral or other place where we worship *will* have an effect on the worship.

Since fundamentally we are spiritual beings, the space in which we live must become ritual space for the soul. Postmodern disciples give sacred signage and shape to their living spaces by the habits and practices they perform there to invite God in. Worship is a way of life, not a wayside on Sunday.

Ritual is not the way, truth, and life, but ritual is a reminder that there is a way, a truth, and a life. Rituals fix you in space and time. Change your rituals and you change your "fixings." Change your "fixings" and you change your realities.

In 1967 the sociologist Peter Berger defined secularization as the loss of "the sacred canopy." In other words, in the modern world we suffered the loss of an overarching religious belief system that provided personal and communal meaning. In historian Christian Smith's recent look at American religion, he says that while we may have lost the sacred canopy, people are now putting up their own "sacred umbrellas."

From a biblical perspective, there are templing "sacred umbrellas" and there are tabernacling "sacred umbrellas": we temple in our homes; we tabernacle in our meeting place. The temple is the most sacred, the most revered residence of God's Spirit. Today God ought to take up residence in the home with one's family, friends, neighbors (including global ones through cyberspace). The tabernacle is the temporary, makeshift place where one puts up altars and conducts worship. This is what the local church needs to be seen as, especially in a highly mobile society where the temple goes with you wherever you go, and the tabernacles change.

In the modern world, the rhythms of the spiritual life were tabernacled but not templed. The festivals, sacraments, liturgies, and pilgrimages took up residence in ecclesiastical ghettos. It is now templing time. The interest in shrines, candles, incense, and mantras is an expression of our need to take these rituals back and make them a part of our templed dailiness. In fact, the world is doing better than the church in wooing outsiders with templing experiences, providing spiritual activities (not necessarily good ones) that can be fitted into everyday life.

Yet the needed templing is different from the manner of Victorian representations and realities. Victorians kept busy through a relentless round of empty, exhausting, genteel rituals. Postmodern templing is more in the manner of most tribal people, whom anthropologists estimate spend 30 percent of their time "working" and the rest of their time "preparing and performing rituals, dances and ceremonies." Why do they do that? Psychologist James Hillman answers, "They do that so their feeling is in right relation with the world they're in."

To mezuzah one's universe is to inhabit an infrastructure of "right feelings" created by social and religious rituals for everyday living. Some spaces will be the spiritual equivalent of Shaker furniture: spare doctrine, perfectly turned rituals, a place for every thought and every thought in its place. Others will be the theological equivalent of highly carved Victorian fantasy furniture: ornate, detailed, unpredictable, highly figural.

To mezuzah one's universe is for the world of grace to intersect with the world of culture in such a way that grace is visible in the whole of life—historically visible as well as religiously viable.

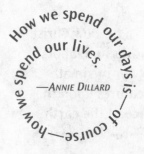

How we spend our days is—of course—how we spend our lives.
—ANNIE DILLARD

Mezuzah Your Home

"So many houses, so big with so little soul." So begins one of the surprise best-sellers of the 1990s, *The Not So Big House* (1998).

Forget all those "Look at me—I've made it" houses built in the 1980s and 1990s that are spacious of things but cramped of soul. Postmoderns would rather have smaller homes with customized details that reflect the values and aesthetics of the owners than huge "McMansions" devoid of character and stories. According to architect Eliel Saarinen, the best architects "always design a thing by considering it in its larger context—a chair in a room, a room in a house, a house in an environment, an environment in a city plan." All of our possessions need to be storied within their larger context—the ongoing story of redemption and transformation as it is lived out in our life mission and in our on-mission family.

Stories sanctify space. The more you live in place, the more your space becomes silted with artifacts. If those artifacts come without stories or purpose, no matter how beautiful or expensive they may be, you are turning your home into a garbage dump. Every room in your home tells a life-or-death story.

What made Mark McGwire's sixty-first home-run baseball worth $1 million? It's the same $5.00 ball that anyone catches. The story is what makes it so valuable. The story is what makes a space that enchants and keeps the bleakness at bay.

Stories are sacred. Storytelling is the most sacred of professions. Stories are what makes the soul healthy or ill, saved or damned. Prozac is really nothing more than a story drug that empties your mind of bad memories and allows the good life stories to take supremacy. To mezuzah our homes is to build a multistoried edifice full of biblical stories coming to life, family stories from the past still kept alive, family stories for the future being created every day.

Stories are our lives' greatest asset.

Mezuzah Your Artifacts

My wife, Elizabeth, and I operate two "advance centers" (our twist on "retreat centers"), one in the hills of West Virginia, the other on an island in Puget Sound. From a new friend I found on eBay, I recently purchased for the Orcas Island Advance Center in Washington a nineteenth-century brass fire devil. It was first owned by Captain A. J. Mandy, a devout Christian and master of the ship *John R. Manta*, the last New Bedford whaler. The devil was attached to the hearth damper. When the damper was closed, the devil was not visible. When the damper was open, the solid brass devil danced in the flames of the fire, giving those gathered around the fireplace occasion to reflect on the consequences of a life at sea lived outside of God's grace and mercy.

I bought more than a damper; I bought a story, I bought meaning. Artifacts like that brass fire devil can be faucets where the divine leaks into the human. Some positive words need to be spoken about the ephemera of everyday life. The world of objects is seen at best as the aesthetics of surface. To engage with the world of surface is to invite ridicule and accusations of materialism. In some circles, the uglier the house, the holier the dweller. Many of our homes are an aesthetic Chernobyl.

Poet Mark Doty conveys something of this in his poem "Concerning Some Recent Criticism of His Work":

> Glaze and shimmer,
> luster and gleam,
> can't he think of anything but all that sheen?

But what's wrong with all that brass and sheen? What's wrong with froth? Surface need not mean superficiality. Besides, there is no shallow end in the pool of theology. There is no edging into God toes first. What appears as surface quickly engulfs you in its bottomless depths. Faith is diving into those surface-depths believing you won't drown.

Every poet strives to achieve the lightness of touch that covers deceptive weight. As a Christian scholar, I enjoy creaming off the froth from a variety of fields as a way of not only leading people to water but also of enticing balkers to drink what's underneath the foam.

- When you move into a new house, have a house blessing and invite neighbors in for a housewarming.
- When you get a car, bless it for God's use. Then treat it with respect.
- When you polish the silver candelabra you inherited from your grandmother, clean the treasure your wife gave you on your honeymoon, or vacuum your mother's oriental rug, offer a prayer of gratitude to God for their influence in your life.
- Every time you open a book, invoke the ancient rabbinic admonition that an hour of study is in the eyes of God as an hour of prayer.
- Every time I open my *New English Bible,* I invoke two prayers. First, a prayer of thanks for William Tyndale, the biblical scholar who gave his life so that you and I can do something we take for granted: read the Scriptures in our own language. Second, a prayer offering my life as a Third Testament to be deployed and distributed in any way God sees fit.

Mezuzah Your Calendar

Your calendar is as much your sacred lair as your "sacred umbrellas" of home or church. In fact, your calendar designs more of your living space than any architect ever could.

Consider beginning the day with chimes. They can be in the form of a whisper or a shout, a clear sound or a muffled ring. But begin the day with prayer. Either a "Good morning, God!" or "Good God, it's morning!" will do. But as soon as you wake up, say a sentence prayer.

Adults have more chores to do than children. Whether at work or at home, the largest percentage of what we do every day is chores. Napoleon spent most of his time on the eve of battle immersed in paperwork. We do chores to be given the right to do what we find pleasurable and creative. Get used to chores and find ways to mezuzah them.

I was glad to learn that, over the last fifty years, the number of people who say grace before meals has increased from 43 percent to 63 percent. It's important to say grace for each meal—if not before, then during or after. To eat is to kill. Whether you're a carnivore, a vegetarian, or a vegan, your very act of eating entails the taking of some life, vegetable or animal. You should be grateful for the life that was given to feed your life, and you should be quick to give thanks to the Source of all life, who made the bounty possible in the first place.

Prayer can mezuzah not just mealtimes but every part of our day. "You say grace before meals. All right," wrote G.K. Chesterton.

But I say grace before the play and the opera,
And grace before the concert and pantomine,
And grace before I open a book,
And grace before sketching, painting, swimming, fencing,
    boxing, walking, playing, dancing;
And grace before I dip the pen in the ink.*

Observant Muslims pray toward Mecca five times daily; why can't Jesus disciples embed their days with the habit of praise and prayer? Three times a day (morning, noontime, evening) I say this prayer three times:

Come and pray in me, Holy Spirit;
Come and pray in me, Holy Spirit;
Come and pray in me, Holy Spirit.

Mezuzah Your Relationships

In every relationship God's living presence can be released or restrained. Disciples mezuzah every relationship with personalized touches that roll out the red carpet of the soul.

- *Mezuzah strangers.* Make everyone feel special in some way. Make every person you encounter leave your presence feeling better, not worse. Give each person some oral applause. Instead of ticking off in your mind what you don't like about that person, which is our natural first reaction, practice the spiritual art of not judging. Try going through one day only accepting people, not judging them. Look only for the positives in other people and let their negatives fall through the cracks of your soul.
- *Mezuzah friends.* Practice the spiritual discipline of secrecy. When you do something good for someone, do it secretly. Make a game of it. See how much good you can get away with and still not be found out. Be a "blessing bomber" who targets friends and strangers alike for gospel grenades of hope, love, encouragement. Pay for someone's meal without them ever figuring out who the benefactor was.

Those who go beneath the surface do so at their own peril.
—Oscar Wilde

S o u l S a l s a

- *Mezuzah meetings.* I know someone who lights a candle every time someone sits down at her desk for an appointment. She says nothing. Just lights a candle. And when the visitor leaves, she snuffs out the candle.
- *Mezuzah creation.* The Spirit of God is laboring on our behalf throughout creation, if only we will open ourselves to receive the gifts: the family dog who slurps your face in the morning; the Steller's jays who nag at you for peanuts; the sycamores who cry for water in these greenhouse times; the flowers whose beauty begs to be smelled and inspected.

God loves stories. —TALMUDIC SAYING God made people because because

Postmodern luxury is about how you spend your free time, and with whom you spend it. Even in the midst of our most luxurious moments, can we mezuzah our universe?

There is an old rabbinic exchange that goes something like this:

Question: "In one breath, speak the Ten Commandments."

Answer: "It's a nice day today."

Mezuzah Your Transitions

Life is filled with transitions and initiatory experiences: graduation from Montessori school to the University of Michigan; birthdays—from one's own to one's great-grandchildren's; years such as five and six, nine and ten, twelve and thirteen, sixteen (you can drive), eighteen (you can vote and go to college), twenty-one (legally, you're in every way an adult). Each transition and initiation needs careful ritual attention, especially when it involves one's children or grandchildren or great-grandchildren.

Native Americans had a unique practice for training young braves. On the night of a boy's thirteenth birthday, after learning hunting, scouting, and fishing skills, he was placed in a dense forest to spend the entire night alone. Until then he had never been away from the security of the family and tribe. But on this night he was blindfolded and taken several miles away. When he took off the blindfold, he was in the middle of a thick woods. By himself. All night long.

Every time a twig snapped, he visualized a wild animal ready to pounce. Every time an animal howled, he imagined a wolf leaping out of the darkness. Every time the wind blew, he wondered what more sinister sound it masked. It was a terrifying night.

After what seemed like an eternity, dawn broke and the first rays of sunlight entered the interior of the forest. Looking around, the boy saw flowers, trees, and the outline of the path. Then, to his utter astonishment, he beheld the figure of a man standing just a few feet away, armed with a bow and arrow.

It was the boy's father. He had been there all night long. Can you think of any better way for a child to learn how God allows us to face the tests of life? God is always present with us. God's presence is unseen, but it is more real than life itself.

If there is one area of our lives where rituals are common, it is in the realm of transition. But many of our transition celebrations deliver little or no depth.

The sign language of the Spirit is different from that of the world. Unfortunately, disciples honor transitions more like the pagans of old than the Christians of old. Take birthdays as an example.

The ancient Romans loved birthdays. Poets celebrated their own birthdays in verse. They even established endowments to enable others to celebrate their birthdays in perpetuity.

We love birthdays as much as the Romans did. The birthday party circuit has become big business. Forget cakes, candles, and party favors—birthday cards alone are a $1.5 billion industry. Some argue that birthdays, even more than Christmas, are holy days for children.

Birthdays now cost hundreds, even thousands of dollars. Gone are pin-the-tail-on-the-donkey and piñatas. Parents almost need to take out second mortgages to pay for birthday parties featuring Reptile Man (he brings live snakes to your child's birthday party) or Cartoon Cuts (girls get manicures and new hairdos; boys get spiked hair and pretend shaves). You name the party—bowling party, pool party, magic party, gym party, horse party, fencing party—the parties are getting larger and more lavish. There are now even professional party givers, many of whom tell war stories of trying to bring sanity back to parents' birthday-bash dreams for their kids.

Our celebrations speak volubly about the desires and drives of our heart. Why are big-deal birthday parties a sign of the times?* Could it be a way of assuaging our guilt that we can't spend more time with our kids? Might parents need these parties more for their own psychological and public relations reasons than for their kids? What does it say about a culture that loves to celebrate birthdays—getting older—while at the same time is obsessed with how "young" we are and how much "younger" we can mummy ourselves? How does a birthday-celebrating culture treat those in its midst with the greatest number of birthdays? (I warned you I have some "birthday issues" to work through.)

Researchers who are interested in these things tell us that 93 percent of USAmericans hear the words "Happy birthday!" on their birthday,

---

*The definitive big-deal birthday bash? Boxer Mike Tyson threw a one-million-dollar thirtieth birthday party for himself at his seventeen-acre, sixty-room estate in Farmington, Connecticut. It featured an unlimited supply of lobster, filet mignon, Cristal champagne, and custom-made cigars.

and 71 percent of USAmericans have the "Happy Birthday" song sung to them on their birthdays. I'm part of the 7 percent and 29 percent. I don't like birthday celebrations one bit. I can't think of anything more egotistical than saying, in the words of Dr. Seuss's birthday greeting, "If I say so myself, 'Happy Birthday to me!'"

Instead of parties that celebrate getting a year older (what kind of a transition is that?) why not throw parties to celebrate getting better—getting more holy, more loving, actually accomplishing something? What about celebrating the sheer gift of life?

- Why don't we pilgrims host a party when we're celebrating the attainment of a higher level of sacredness in living or progression to a higher plane of biblical living?
- Why don't we pilgrims send our parents and grandparents a handmade note and gift on our birthday, thanking them for this precious gift of life? One note like this I sent to my mother (who lived with me the last eleven years of her life) I found in her purse when she died.
- Why don't we disciples celebrate our elders with a countdown? For church members or ancestors in their nineties or older, start a countdown before their birthday equal in number of days to the number of years old they are. In other words, if Grandmother is ninety-three, start ninety-three days before her birthday sending her something special in the mail each day until the final birth day.
- Instead of a "give me presents" party, why don't we disciples host a "save the wetlands" party and take a field trip to a local endangered wetlands (or prairie, bay, desert, etc.)?
- Why don't we pilgrims write an original composition that can be used annually to celebrate someone's creation? One family with a child named Grace composed for her this song, which they sing to her on every birthday:

  > Amazing grace, how sweet the sound,
  > Your name fills us with glee!
  > Your spirit blessed, your light profound,
  > A gift to all you see!

- Instead of having the birthday person sing for his or her supper, why don't we disciples ask the person to answer questions for supper? Here are some examples from a self-esteem resource:

1. What is one of the funniest things that happened to you last year?
2. What is one of the most frightening things that happened to you last year, and how did you overcome the fear?
3. To whom did you get closer last year? Or to whom did you want to get closer?
4. What is one of the most important lessons you learned last year?
5. What was one of the biggest risks you took last year?
6. What goal would you most like to achieve this year?
7. Where would you like to travel this year?
8. If you could go back and live one day over again from last year, which day would it be and why?
9. What hobby would you like to take up this year?
10. If you could learn from any teacher in the world, past or present, whom would you study with this year?

One last example of another mezuzah transition. It is customary to provide kids with transition objects for their pilgrimage, usually gifts that have no particular meaning. But instead of a traditional going-away gift, one father snuck into his oldest son's pocket "something for later" during the tearful farewell of going off to college.

During the long drive to school, the freshman fished out of his pocket a hundred-dollar bill wrapped around a cassette tape. When he inserted the tape into the car's tape player, he listened as the entire family related what they would miss about him, what they wouldn't miss about him, how they thought he might change, what fears they had about these changes. He played the tape the whole drive to college.

The first month of college, he listened to the tape many times. The second month, fewer times. The third, fewer and fewer. Yet eventually that tape became an icon of his family's liberating love and his leaving home to become an adult.

Postmodern culture suffers from a content deficit. To mezuzah our universe is to release the depth charges in life. To mezuzah our universe is the embedding of daily life with embodied meaning. To mezuzah our universe is to live in a God environment.

1. We all know that Roman Catholics and members of some other religious traditions make the sign of the cross from forehead to breast and from shoulder to shoulder. But historians tell us that this practice developed out of a very early and widespread Christian tradition of using a thumb or finger to trace the shape of small cross on one's forehead or an object. Second-century church leader Tertullian had this to say about the practice: "In all our travels and movements, in all our coming in and going out, in putting off our shoes, at the bath, at the table, in lighting our candles, in lying down, in sitting down, whatever employment occupieth us, we mark our foreheads with the sign of the cross."

   What spiritual advantages might redound to Christians who returned to this practice?

2. At the Web site for Scope Systems (http://www.scopesys.com/anyday/), you can pick your birthday and find out who was born, who died, who was reported missing in action, what happened historically, what holidays are celebrated, and what religious traditions have observances on that day. Check this one out too.

3. For an excellent mezuzah resource, see Ann Hibbard's Family Celebrations at Birthdays and for Vacations and Other Holidays (Grand Rapids: Baker, 1996). Although short, it has a marvelous section on "Family Devotions for Birthdays."

4. Internet birthday sites are hot. Here are some e-mail card sites to look at (not in any particular order):

   Warner Brothers (http://www.wbwebcards.com/cmp/crd-bday.htm/)
   Blue Mountain Arts
        (http://www.bluemountain.com/eng/brth/index.html/)
   Postcards from the Edge (http://edge.com.sg/cards/birthday/)
   Viet San Diego Online
        (http://www.vietsandiego.com/ecards/birthday.html/)
   PBS (http://shop.pbs.org/RoT20gSkbP/giftshop/postcards/)

Awesome Cyber Cards (http://www.marlo.com/birthday.htm/)
BC Yellow Pages
   (http://www2.mybc.com/aroundtown/ecards/bday/birth-
   day.html/)
AdOnWeb (http://www.adonweb.com/cards/bday/)

5. A contrasting voice to mine comes from the late Henri J. M. Nouwen, who insists that "celebrating a birthday is exalting life and being glad for it." One way to live in the present, says Henri Nouwen, is to celebrate birthdays:

> Birthdays need to be celebrated. I think it is more important to celebrate a birthday than a successful exam, a promotion, or a victory. Because to celebrate a birthday means to say to someone: "Thank you for being you." Celebrating a birthday is exalting life and being glad for it. On a birthday we do not say: "Thanks for what you did, or said, or accomplished." No, we say: "Thank you for being born and being among us."
> On birthdays we celebrate the present. We do not complain about what happened or speculate about what will happen, but we lift someone up and let everyone say: "We love you." . . . Celebrating a birthday reminds us of the goodness of life, and in this spirit we really need to celebrate people's birthdays every day, by showing gratitude, kindness, forgiveness, gentleness, and affection. These are ways of saying: "It's good that you are alive; it's good that you are walking with me on this earth. Let's be glad and rejoice. This is the day that God has made for us to be and to be together."

To your way of thinking, what are the pros and cons of Nouwen's views on birthdays stated here and those of my views stated above?

6. Nouwen also told the story of his friend who every birthday gets forcibly carried up to the bathroom, dumped into a tub full of water, and playfully "re-baptized." Is this an example of a mezuzah ritual that countermands the world's celebrations? Would you try it with someone?

7. Watch the Antiques Road Show on television. To what extent do the experts factor the objects' stories ("provenance") into their appraisals?

8. Q: What is the probability that at least two members of a Sunday school class of thirty were born on the same day of the year?

   A: 70.63 percent

   Two physicists have computed further that the probability of two students in a class of sixty having the same birthday is 99.41 percent, and for a class of eighty, a probability of 99.99 percent. In other words, randomly select eighty people and there is almost a certainty that two people will have the same birthday.

   In fact, in a church of eighty people, there is a 10.3 percent probability that there are seven pairs of people with the same birthday. Check it out in your own congregation.

2

Make a Moment

SOUL ARTISTS TURN EVERY DAY EVENTS AND EVERYNIGHT
ESCAPADES INTO MEMORIES THEY CHERISH.

The quality of a godly life does not depend on its number of great happenings or big actions but on what happens in it one small moment after another. The soul is made up of an awful lot of moments and a lot of awful moments.

How goes it with your soul? Are you living a truly momentous life? Or are you living unmomentously? Are your year's supply of "525,600 Minutes"—as the hit musical *Rent*'s theme song, "Seasons of Love," puts it—a never-ending chain of meaningless moments, a drizzle of days? Or is each minute you live intensely and rapturously alive?

There are many ways to live so that you won't have to develop an inner life. Some people live lurching from moment to moment. Others live hanging on the spur of the moment. Still others live duly "one day at a time." And others live immersed "in the moment."

Living momentously means capturing life's moments whole, or at least in part, and framing those moments into holy form in such a way that ever thereafter the frame reads, "God was here." Making a moment is the art of sky-punching, penetrating the heavens to open earth to larger shafts of divine light.

Magnetized Moments

The art of making a moment into something holy is the art of magnetizing moments with the Spirit. To make a moment is not to manufacture a moment or concoct a split-second spirituality. It is rather to identify a moment in such a way that it can become a conscious moment, an enjoyed moment, and an enduring moment that redounds to the glory of God. When a moment is magnetized by the Spirit, it becomes whole, holy, and eternal.

I have so much to do today, I need to meditate twice as long.

—GANDHI

Two primary demagnetizers inhibit the magnetic forces of the Spirit:

- The first is a greed for large-scale epiphanies.
- The second is a preference for living other people's moments rather than our own.

Charles Eames, whom some argue was the greatest furniture designer of the twentieth century, said there are two questions one should ask about every small town: First, "What is the quality of their bread?" Second, "What is the quality of their parades?" Humble experiences like sniffing the aroma of home-baked bread and cheering on Main Street parades are what make up most of the good stuff in life.

The kingdom of God is not some marbleized Jerusalem we build "out there" somewhere. The kingdom of God is among us, around us, and within us. Look at the world of a flower. Look at a loaf of bread. Life's magic, miracle, passion, and promise are gifts that fall right in our laps and find their way right into our hands. Our problem is that we are less open to the unexpectedness of the everyday in our quest for the extraordinary and extreme. In fact, it's the pleasures of the moments that provide consolation against the drone and droop of the hours and the days.

Life's treasures are buried right under our noses. Can we relish the wonders of small-scale epiphanies and everyday events? The discovery in Newark Airport's Terminal B of a daily delivery of fresh flowers to a men's room? The discovery that plants can count? Each leaf of the Venus's-flytrap has three hairs. If an insect touches two of them—any two of them—the leafy trap snaps shut. If an insect touches just one—any one—nothing happens.

There are so many discoveries to be made of this ever-changing world. Life isn't somewhere else. Life is here—all around you and inside you, a succession of astonishments. True artists write hymns to ordinariness. True artists find meaning in the small wonders of life. The art of godly living is making every event a real do, making every moment count, even turning "senior moments" into "God moments."

The second obstacle to magnetized moments is our preference for copies over the original. David didn't allow Goliath to define who he was. One of the hardest challenges in life is not to allow our Goliaths— boss, spouse, church—to define us. The modern church arguably has been more in the business of forcing individuals to become as standard as those mirrored molecules found in nature than has any other sector of society. How many have "succeeded" in the church while at the same time refused the bridle imposed as its price for success? The history of the Christian church boasts a rich and idiosyncratic cast of characters— quite a contrast to many of the fitted waxwork leaders of today.

> All happenings, great and small, are parables whereby God speaks. The art of life is to get the message.
> —MALCOLM MUGGERIDGE

Christianity in the West was built by adventurers; it is being lost by back-covering, back-scratching look-alikes.

Like a nail hammered back into a board, our kinks and quirks are pummeled out of us as soon as they stick out. We come to fear the honest living of our own moments. We come to live vicariously, inhabiting the hyped moments of stars or the hyper expectations of others. We pay public figures big bucks to live our private lives for us. Our investments in celebrities entitle us to pinch, tickle, and torment them, even to see them in their grief and briefs.

God has called each one of us to move "beyond category," to borrow Duke Ellington's highest term of praise. When your soul is "beyond category," you are living an "inspired life." You are living in a state of "in-spiration"—having the Spirit breathed into you—and your soul is in tune with the music of a God who is composing the score of the universe. For too many Christians, the music has stopped.

Landmark Moments

Postmodern disciples can make a landmark moment. And these moments don't necessarily get their red lettering because they were good ones; bad moments can become landmarks too.

Disciples of Jesus are to have rocklike qualities. But Peter showed us that if we are rocks, we are rocks that rock—we move, we fall, we shatter, we break, we fail.

There is one day in your life that will be your best day. There is one day in your life that will be your worst day.

It's important to know when you're having one of life's best moments. And worst. Landmark both.

It's important to know when you've preached your best sermon. And worst. Landmark both.

It's important to know when you've eaten the best peach you'll ever eat. And worst (which I think I just did). Landmark both.

My mother made a landmark moment of her worst meal—a meal she ate with an Appalachian mountain family with whom she was doing home mission work. The milk was full of flies. The meat had maggots all over it. But Mother ate it all and framed her worst meal as a landmark moment that served to instruct her three boys: sometimes the milk curdles and the honey sours on the milk-and-honey path of true discipleship.

Memory Moments

Erwin R. McManus is the talented pastor of a church that holds a Sunday evening service, which they call Urban Mosaic, in a Los

Angeles nightclub. He has a saying that goes like this: "The truth is out there, but how do you download it? . . . More and more people are choosing to buy memory rather than make one."

To make a memory moment is to "re-member" the soul. The word *remember* means both "to mark" and "to put together," as in putting together the members, or parts, of a body. In terms of the soul, what do we mark and put together? Memories and stories. If the phrase "remember when" is not on your lips many times a day, if you are not constantly recalling back to life meaningful memories and stories, your soul is being starved to death.

Memory is the humus of the soul. Memories fall to the ground and fertilize the soil so that the soul can grow. When there is no sun and no rain, the soul can still grow from the soil being enriched by all that humus. When I'm lonely, a piece of music coupled with a memory moment can turn me into a person who no longer possesses the key to his heart. When I'm depressed and dangerously low on currencies of hope and faith, I make withdrawals from my memory bank that keep me going until my faith-and-hope crisis has ended.

The art of moment making is the making of deposits in the first place so that you can make withdrawals later, even when you're wearing a salt-smeared face. Or in eight words I have memorized from the "war poet" (who didn't write about war) Edward Thomas, in his last poem written from the trenches: "Despair is but hope blinded by its tears."

A team of researchers at St. Olaf College in Northfield, Minnesota, say that the sharing of such stories may actually bring health benefits. They soothe the soul and provide markers for the mind in its passage through time. Postmoderns care little for high fashion. They care deeply for high integrity. And what gives anything integrity is not a state of perfection but a story that proves its authenticity.

The role of aroma in marking moments is becoming more significant to my soul with every passing year. Smell molds the building blocks of memories. To mark a memory with a smell is to tattoo that memory on the soul.

More than we care to recognize, smell is one of the things that unites us as USAmericans. Miller Lite did a survey and found that the number one smell in the country, the one that makes us most think of "America," is smoky barbecue. Apple pie came in second, followed by the ocean and, in fourth place, garbage. (Where is the coffee?)

Ever since God marked Jesus' birth with the smell of frankincense, fragrance has played a powerful role in the Christian church . . . up until the modern period. Before the modern era, foul smells were an indication of ungodliness; sweet aromas, the mark of holiness. A mystical

We are the aroma of Christ to God among those who are being saved.
—Paul (2 Cor. 2:15 NRSV)

Make a Moment

33

odor signaled the presence of the Holy Spirit, and aromatics were alleged to have both preventative and curative functions. The Enlightenment world deodorized smell and associated it with madness or depravity.

Once again, the postmodern world is much more like the medieval world, where the church honored the tenets of the "odor of sanctity." The postmodern world is coming alive with smells. Healing powers are once again being attributed to smells, and while some of aromatherapy can be downright kooky, other parts of it are right on target (for example, pumpkin pie and lavender are natural Viagras). It is no longer superstitious nonsense that there are certain problems you can smell before you can see them (dogs and cats telegraph fires first because of this).

The business world is practicing "aroma persuasion." Houses sell faster, for example, when a loaf of bread is baking in the oven while interested buyers visit. I practice aroma inspiration when I meditate and write. Incense is more than a symbol of prayer. Its smells help usher me into the presence of God. When I need to write for marathon sessions, I stock a supply of "burnt offerings"—scented candles, incense sticks, aroma votives—with different smells taking me through different writing stretches.

To help mark my memories, I have different scents for different places. A "when I'm traveling" cologne to help keep my memories on the road green. A "teaching at Drew" scent that I associate with students and colleagues. A "Wintercadence" (Canaan Valley, West Virginia) scent. A "Dolphin Cay" (Orcas Island, Washington) body shampoo that sprays the ocean on me. Fragrances are one way I keep my sanity, care for my spirituality, and continue my soul's journey.

One church in Venice, Italy, to stay above the water, rests on 1.1 million wooden piles driven down into the sediment. One soul, to stay afloat, rests on a million piles of memories driven deep into life's alluvial deposits. With or without the aid of your nose, capture the moments of your life so that later you can re-member them, enriching your soul's progress.

Angel Moments

Into every life an angel will come: it may be angel money, angel presences, angel warnings, angel consolations. But angel moments will occur.

Some of the times I feel angels the most are when I'm preaching. Every preacher is my witness: there are certain people (known and unknown) from whom you gain strength and energy while you're preaching; there are other people who suck the energy right out of you

SoulSalsa

with their yawns, frowns, and guffaws. One of the first things I try to do in a sermon is quickly locate where are my "hot spots," my "dead spots," and my "spirit vampires."

It is a matter of honor for me to thank after the sermon those "angels" who lifted me up and carried me home. I used to say when I finally located them, "Thanks for being a hot spot of divine energy for me during that sermon." But in the interest of not being misinterpreted, I now thank my "hot spots" for either sprouting wings during worship and becoming my "angel presence" or for being a "Barnabas force" of encouragement and energy.

If you're a teacher, what kid was your angel presence today?

If you're a salesperson or checkout clerk, what customer cheered you up and calmed you down?

If you're a police officer, what run-in with an angel made your day?

God's angels may need no wings, but they do need acknowledgments.

If I had known what it would be like to have it all, I might have settled

—LILY TOMLIN

Prayer Magnets

The making of moments encompasses the whole universe of human experience: birth moments, healing moments, forgiving moments, loving moments, silent moments, defining moments, fork moments (what our ancestors called "choosing times"), mystery moments, etc. What is it that magnetizes human experience and makes it into a moment?

Our direct uplink (or better, surroundlink) to the Almighty is called *prayer*. Prayer is the primal and primary religious act. Prayer is the trigger mechanism that releases God's will in our life and world. Prayer is the art of hole-punching the sky so that "as it is in heaven" becomes an earthly reality. As with all high-powered, high-voltage sources, prayer mandates certain vectors.

The *first prayer vector* is one we largely abandoned in the high modern world: when you pray, change your posture.

Parents tend to teach their children correctly: pray with body before mouth. Just as a child learns to make signs with hands before opening mouth, so all children of faith must learn to change posture before entering into a season of prayer. Whether it's a move to a standing, sitting, kneeling, bowing, or prostrate position, the change in posture signifies a change in one's stance in relationship to the divine and a readiness to open channels to the most powerful force in the universe. In fact, in some cultures it's the tradition to stand in prayer before eating.

The *second prayer vector:* when you pray, prepare to be changed. God gives us the means for our mission, not the means for our cravings and lusts and wishes. When you pray for the means to do what God is calling you to do, that prayer is answered. Watch out.

You can't pray for people without being changed by those prayers. A pastor taking another parish spoke these words of warning to the congregation in his good-bye sermon:

> Sometime I'd like to hear someone say, "Pray for me," and have the person they're asking say, "No, I'd be afraid of doing that. It would require us to become too connected. If I prayed for you I would no longer be able to objectify you and it would change our relationship in ways I would find unsettling. Praying for you would also pull me out of my narcissistic selfishness and force me to contemplate the ineffable power of God in my life which would also be uncomfortable. So thank you, but I just can't."

To pray for someone is to enter into a reciprocal relationship of life transformation.

The *third prayer vector:* each one of us will pray differently. No two people have the same devotional life. Each one of us connects with God differently.

A Methodist woman wrote John Wesley for some spiritual counsel. She confessed to being dry spiritually. She was rising at dawn to do her devotions. She was reading the Bible and going to church and doing all the right things. But her faith had grown cold. What should she do?

Wesley wrote back matter-of-factly: Try rising before dawn. Some of us need to work harder at these things than others.

We disciples have at our feet a lot of runways from which to take off in prayer. Some work well for one kind of person, and some for another. A few prayer initiatives that have launched me spiritually are prayer walks, concerts of prayer, on-site prayer, prayer partners, prayer warriors, and ancient prayer rituals.

The *fourth prayer vector* is to pray without ceasing. This means first and foremost a life steeped—and steepled—in prayer. In the early church they prayed the Paternoster (the "Lord's Prayer," or what I call the Disciples' Prayer) three times a day. It was a daily, not a Sunday, prayer. I am a big fan of short, sharp prayers, books of which were called in the sixteenth century a "quiverful" (*pharetra*). How full is your "quiver" of sentence prayers? Take out one arrow from your quiver when you leave hotel rooms and let it fly. As you look back to see if you left anything, pray for the next person who will occupy the room after you check out.

The *fifth prayer vector:* make all of life a prayer vector. The greatest ambition of my life is not so much to *pray* the Lord's Prayer as it is to *become* the Lord's Prayer. The ultimate in answered prayer is for all of life to be made into a moment.

This is the definition of "having it all." Of course, no one can literally "have it all." All you can have is what you are willing to sacrifice for, value most, pray about, and pay the price for. When everything I do becomes a prayer offered to God, then I will go from praying the Lord's Prayer (Disciples' Prayer) to becoming the Lord's Prayer. That's the ultimate in "having it all."

God did not give us a spirit of timidity, but a spirit of power, of love and of self-discipline.

—PAUL (2 TIMOTHY 1:7)

1. When was the last time you felt "all prayed out"?

2. Consider this quote from novelist/poet Madeleine L'Engle. Where does it ring true? Where might it not ring true? She says:

   The Trinity is limitless and we mortals want limits, limits to what is demanded of us, limits to God's love, limits to those God is willing to redeem, limits to those who are going to be saved. Redemption is Trinitarian, and it is not just for us human creatures; it is for all of Creation. . . . We will truly understand the Trinity only when there is total reconciliation.

3. If you haven't seen the musical Rent, learn more about it from its official Web site: http://www.siteforrent.com/. Listen to the song "Seasons of Love" (downloadable from the Web site). To what degree do you think Rent was the Godspell of the 1990s?

4. What are your favorite "remember when" stories that you tell your kids or friends? What are you really trying to get them to re-member (put back together)?

5. As you read the following quote from Dow Edgerton, think about what you have planned for tomorrow.

   To live an ordinary day. . . . But what could be harder to do? Who can claim to have done so much? A pilgrimage may be easier than a day! A great quest may be easier than a single day! Some task which is dangerous, demanding, and full of the bright din of conflict may be easier than the ordinary day.

   What can you do to make tomorrow, an ordinary day, more spiritually rewarding than a pilgrimage, more adventuresome than a great quest or risky task?

6. In the medieval monastic tradition, the head was tilted downward toward the heart to show the primacy of the heart to the head. Try praying this way.

7. Journalist/novelist Daniel Defoe tells of attending a worship service in 1722 in which "the whole church was like a smelling-

---

The pleasure of perfume [is] among the most elegant and also most honorable enjoyments in life.

—PLINY

bottle; in one corner it was all perfumes; in another, aromatics, balsamics, and a variety of drugs and herbs; in another, salts and spirits."

How would you have liked to walk into that church? How can you incorporate smells into your own worship experiences?

8. Listen to Steven Curtis Chapman's "Let Us Pray," off his Signs of Life album. Or at least read the lyrics at http://ltd.sim-plenet.com/scc/albums/signs.htm#5/.

9. Karen Neudorf is the visionary editor of the postmodern Christian journal Beyond Magazine. In a recent editorial entitled "Life and Belief in One Dimension," she writes:

> We draw straight lines. Perhaps this, in our limited knowledge, is the shortest distance between two points. Perhaps it is a perilous tightrope stretched between Point A and Point B. So many lines drawn in the sand. So many voices saying, This is the way; this is what living was meant to be.
>
> I have tried to lay my body down on this thin straight line. I suck in my breath, draw my arms tight to my side like a stiff stick drawing and hope I look at ease in this narrow life, this rigid belief system. I would smile but that might throw me off balance, a lopsided grin knocking me to the ground and then everyone would know, "She doesn't fit with us. She's not going to make it here."

Can you hear the cry of postmoderns in this quote? Where are you hearing this cry inside of you? Around you? In your church?

One ought, every day at least, to hear a little song, read a good poem, see a fine picture, and if possible, to speak a few reasonable words.

—GOETHE

3

Think Methuselah

SOUL ARTISTS PREPARE THEMSELVES FOR A LONG LIFE.

Sometimes we stare so long at a door that is closing that we see too late the one that is opening.

—ALEXANDER GRAHAM BELL

Postmoderns know a reality in which life expectancy is increasing steadily with no end in sight. It gives new meaning to the phrase "long-term plans." If we're wise, we're laying track for multiple-decades productivity while taking with us a recognition of our own mortality. No matter how old we get, the percentage of people who eventually die is still hanging right up there at 100 percent.

Biblical spirituality is not so much an age-defying spirituality as an age-affirming spirituality. Whatever age, stage, or state we're in, therewith to be content. Therewith to be on a mission.

Mission-Driven Living

I am a Boomer. I divide a Boomer life into three stages, each roughly comprising thirty years.

- The question of the first stage is "Where do you go to school?"
- The question of the second stage is "What do you do for a living?"
- The question of the third and last stage is "What difference are you making for God?"

Although all three questions are really asked in each stage, the question that ties all of them together into one question is this: "What's your mission in life?"

You will suffer and die in life. The question is whether or not you will suffer and die for a mission. Or in the words of one of my favorite literary critics, Richard Ellmann, "If we must suffer, it is better to create the world in which we suffer, and this is what heroes do spontaneously, artists do consciously, and all men do in their degree."

We are all, in the words of poet Carl Sandburg, "riding on a limited express." But the time we're spending on that "limited express" is getting longer and longer. By the time you read this, more people will be over forty than under. And by 2005, one in four USAmericans will be over sixty. Between 1960 and 1994, the "oldest old" (eighty-five and older) increased by 274 percent. The fastest-growing age-group of the USAmerican population, proportionately speaking, is that of centenarians—our seventh-generation ancestors.

We have seen the future, and it is . . . Methuselah.

An Age of Methuselahs

It used to be that everyone who wanted one got a televised one-hundredth birthday greeting from Willard Scott. Now Scott can handle only a fraction of the requests he receives. Ninety-year-old management guru Peter Drucker has been pointing out this fact to us for years: it is unprecedented in history that older people will outnumber young people because of a collapsing birthrate and increasing longevity. Our kids born in the 1990s may well live to see a third of the twenty-second century. They are not twenty-first-century kids but twenty-second-century kids.

The days of the psalmist's years may have been "threescore years and ten" (Psalm 90:10 KJV). But the days of postmodern lives are more three-digit than two-digit, more Moses (120 years) and Abraham (175 years) and, if some molecular biologists are to be believed, even Methuselah (969 years). By 2002, the human genome will be completely known. Given genetic engineering (and that's not as big a given as most think, especially since the number of rheostat genes appears to be under a dozen), this means that the greatest limit to longevity will be mishaps and tragedies. Get used to Methuselahs. And to the laughter of Sarahs, as women in their fifties and sixties (now) and seventies (soon) discover they're pregnant.

Julius Caesar once remarked that every year he found himself one year older but the age of the crowd in the street always seemed to remain the same. No longer. The age of the crowd seems to grow right along with me.

The most widely exhibited living American artist is a ninety-year-old Baptist country preacher from Georgia named Howard Finster. Now a New York art world celebrity, this Grandma Moses of the 2000s has appeared on the *Tonight Show* and in *Rolling Stone* magazine, and he was honored in 1990 with a Smithsonian exhibition.

He didn't start painting until he was sixty-five, after having pastored churches for forty years. His plunge into being a full-time folk artist took place at a Sunday night service. After preaching 4,625 sermons as

For to me, living is Christ and dying is gain.

—PAUL
(PHILIPPIANS 1:21 NRSV)

well as officiating at 400 funerals and 200 weddings, he decided that the time had come to survey his congregation about what they remembered him saying. To his dismay, he discovered that no one remembered much of anything he had said, including what he had preached on that morning. Finster recalls, "I said to myself: 'They're not paying much attention to me. What am I gonna do? Lord, I want to preach all over the world and reach more people.' Then God called me unto sacred art, got to putting messages on it."

The "it" Finster started "putting messages on" was objects from everyday life. With material culture as his canvas, Finster now has more than forty thousand original compositions, each one a living testimony that anything can become art and anyone can become an artist. His junk "garden" and galleria eighty miles north of Atlanta (in Pennville, Georgia) is a mecca for those following the formula for mission living found on Winifred Holtby's gravestone:

> God give me work
> Till my life shall end
> And life
> Till my work is done.

Finster is the postmodern norm, not the exception.

- Portuguese novelist Jose Saramago, Nobel laureate in literature in 1998, didn't really start writing until he was sixty.
- Surgeon Michael DeBakey regularly performs three-hour heart operations at the age of ninety.
- Emma Gershtein, still writing, won the Little Booker Prize in 1998 when she was ninety-five.
- Southern monument Eudora Welty published *One Writer's Beginnings* when she was seventy-five.
- Novelist Penelope Fitzgerald won the American National Book Critics' Circle Award for her ninth novel, *The Blue Flower.* Her first novel, *The Golden Child,* was published when she was sixty-one.
- One of my favorite writers, the Canadian Robertson Davies, wrote his last novel, *The Cunning Man,* at the age of eighty.
- Frank Lloyd Wright designed Fallingwater at sixty-nine and the Guggenheim Museum at seventy-six, and did his most productive work between eighty and his death at ninety-three.
- Cecil B. DeMille produced and directed his most famous film, *The Ten Commandments,* at age seventy-five.

- Claude Monet created the last of his famous water lily paintings shortly before his death in his eighty-sixth year.
- Guiseppe Verdi wrote two of his greatest operas after eighty.
- Michelangelo was appointed chief architect of St. Peter's in Rome at age seventy-one—and continued in that position until his death at eighty-nine.
- Ray Kroc, Colonel Sanders, Grandma Moses, Emily Post, Ferdinand Zeppelin—all of them didn't start doing what they became famous for until they were in their late fifties or sixties.

I was born in the year of our-Lord-only-knows. Moderns changed *names* on birth certificates. Postmoderns want to change *dates* on birth certificates. Especially us graybeard Boomers now in the midst of "mid-youth" (middle age).

The thing that is making it possible for us to think Methuselah is both a blessing and, in the wrong hands, a curse. The biggest wall that came tumbling down in the twentieth century was not the Berlin Wall in 1989 but the wall of the human body that was chipped away at, hammered and shattered into oblivion by a variety of technologies (starting with pacemakers in the 1950s) that had a multiplying effect throughout the century until traditional notions of flesh and machine, born and made are now forever changed.

We all can be fleshed cyborgs now. Soon we will be cyberspatial cyborgs. The interconnectedness between humans and machines is now irrecoverable, as the boundaries between the vital, the viral, and the virtual are dynamited almost daily.

As with all the lifeware design components, there is a double ring to thinking Methuselah. First, we live to live forever. At the same time, we live to die tomorrow.

Live to Live Forever

To live to live forever is to abolish the concept of middle age. Increasingly, what is being defined as "old" is getting older. Where "old" used to be defined as over sixty, now 32 percent say that "old" is over seventy, 15 percent say it is over eighty, as 37 percent argue that "age is only a state of mind." When "middle age" becomes something between thirty and seventy-five, it becomes a meaningless category. That's why what used to be called "middle age" I call "mid-youth." When the seventy-four-year-old Illinois Republican Henry Hyde deflected the uncovering of a five-year illicit relationship during his forties with a dismissive "the statute of limitations has long since passed

> Youth is something to be endured while you wait for your forties, fifties, and sixties.
> —RETAIL CONSULTANT CANDACE CORLETT

on my youthful indiscretions," he had it exactly right. Your forties any-more *are* "youthful."

The ancient philosopher Horace had a saying for which he was famous: *"Damnosa quid non imminuit dies?"* It means "Time corrupts all. What has it not made worse?"

I was born yesterday, Horace, but I wasn't born last night. You've got this one wrong. Not true then, not true now. Forget all the jokes about the three kinds of seniors (the go-gos, the slow-gos, and the no-gos), or the milestones in memory loss ("first you forget names, then you forget faces, then you forget to pull your zipper up, then you for-get to pull your zipper down").

We are now living in a time when people can be "aged to perfection" in every way—physically, mentally, and spiritually. Just as the health industry is moving from treating disease to creating health, so the church must redesign itself as a place that creates wellness rather than attends the sick. And wellness incorporates body, mind, and spirit.

BODY

Elizabeth Somer calls pursuing physical wellness "age-proofing" your body. Most age-related diseases are avoidable (70 percent of can-cers are lifestyle-related), and many of the body's aging switches are within our control to turn on and off. For example, diet, exercise, and intimacy are three aging switches we can manipulate to forestall aging. The National Institute on Aging says that 80 percent of older people's health problems are not aging-related but due to improper eating, men-tal, and exercise habits over the course of a lifetime. Dr. Franz Ingelfinger, onetime editor of the prestigious *New England Journal of Medicine,* flips the focus and ends up with an even higher figure. He says 85 percent of illnesses fall within the body's power to heal.

We have medicalized aging to a degree larger than anyone antici-pated—all the way from Viagra (sexual decline) to DHEA (growth hormones) to antioxidants (beta carotene, vitamins C and E to combat damage done by free radicals). Etienne Baulieu's antiaging pill may be even more controversial than his abortion pill, RU–486. In some ways these three words—Valium, Viagra, vitaceuticals—say it all about life in the future.

MIND

Mentally, we can be "aged to perfection" too. Some Boomer some-where is turning fifty every fifteen seconds. When the statistics tell us that 6 percent of Boomers had already retired as of 1998, they fail to show that the kinds of "retirement" Boomers are looking for is less a change in situation (as with their parents) as a change in state. Boomers are not looking to retiree-rich counties in which to retire but to small towns or rural counties. The hottest "retirement" spots in the country are college towns where Boomers can go and do everything but retire. Whereas late moderns slithered off to adults-only communities where they could spend their reclining years breathing each other's fumes, postmoderns want their best years filled with the best in intellectual stimulation, cultural enrichment, and seven-generational incitements. This is why college towns are sprouting "age in place" retirement communities and assisted-living facilities to provide knowledge workers with the knowledge "retirements" they want.

This does not mean the work we do and the missions we go on in our nineties or later will be the same as what we did in our fifties and sixties. Composer Igor Stravinsky and poet/preacher Richard Young are my models. In his senior years Stravinsky recognized his limitations and began to focus on what one critic has called "making beautiful objects." In Stravinsky's last works (for example, *Requiem Canticles*), "the intellectual fire is still there, but most of the physical energy is gone; it is condensed into a single gesture, a single chord." Similarly, in his later years Young produced a series of single-paragraph sermons that were densely epigrammatic. The bravado of bigness was gone. The perfection of exquisitely crafted smaller works was now on exhibit.

Never eat anything at one sitting that you can't lift.

—*Miss Piggy*

SPIRIT

In addition to body and mind, spiritually we can be "aged to perfection." Paul promised as much in 2 Corinthians 4:16–17, where he testified that when he was at his most impaired physically, he could be at his most accomplished spiritually. The best example of this double ring in which our inner nature can be renewed each day even as our faces become creased and our ears stopped up is Billy Graham. I want to age like Billy Graham has aged. With every passing year he has gotten better, more forgiving, more loving, more global, more grand. In an interview late in the 1990s, a Parkinson-afflicted Graham demonstrated how optimal our state of spiritual functioning can be when our bodies are at their least optimal:

> I believe the overwhelming message is the grace and the love and
> the mercy of God, and that's what I emphasize a lot more than
> I did in the earlier years. I think the Lord just gradually changed

me as I began to study the Scriptures. I began to see how much of the emphasis is on God's love and mercy and grace. I'm not going to heaven because I'm good. [That was the mistake the Pharisee in the parable made.] I'm not going to heaven because I've preached to a lot of people. [That's the mistake a lot of preachers make.] I'm going to heaven because of God's grace and mercy in Christ at the cross. And grace means unmerited favor. Something I didn't deserve. I haven't worked for. It's a free gift from God to me.

Live to Die Tomorrow

"Life is death we're lengthy at," wrote Emily Dickinson. We learn to face the "facts of life." We must also learn to face the "facts of death." For Jesus, the secret of life is death. To come to terms with life is to come to terms with dying, the last life experience.

If there is one thing harder than the art of living well, it is the art of dying well. "Who ever succeeded in draining the whole cup with grace?" Carl Jung once asked.

Lots of people have. Especially Jesus' followers. John Wesley bragged about the people called Methodists, "Our people die well."

Life isn't always chronological. The seasons of life don't always come in linear order. In life as well as in global-warmed nature, sometimes summer follows autumn, and winter, spring. An experience of life-threatening illness may be followed by a period of excellent health, thanks to a new treatment. A child may learn the word *chemotherapy* while missing kindergarten. But whatever season comes first, the grand closing of winter always comes. However long your gift of years, life is short. The cancer comes, the cookie crumbles, the bough breaks . . .

The more you shake life, the more the dead falls off. The great spiritual masters have recommended a variety of life-shaking, *memento mori* techniques, or as we would put it today, "Put death in your Day-Timer." Fifteenth-century monk Thomas à Kempis offered this advice:

If you have ever seen a person die, reflect that you too must pass the same way.... How happy and wise is that person who strives now to be in life what he wishes to be found in death.... Ah, dear friend! from what great danger can you free yourself and from what great fear can you be freed if you will always be apprehensive and respectful of death.

Our ancestors' death-in-your-Day-Timer exercises included actually sleeping periodically in one's casket or lying in bed imagining that the bed is the casket. From the perspective of one heartbeat away from eternity, one achieves rapid clarity about what really matters. Paradoxically, contemplation of the bitters at the bottom of life's cup makes the cup of life all the sweeter. Death's great gift may be a vision of what matters most in life and what the mission of one's life is all about. We only get a certain amount of life energy to spend; how will we spend it?

The Sunset Effect

Centenarian gardener Marie Aull taught me most of what I know about the outdoors. She always worried when a tree burst into brilliant bloom. Just before a tree dies, she warned, its last bloom can be its most glorious—and trick you into thinking it's still healthy.

This is called the "sunset effect." It happens culturally as well as biologically. Take two examples. First, as the industrial age ended, our skyscrapers got more desperate, more arrogant, more pointless: 1,482 feet in Kuala Lumpur, 1,837 feet in Melbourne, 1,863 feet in Hong Kong. To look at these towers alone would give the impression, not of a new era dawning, but of an old era at its best and brightest. Second, as the modern era ends, there is a revival of reading the likes of which we have not seen before. The historian of the book Alberto Manguel argues that "before most great changes in technology, the previous technological form experiences a flourish, a last-minute exuberance. After the invention of the printing press, the number of manuscripts produced in Europe increased dramatically, and canvas painting mushroomed immediately after the invention of photography." It is Manguel's contention that the burst in book reading may be evidence of a similar "last-minute exuberance" before the rise of more electronic, experiential, interactive, and image-based reading habits.

Each one of us can go out in a blaze of glory if we master what the ancients called the *ars moriendi*, literally, "the art of dying." I call it the art of happy endings.

First, know the signs of ending. Whereas past endings took months and even years, the transitions from "on earth" to "in heaven" are now taking only days and weeks. We can expect to live full, abundant lives almost up until the very moment of our death. If "old age" means being diseased, failing, indisposed, and infirm, then the period of "old age" is now so short that it's an eye blink in a lifetime. But rapid decline makes reading death's early-warning signals more difficult than ever, not less.

Eighty-five is nothing.
Eighty-five is young.
Eighty-five is 15 years
away from 100.
—Dr. Thomas Perls,
geriatrician, Beth Israel
Deaconess Medical Center
(Boston)

Think Methuselah

47

Second, give the ending of your life a godly meaning and moral consequence for all who are touched by it. Use your dying as a "teachable moment" for the loved ones who are going through the wrench of losing you.

Third, put the past in context, and if need be, set the past straight. They say that you see your whole life flash before your eyes before a sudden death; do the same thing deliberately if you're dying more slowly. What threads are left dangling that you can still tie up?

Fourth, tell stories to nearby loved ones and visitors about the divine coherences in your life. You won't understand all of what God intended for your life until you've gained the perspective of Abraham's bosom, but the deathbed isn't a bad place either to trace the working of God in your life—and to testify to it.

Fifth, commission heirs, bless the succeeding generations, bestow your mantle, and bequeath your treasures. When the patriarchs were dying, they established both the birthright and the blessings—material and spiritual legacies that would outlast them.

Sixth, offer testimonials to future vistas and give reasons for the hope that is in you. As your thoughts turn to the room Jesus has prepared for you in his mansion, share this with others for their strengthening.

And finally, make your peace with God and with others around you.

Trust and Obey

To think Methuselah is to trust God. And part of trusting God is reveling in the wonder of how our body is made, how it works, and how long it lasts. One of my favorite meditations is to marinate my mind in the mystery of how a single cell can give rise to a human being with 2 to 3 million sweat glands, 7 billion capillaries, 25 trillion red blood cells, 60 trillion cells, 5 million hairs on the body, and 170,000 hairs on the head if you're a redhead, 185,000 if you're blond, and 200,000 if you're brunette or black-haired.

How long our genetic whirlpool will allow all these cells to talk to each other and work together is anyone's guess and God's surprise. But one day a particular system will break down. One day an organism will lose the struggle against a competing organism. Disease has functions as well as causes—the germ wins, the body dies.

For the disciple of Jesus, death has meaning for the body but not for the soul. The soul lives forever. We shall never die. "Death, that old snakeskin," writes poet Irene Zimmerman, "lies discarded at the garden gate."

So, what is death like? The best answer I've ever encountered came via popular culture. When a dying character in a popular TV program

Your tears come easy, when you're young, and beginning the world. Your tears come easy, when you're old, and leaving it.

—GABRIEL BETTEREDGE IN THE MOONSTONE

(I think it was *Seventh Heaven*) asked someone what death was like, that person gave a reply that keeps ringing doorbells to eternity in every cell of my body, mind, and spirit.

The respondent said death is like when you're a child and you get sick and feverish. You go to bed at night sweating, shivering, feeling wretched enough to die. The next morning you awake, your fever is broken, and you are feeling much better. You feel secure, snug, and strong—and suddenly you realize why. You're now in your parents' bed. In the middle of the night someone came to get you to take you home.

You can't turn back the clock. But you can wind it up again.
—BONNIE PRUDDEN

There are no final missions.

—JONATHAN ALTER,
COMMENTING ON JOHN GLENN'S
STINT AS AN ASTRONAUT
IN HIS SEVENTIES

I meant to write about death, only life came breaking in as usual.

—VIRGINIA WOOLF'S
SELF-CHOSEN EPITAPH

SPIRITUAL PRACTICES AND WEB INTERACTIVES

1. Check out the Web site of centenarian expert Lynn Peters Adler (http://www.adlercentenarians.com/) and read about the life of the person in the "Centenarian Spotlight." How is this hundred-plus USAmerican a blessing to those who know him or her?

2. "The true wealth of nations," Theodore Roszak insists, "lies not in bank vaults and missile silos, nor in chips and nets, but in the compassionate hearts and noble minds of their citizens." To what extent is he correct? How wealthy are we?

3. Here is Presbyterian elder/U.S. Senator/astronaut John Glenn reflecting on his first Project Mercury orbital flight, 20 February 1962:

> Death was possible. I thought we'd be lucky if we didn't lose one or two. . . . I have since been asked why I did it. I did it because it was important for our country. . . . While I wasn't rushing to leave this life any more than anyone else, I have always felt that it is more important how you live your life than how long
> you live.

Do you agree with his last sentence?

4. Thirty-seven percent of USAmericans say age is unrelated to chronology but is a state of mind. Twenty-three percent of USAmericans dread getting older, and about equal numbers fear aging as much as they fear dying. Where do you come down in these statistics?

5. Some say you get old only when you look to the past more than you look to the future. True or false? In practical terms, what does it mean to look to the future?

6. Log on to the Web site of the World Health Network (http://www.worldhealth.net/) and take the Official Longevity Test to get a perspective on how long you might live. You can get other perspectives on the same thing from MoneyCentral's Life Expectancy Calculator (http://moneycentral.msn.com/investor/calcs/n_expect/main.asp/) and the gruesome Death Clock (http://www.deathclock.com/).

7. Do a Bible study of Mark 7:9–13. What escape clause were Jewish leaders using to evade supporting their parents in their old age? What does the Bible have to say about the sense of honor that is due the aged?

8. Check out www.deathclock.com. Enter your birth date and gender, and get your date of death.

   A more sophisticated one with greater detail is http://money-central.msn.com/investor/calcs/n_expect/main.asp.

9. Here's a bibliography of resources on thinking Methuselah:

Henry C. Simmons and E. Craig MacBean, Waltzing Methuselah: Practical Steps to Paying for a Longer Life (Richmond, Va.: Prime, 1968).

Michel Allard et al., Jeanne Calment: From Van Gogh's Time to Ours, 122 Extraordinary Years (Thorndike, Maine: Thorndike, 1999).

Lynn Peters Adler, Centenarians: The Bonus Years (Santa Fe: Health, 1995).

Michael Fossel, Reversing Human Aging (New York: Morrow, 1996).

Ronald Klatz and Robert Glodman, Stopping the Clock: Why Many of Us Will Live Past 100—and Enjoy Every Minute! (New York: Bantam, 1997).

Marvin Cetron and Owen Davies, Cheating Death: The Promise and the Future Impact of Trying to Live Forever (New York: St. Martin's, 1998).

Theodore Roszak, America the Wise: The Longevity Revolution and the True Wealth of Nations (Boston: Houghton Mifflin, 1999).

For an example of a sixteenth-century antiaging publication, see Luigi Cornaro's Discorsi Della Vita Sobria, available in English as The Art of Living Long: A New and Improved English Version of the Treatise by the Celebrated Venetian Centenarian Luigi Cornaro (Milwaukee: Butler, 1916).

Pick one of these resources and mine it for what it can teach you about living the years that are still stretching out ahead of you. For fun, you might also want to read a new science fiction thriller by Sal Destefano called The Methuselah Gene (Philadelphia: BainBridge, 1999).

Here lies
Ezekial Aikle
Age 102
The Good Die Young
—EPITAPH IN EAST DALHOUSIE CEMETERY, NOVA SCOTIA

4

Bounce Your Last Check

SOUL ARTISTS RECEIVE GOOD THINGS GRATEFULLY
AND GIVE IT ALL AWAY IN THE END.

A middle-aged patient was sitting in a waiting room, anxiously waiting to discover the results of his biopsy. The minutes that passed seemed like hours, and the hours like weeks. Did he have it or didn't he? Just when he felt he could take it no more, he heard a voice: "The doctor will see you now."

As he walked into the doctor's office, he blurted out: "Am I going to die?"

And the answer to that question is yes.

We are all going to die. Many of us are living as if we are immortal, but we are all going to die. The only question is, what will we leave behind when we die?

If you dance the soulsalsa in this new millennium, you will leave nothing behind. By the time you die, you will have given away whatever you had. Time it so that the last check bounces.

To die broke was industrialist Andrew Carnegie's dream at the turn of the *last* century. Today it is Bob Buford's dream. It is Tom Monaghan's dream. Buford is a Texas media mogul, best-selling author, and the founder of Leadership Network. He recently sold his business and created a plan to give all his money away before he dies. Monaghan is a Michigan pizza mogul, the founder of Domino's Pizza. A devout Roman Catholic, Monaghan has dedicated the rest of his life to working full-time for God.

Carnegie made it into a maxim that "the man who dies . . . rich, dies disgraced." He himself practiced this maxim, leaving nothing behind. He slept all his life on a poor boy's metal cot; he never wanted to forget from whence he came. Carnegie expressed his wealth ethic in terms of trusteeship:

This, then, is held to be the duty of the man of wealth: To set an example of modest, unostentatious living, shunning display or extravagance; to provide moderately for the legitimate wants of those dependent upon him; and, after doing so, to consider all surplus revenues which come to him simply as trust funds, which he is called upon to administer . . . to produce the most beneficial results for the community.

To bounce one's last check is to die vertical, not horizontal. To die vertical is to take a stand and to declare your values even when you die. To die horizontal is to allow others to declare your values for you and to let them take whatever stands they want to take with your money (most of the time the "stands" they take are for themselves).

In the words of the Welsh poet David Whyte, "I don't want to have written on my tombstone, when finally people struggle through the weeds, pull back the moss, and read the inscription there, 'He made his car payments.'"

Postmoderns deserve a new vision of a discipleship where one's "savings" is more a deposit than a deal. If postmoderns are not to vanish into the crevasses of careerism, a theology of receiving must come before a theology of giving.

The BMW of the next decade will be the personal charitable trust fund.
—PAUL SAFFO, INSTITUTE FOR THE FUTURE

Trustees

Jesus discipleship entails a trusteeship ethic, not a stewardship ethic. In fact, the two New Testament Greek words translated most often as "stewards" (*epitropos* and *oikonomos*) are better rendered as "trustees."

A theology of giving seduces us into believing that our "gifts" to God are ours to begin with. The truth is just the opposite. Everything we have is a trust from God. Everything. A stewardship ethic is based on giving to God a portion of what is yours. A trusteeship ethic is based on receiving for oneself a portion of what is God's. And that's why we need a theology of receiving.

I remember one of the first songs I learned at Pine Grove Camp Meeting (a Free Methodist camp meeting at Saratoga Springs, New York):

He owns the cattle on a thousand hills,
the wealth in every mine.
He owns the rivers and the rocks and rills,
the sun and stars that shine.

The music was dreadful; the theology was flawless. God owns everything: the cattle, the car, the IRA, the TIAA-CREF. You and I own nothing.

Not even ourselves. Who owns you? Does your job own you? Do your "possessions" own you? Do you own you? Or does God own you? To render to Caesar what is Caesar's, and to God what is God's, doesn't mean that what Caesar gets isn't God's.

We prove our nonownership when we die. You can't take it with you because it isn't yours to begin with. Jesus' words to the rich young ruler—"You must give it all away"—are words Jesus speaks to every one of us (compare Matthew 19:21). None of us gets out of life without giving it all away—to someone, somewhere, somehow. We leave as bare as we came.

Trustees are the legal entities of an institution or estate. Trustees "own" nothing. But they are legally accountable for everything. An estate trustee is judged not by the question, what percentage do I give away of what is mine? but by the answer to the question, what percentage do I receive for myself so that the estate might grow and prosper and do good? A trustee ethic begins with a theology of receiving and ends with a theology of giving.

Giving It All Away

In many Native American cultures, the *potlatch,* or giveaway, was at the heart of their economic system. One gathered wealth not to accumulate for oneself but to give it away and invest it in others. The richest person in any community was the one who gave the most away. Only a theology of receiving can get the postmodern church beyond a tithing system's 10-percent tip to God (what waiter is honored by that gratuity anyway?) and toward a *potlatch* discipleship.

In 1999 my wife and I finally concluded our nine-year authorship of a preaching resource called *Homiletics.* It amounted to twenty-five double-spaced pages of fresh material a week, fifty-two weeks a year. That's over a thousand pages of original copy a year. When I first began this project, I tried to save the best material for myself. What I "gave away" to other preachers was what I didn't want myself or what I decided not to use. Only deadlines could rip away my most precious "stuff." But I clung with all my might for as long as I could.

Two things changed me into a "give it all away" *potlatch* disciple. The lectionary text for one Sunday included the manna story. The Israelites had to learn their absolute dependence on God for their *daily* food, trusting that God would supply their every need. I now refer to my writing of *Preaching Plus.com* as my manna project.

Erma Bombeck was a second influence in helping me get into a "give it all away" mode. Bombeck was often asked if she saved up her best ideas for the next column, or how she parceled out and dribbled out her best ideas. Before Bombeck died, she answered these queries in a column called "What's Saved Is Often Lost." I've never forgotten those words.

Thanks to the manna metaphor and the "what's saved is often lost" mantra, I went from hoarding my best stuff until the bitter end to leading off with my best stuff. Every issue of our new preaching resource, *Preaching Plus.com* becomes a manna experience.

A Useful Pair

Ever since my graduate school days, William Rainey Harper, biblical scholar and president of the University of Chicago, was one of my heroes. He was known as a fantastic fund-raiser. One evening before he gave a banquet address, he was introduced playfully as "the greatest beggar in the world." Harper got up to the podium, thought for a second, and said slowly: "I have never begged a dollar in my life. But I have given many people great opportunities for usefulness."

When I was president of United Theological Seminary in Dayton, Ohio, one of my favorite treks was to Columbus, Indiana. There lived Fran and Chuck, both in their eighties, who were major donors to the seminary. A couple times a year my job was to give Fran and Chuck a "great opportunity for usefulness." I would take them out to lunch and dinner, spend a pleasant afternoon telling stories about what was happening in the world of theological education, and work into the conversation my case for increased levels of support. Before I left in the evening to drive back to Dayton, I usually received a check for the annual fund. The first ones started out at $5,000. By the time I left United to go to Drew, their checks were in the amounts of $15,000 and $20,000.

United was one of their smaller charities. Fran and Chuck spent their last years having the time of their life. They sat on a back porch in Indiana and waited for the world to come to their door. And the world did. Heads of universities, ministries, and charities from around the world traveled to Columbus, Indiana. Some of the biggest names in education, the arts, and the church drove into an unassuming retirement community, spent the day with two enchanting individuals, and paid for all their meals. Fran and Chuck were besieged with gifts. Their walls were crowded with pictures of world leaders. Their calendar was crowded. They never cooked. Every day was different.

Fran and Chuck decided that they were in a time of life where they could live off a reverse tithe, no more than 10 percent of their income.

Give as you have received.
—JESUS
(MATTHEW 10:8 PHILLIPS)

Their goal was to spend as little as possible on themselves and to give away as much as they could on causes they believed in. Some of my peers were receiving checks of $50,000 or more when they came to call. Some got only $1,000. But here were an elderly couple whose last years were their best years because they got a theology of receiving right.

Freely, Freely

When I write a check or set up an automatic withdrawal or toss some cash into the offering plate, I am not disbursing my assets but God's. I am making a theological decision about how much to receive for myself of what is God's based on Jesus' admonition "Freely ye have received, freely give" (Matthew 10:8 KJV). How do we make this decision?

One thing to remember is that our God is an extravagant God (Ephesian 3:20; Philippians 4:19). God has lavished on us an incredible trust. Will you become God's trustee? Will you receive the estate God has in store for you?

I'm not ascetic. I don't romanticize poverty. I enjoy life. I champion an elegant spirituality.

"Elegant" is now a technical term among physicists used to advocate certain theories. To clinch a case, they say, "It's an elegant formulation." By this they mean that it is internally consistent, analytically comprehensive, coherently polished, beautiful of design and expression, respectful of mystery, and capable of engendering wonder and awe.

Jesus champions for us an "elegant" life. We were meant to be well dressed in the universe. The messianic banquet features a menu filled with "good things": riches, richness, culture, art, beauty, jubilation.

"Pennyless at the Wishing Well"

Riches, like leeches, can suck your soul dry and leave you bloodless. Have you noticed the statistics? The richer people get, the stingier they become.

Ask any waiter. Who are the worst tippers? The rich.

Disciples ought to be the best tippers (especially at breakfast, when the bills are the smallest and the waiters work the hardest). Why not even tip exorbitantly every now and then? Tipping is a silent "inasmuch" witness. Besides, disciples need the discipline of giving something away every day—even if it is only a smile. Or time.

A woman with expensive rings all over her fingers showed John Wesley her hand and asked: "How do you like my hand?"

56

SoulSalsa

Wesley replied sweetly, "You have a beautiful hand, my lady," saying nothing about her jewels.

The beauty is in the hands, not the jewels. My holiness ancestors didn't wear jewelry. They used the money that they would have spent on jewelry to give to the poor. They believed that the adornments of the body muster no luster alongside the adornments of the Spirit. As a way of honoring my ancestors and living in their spirit, I wear no jewelry. In spite of what some book covers may portray (it's amazing what an airbrush can do), I have never worn and never will wear jewelry on my hands.

For a culture of greed diseased by success, the only line worth reading is the bottom line. But disciples don't live "by the numbers." Disciples live by the Spirit. Bottom-line living goes over the line.

There is no cause-and-effect relationship between well-off and well-being. Over the past thirty years, our material standard of living has skyrocketed, with no measurable increase in any standards of happiness or peace. Just the opposite. The verdict is now in. The studies are unanimous. The more you strive for success, fame, money, and power, the less likely you are to be happy. Even if you win the success, fame, money, and power, you lose. Living well is not the same thing as being well-off.

God wants us to receive for ourselves an abundance (John 10:10). In Luke 18:30 Jesus promises those who would abandon everything and follow him that they should receive "many times as much" (NIV) with respect to their earthly needs and human friendships. When we pray "Give us this day our daily bread," St. Jerome contends, we are not praying for a prison diet of bread and water but for an abundant supply of whatever it takes to make us good and faithful trustees. The word the Evangelists used for "daily" (epiousios) actually conveys, Jerome insists, the meaning of abundance (supersubstantialis). We can feel free to take from the trust far beyond what we deserve or need for mere subsistence.

A fuller definition of "abundance" is given in Proverbs 30:8, a key text in any theology of receiving. "Give me neither poverty nor riches; feed me with the food that I need" (NRSV). Or as another translation puts the last clause, "provide me with food sufficient for my needs" (AT). The ethical axis does not tilt either toward sparsity or superfluity. Its poles are at one end selfishness and at the other end obedience. Jesus does not call trustees to asceticism or to affluence; Jesus calls his trustees to obedience.

At God's Table

The ethical axis in a theology of receiving is one of necessities versus luxuries, what I need as opposed to what I want, and when in doubt, erring on the Philippians 2 side of self-limitation and other-generosity because God tilts in the same direction. Clement of Alexandria compared a person's possessions to a person's shoe size. Possessions must fit the person—they will be cumbersome and uncomfortable if too large, painful if pinched.

Each soul has a different size. That is why, according to the parable of the talents (Matthew 25:14–30), inequality does not spell injustice. We all share as equals. But we are not all given equal shares. It is not wrong for one person to have more than another person, because each person has many different needs, some of them more costly than others.

The soul can be an expensive thing to grow. It may need books, music, art, travel, and beauty. Some souls even need opera. Jesus made all these things a part of the daily bread that we can receive freely.

Because God called the world good, the Hebrews believed that all of creation was to be enjoyed. They reveled in lots of children, animals, art, friendships, beauty, big parties, knowledge. When we get a taste of the new life in Christ, or what Paul referred to in Ephesians 3:8 as "the unfathomable riches of Christ" (NEB), there is an intensification, not a diminishment, of the colors of art, science, culture, and nature. The gospel of Jesus Christ gives us eyes to see new beauties in earth, sea, sky, and human experience. In the words of the old George Wade Robinson hymn:

Heav'n above is softer blue
Earth around is sweeter green;
Something lives in every hue
Christless eyes have never seen.

A colleague of mine is a world-class art collector and dealer. Few people in the church know of his global wheeling and dealing. He has an eye for beauty and has purchased the work of fledgling artists who went on to become some of the greatest artists of the twentieth century. Up until the late nineteenth century, America's religious leaders used to be some of the nation's major art experts and collectors.

The church is ideally the place where rich and poor will reconceive themselves in light of each other. It will end up being a place of abundance. Just as in the early church, churches today should have no poor among them. Its rich will have learned to recite the trustees' prayer—*God, help me handle possessions with a light touch*—and to live a life where not the one with the most toys wins but the one who bounces his or her last check wins.

You cannot serve God and money. But you can sometimes serve God better with money than without it. A disciple's theology of giving will not be based on guilt or scorn for possessions or some abstract principle of "unto the least." Rather, a theology of giving will be based on a spirit of compassion, love, and a trustee's accountability for creation and the common good, which has absolute preeminence over property and class.

Jesus invites all to come to his banquet. It is at the Lord's table that we get the right hungers—that we learn to hunger and thirst after righteousness.

We *do not* come to the table in a spirit of guilt that we in the West are 150 times richer than the world's poorest. Too many religious people want to pick up money without touching it.

We *do not* come to the table in a spirit of glee that we're so well off.

We *do* come to the table in a spirit of gratitude for the abundance God has entrusted to us.

We *do* come to the table with determination to see that we invest God's estate and our soul energies wisely so that others can share in the abundance God has promised for all.

Five hundred dollars can improve the standard of living of a family of five by 50 percent within one year. Ethicist Ron Sider has figured the total income of self-professed Christians around the world to be around $10 trillion. According to his calculations, if this one group donated just one percent of their income for microloans, the condition of the world's poorest one billion could be improved by 50 percent within one year. If microloans can have mega impacts, imagine the changes that a trusteeship ethic would make.

There need be no poor at God's table if more of us were to bounce our last check.

Giving up everything gives everything its significance.

1. In a Fortune magazine article entitled "Should You Leave It All to the Children?" the response by Warren Buffett—an investor worth a couple billion—is most interesting. He says that setting up heirs with "a lifetime supply of food stamps just because they came out of the right womb" can be "harmful" for them and is "an antisocial act." To him the perfect amount to leave children is "enough money so that they would feel they could do anything, but not so much that they could do nothing."

   What do you think? What does your will say about your values?

2. Sing the doxology "We Give Thee but Thine Own." What is the theology of this doxology?

3. Consider this quote from John Wesley:

   Gain all you can, without hurting either yourself or your neighbour, in soul or body, by applying hereto with unintermitted diligence, and with all the understanding which God has given you. Save all you can, by cutting off every expense which serves only to indulge foolish desire, to gratify either the desire of the flesh, the desire of the eye, or the pride of life. Waste nothing, living or dying, on sin or folly, whether for yourself or your children. And then, Give all you can, or in other words give all you have to God.

   Do you think you could live like this: make all you can; save all you can; give all you can?

4. The currency of the future is time more than it is money. Listen as David A. Cooper makes this case:

   In my late teens I had gained an insight that had proven enormously rewarding throughout the rest of my life. It was this: The most valuable commodity in the world is time. Other people work for material benefits; I worked to buy time. Things are of little consequence to me, except for life's necessities, while time is always precious. Thus my life's

SoulSalsa

pattern had been to work intensely for periods of one to three years, and then to give myself as much time as my savings would allow. This rhythm afforded me a wide variety of experiences, and an earnest exploration into the inner being. The result had been the ripening of an ever-growing faith that became the foundation of my spiritual development.

Is time a more precious commodity in your life than money? Are there time vampires in your life?

5. What can you do in your own life to maximize the amount of God's trust that you can distribute? Add to these ideas:

- Celebrate events with gifts of time and labor instead of high-priced presents.
- Make your own original clothing rather than buy designer outfits.
- Cook at home more and invite friends in to join the cooking.
- Drink from the same well: purchase from a common neighborhood pool high-ticket lawn implements and other items that everyone can borrow and share.

6. Can you guess what place money occupies among the most common sources of marital strife in the U.S. today? Check the source note in the back to find the answer.

7. To what extent have issues of possessions and clothing become less matters of status than identity?

It's silly to pretend that you can be talented and rich and not messed up. Usually, the three go together.
—Cher

5

Never Graduate

How can you graduate when the most basic meaning of the word *disciple* is "learner"? A disciple of Jesus is a lifelong learner. A disciple's hunger for truth is never satisfied. A pilgrim never quits the pilgrimage.

To be made in the image of God means we share intelligence with God. One of my favorite rebels in the history of the church was Cornelius Jansen (1585–1638), the founder of the Jansenist movement in France, which was ruthlessly persecuted in the eighteenth century. Much like John Wesley and the Methodists in England, Jansen took seriously our "shared intelligence" with the divine. In his opposition to the rationalist captivity of the Catholic Church, he read everything he could get his hands on, sometimes more than once. He aerated his mind with the complete works of St. Augustine at least ten times.

Jansen died my favorite death. He died after contracting a disease from the dust of old books.

This passion for learning, and for the knowing beyond knowing, is a direct inheritance from Jesus himself, who opened up along the shores of Galilee, not Oxford, the first "All Souls College." Jesus practiced learning as both a form and function of spirituality.

First, Jesus shifted us from a "teacher-teaching" model to a "learner-learning" model. To be sure, teaching something may be the best way of learning about it. And learning skills are teachable. But the shift from a teaching model to a learning model was so far ahead of its time that its implications are still being discovered today.

The postmodern learning model is lifelong self-directed learning (sdl). Sdl is more than moving from classroom-based learning to computer-based learning or multimedia learning or experiential learning or project-based learning. Self-directed lifelong learning is being free to assess our own needs and explore our curiosities, with direct access to resources to meet those needs, and with critical evaluative skills to assess how well we are doing. Self-directed learning is also knowing one's natural mode of learning—whether visual, auditory, or kinesthetic—and one's primary learning track.

Second, Jesus taught that whenever we discover truth, it is God who has taught us. No book is so bad that you can't get some truth out of it. No person is without some truth to teach us. No situation is without its truth. God is instructing us in the soul sciences and soul arts every second of every day.

That's why we should greet everybody as if they were the most creative, exciting people we had ever met. Because they are. They have something to teach us. After (or better, during) any of these schooling moments, I write my learning down on whatever is handy—newspaper, envelopes, gum wrappers, Kleenex, skin. At the end of the day my pockets get emptied of my "treasures," and my "treasures" are banked into their interest-bearing files (computer, manila) or notebooks. I have yet to do what Henry David Thoreau did one day when he forgot to bring his notebook on his walk: he stripped off some birch bark and used it for paper instead. But Thoreau was right: "The writer who postpones the recording of his thoughts uses an iron which has cooled to burn a hole with."

One's life begins to slope downward when one becomes an "expert." Postmodern pilgrims are not "experts" in anything. Pilgrims are students of everything and everyone. Pilgrims never graduate. We are students sitting lifelong, and one day eternity-long, at Jesus' feet.

Moon's Eye

Postmodern culture is altering forever what it means to *know* something. In classical physics one could "know" something by taking that thing apart and achieving distance from it. The modern scientific method taught us to look at things with a moon's eye, unblinking and remote. But now the postmodern scientific method of "knowing" something requires us to enter into a relationship with it, which in turn alters the character of what it is we are knowing. In other words, postmodern scientific "knowing" is much more what the biblical world understood by "knowing" than it is what the modern world understood.

The first person to challenge my moon's eye reading of the Scriptures was biblical scholar Walter Wink. His declaration of bankruptcy for much of Sunday School Bible study can be found in his book *The Bible in Human Transformation: Toward a New Paradigm for Biblical Study* (1973). Wink's critique of the ways in which Bible study has become intellectual and cognitive, separating "theory from practice,

Every natural object is a conductor of divinity.

—JOHN MUIR

mind from body, reason from emotion, knowledge from experience," is as timely today as the day it was written.

When my brothers and I reached the age of five, my mother enrolled us in Bible Memory Association (BMA), a twelve-week Bible memorization program founded by Dr. W. A. Woychuck. A "hearer" appeared at our house every Friday evening. If we recited to the "hearer" the assigned verses without error, we were granted special weekend privileges. If we were able to recite all 144 verses perfectly at the end of twelve weeks, we got a free week at a summer BMA camp.

In the nine years I was in this program I learned a variety of memorization techniques that helped me get through college, seminary, and graduate school. I no longer need this ditty to remember the gospels:

Matthew, Mark, Luke, John;
hold the horse while I get on.

But I still can't name the twelve disciples (or my ABCs, for that matter) without singing them.

It was only after many years of struggling with the Scriptures that I learned to read the Bible like Ezekiel. During his call to become a prophet, Ezekiel was handed a written scroll and told to eat it: "Son of man, eat what is offered to you; eat this scroll, and go, speak to the house of Israel" (Ezekiel 3:l RSV). This is what it used to mean to "read" a text: to "eat" it and make it one's own.

I know of no more powerful image than this of the necessity of the Scriptures being digested within one's being and circulating throughout one's life to modify everything one thinks and does. It is one thing to memorize a biblical story; it is quite another for that memorized text to morph into a memorialization of one's own personal experience.

We've got a problem when only 11 percent of those who call themselves Christians read the Bible. I am obsessive about reading a portion of Scripture every day. It doesn't have to be a long passage. I don't have to swim the Channel every day. But at the very least I do have to get my feet wet daily.

All of us are obsessive-compulsive about something. Charles Dickens was obsessive about always facing north when writing. Why can't postmodern pilgrims be obsessive about a daily dip into God's Word? The Scriptures are our very staff of life.

The founder of the Navigators, Dawson Trotman, offered a "handle" on how to integrate Scripture into our daily lives. He suggested we look at our hand and its five fingers as symbolic of how God's Word comes to us: hearing, reading, studying, memorizing, and meditating. Regardless of which five of the fingers one uses at any one time, with-

SoulSalsa

out taking stock of scriptural passages and patterns, visions and vibrations, one cannot achieve true intimacy with God. Postmodern pilgrims swallow *The Book*—hook, line, sinkers, and stinkers.

Postmodern learners also must be content to "know in part" (1 Corinthians 13:9), to embrace a theology of the dimly seen, and to "speak of things we do not understand" (see Job 42:3) if we are not to come down with a case of arrested spiritual development, premeditated theology, or premature piety.

When novelist Gertrude Stein famously said of Oakland, California, "There is no 'there' there," she was not registering a commentary on her hometown but was recording her dismay that the house in which she was born had been torn down. All her familiar landmarks had changed.

It's only gotten worse. Less than twenty-five years after the first test-tube baby (1978), we are now living in a world where a woman can give birth to her own grandchild, people can have children after they have died, a child might have as many as five "parents," and an aborted fetus is the biological mother of a child. It can only get stranger when, according to futurist Graham T. T. Molitor, "the world's fund of information is doubling every two to two-and-a-half years. Scientific information doubles every five years, and scientific knowledge doubles every ten years. Literature doubles every ten to fifteen years; scientific articles double in four to five years.... As much as 97 percent of world knowledge will be accumulated over one person's lifetime."

We are living in perfluity, awash in a gulf of information that is now only a small sea compared to the ocean it will be for our twenty-second-century kids. The future is not in electronics but in photonics. Forget "Moore's Law," which has microchip power doubling every eighteen months. The new law is "the Law of the Photon," which says that bandwidth (the carrying capacity of a communications line) triples every year.

The explosion of bandwidth among electronic information vehicles—cable TV and cyberspace—has extended the central nervous system of the human species to the point where we are able to process huge amounts of information at blinding speeds. In spite of all the "drowning" metaphors, fewer than one in three say they are suffering from information overload, and more than two-thirds are happy with their multiple information sources and wouldn't change anything.

Robert Metcalfe is founder of 3Com and the discoverer of "Metcalfe's Law," which states that a network's value increases exponentially as the number of users on the network increases geometrically (Utility = users^2). Metcalfe predicted in 1996 that the Internet was a fad

> Progress is impossible without change; and those who cannot change their minds cannot change anything.
> —GEORGE BERNARD SHAW

Never Graduate

65

and would crash. He later was forced to eat his words (literally—the column in which he wrote those words).

In this kind of a world, how can anyone ever graduate from anything? In that kind of world there *is* a substitute to experience. That substitute is constant learning. Nobel laureate F. A. Hayek was once asked why he didn't review John Maynard Keynes's *General Theory of Employment, Interest, and Money* (1936). There was no point, Hayek replied. "By the time I would have finished my review, he would have changed his mind." Ironically, the two places least likely to change their mind, make changes, or turn something off are the two major seats of learning: the worlds of academe and the church.

Some futurists are estimating that 95 percent of the jobs today's high school students will hold in their lifetime have not even been invented yet. Here are some of the job titles of the future, according to Danish futurist Rolf Jensen:

- Director of Mind and Mood
- Vice President of Cool
- Chief Imagination Officer
- Creatologist
- Intangible Asset Appraiser
- Director of Intellectual Capital
- Visualizer
- Assistant Storyteller
- Chief Enacter
- Court Jester

In a world that is constantly changing, one cannot prepare for careers, only competencies. The best one can do is to keep on the cutting edge of one's own area while learning new skills in other areas.

It is the same with spiritual intelligence. We are always in a state of growing "in the grace and knowledge of our Lord and Savior Jesus Christ" (2 Peter 3:18). Each of the stations of my pilgrimage occasions restless insights into the divine that are fluid. Not fixed, not flexible, but fluid. I boast no immaculate perceptions. My favorite philosopher (Cicero) hated the secret ballot. My favorite Protestant Reformer (Luther) hated Copernicus. No one gets everything right. To wield the sword of the Spirit—which is more powerful than any physical sword—is to brandish a blade that cuts both ways: it heals us at the same time it cuts away our divine pretensions and human arrogance.

One of the rules of the Benedictine order is to convert continually. Pilgrims must always be open to change, to turn and re-turn constantly so that, in the words of my friend Landrum Leavell III, "the Son is in your eyes."

In 1999 John Stanford, the superintendent of the Seattle school system, was brought down by leukemia. But before his death, he inspired the people of Seattle to believe in the public school system again, and to work to change it. When people asked him how he was doing, or how the schools were faring, he would say, "Perfect—and improving."

When people ask, "How goes the state of your soul?" or "How's your walk with God?" is there any better response than "Perfect—and improving"?

Being a Mysterian

I am a mysterian. The word *mysterian* is a recent coinage of the American philosopher Owen Flanagan. Its technical meaning is the espousal of the position that no physical theory can ever solve the riddle of consciousness. I use the word in a much looser sense: there are some aspects of life that never yield to scientific investigation. Or in its most precise looser formulation, a mysterian believes in the paradox that the more we know about life, the more we know we don't know.

I read the sciences like a scientist. They have their truth. But the truths of life are deeper and more complex than the truths of physics or the truths of biology. The notion that science is the truth, or is the path to truth, was the greatest heresy of the modern world. It is what led Thomas Paine to announce in 1793 that the discovery of a plurality of worlds "renders the Christian system of faith at once little and ridiculous and scatters it in the mind like feathers in the air."

Quite the contrary. Biblical faith is built on the assumption of a plurality of worlds—heaven, earth, hell—and a plurality of worlds within worlds ("in my Father's house are many mansions," John 14:2 KJV reads, and "hell has as many mansions as heaven does," comments Drew Professor Lynne Westfield). If the God who created the Milky Way, which boasts 100 billion stars, also created billions of similar galaxies that make up the universe, it seems almost incredible to imagine that there aren't other forms of life out there. While the theological implications of the search for extraterrestrial life are significant, the notion that any scientific discovery, even this one, can negate faith is a condescension truly breathtaking.

As any reading of Galatians makes plain, Jesus' work of redemption has as much to do with saving humanity for a new future as it does with restoring humanity to a lost past.

A single word even may be the spark of inextinguishable thought.
—*Percy Bysshe Shelley*

N e v e r   G r a d u a t e

Leaders "Must Be Readers, Perceivers, Sensers, Listeners, Observers, and Internet Surfers"

The magic of learning will be different for everyone who strives to live soulfully. There is no one formula for keeping the soul's firepower fully loaded. In fact, that is the magic of leadership. And no magician tells his secrets. Always keep it a mystery how you are able to do what you do. When the mystery is gone, the magic goes with it.

But there are some things all of us can do to keep the soul on the edges of learning. The most important of which is to learn without ceasing.

Until the Renaissance, every room in a house was public, including the master bedroom. The concept of a "study," a private space for studious leisure, was an Italian invention made famous in part by scholars like Machiavelli, who would ceremoniously robe before entering their *studio* to stand on the shoulders of those who had gone before.

When I commune with the ancients in my hexagonal cave annex to Dolphin Cay, I light candles. But in many ways every space where I can open up a book, magazine, or my IBM ThinkPad is my "study." Since most of my learning takes place on the road, airline terminals are probably my most-used *studio*. My biggest problem in these mobile *studios* is finding (and sometimes fighting over) the electrical outlets at terminal gates. I can only imagine what rage led one road warrior to rig an outlet at Terminal A in Atlanta to explode when the next person (who happened to be me) plugged his computer into it.

My spiritual forebear, John Wesley, argued for an intellectual backing to belief that required five hours of study a day. I try to follow the same rule of thumb, spending five hours out of the twenty-four every day in study.

This study includes not just reading print (books, magazines, newsletters) but also listening to audio sources (radio, CDs, tapes, albums), watching video streams (movies, television, www), using software (CD-ROMs, computer games), and increasingly, spending time with a browser exploring a virtual library of spiritual resources on the Web. Internet technology is not somehow going to save the world, but it isn't going to destroy it either. The Web will be the urn that contains the world's memory. I have working in my office at Drew a home-schooled fifteen-year-old who is teaching me how to use the Net for online study and online courses. The Bible is right: a little child shall lead us into the future.

It requires self-discipline to utilize any of these media, especially when popular culture is involved, to build up reserves of learning, not just for entertainment purposes. But as Leith Anderson has pointed out, "Life-long learning is far more a mindset than a regimen. Life-long learning grows out of curiosity, inquiry, hunger for truth, fascination with ideas, interest in people and a personal discipline to choose intellectual exercise over intellectual satisfaction."

A good soul makes music. The role of a book, a movie, a CD, a word, an image is to give rhythm so the drummer is no longer distant and the music can start. Everything that exists can set the soul to singing. Since I am convinced we are living in a time when God is more active in the world than in the church, the music of my soul starts playing more often when I read a scientific treatise than a theological text. Bioinformatics is more a learning experience than systematic theology. The business magazine *Fast Company* sets my soul vibrating more powerfully than religious magazines or so-called spirituality newsletters. I have never failed to find something that changes the way I look at postmodern culture from an issue of *Utne Reader*. That's more than I can say for most religious journals.

Because of this massive inundation of learning, postmoderns need certain rituals that slow down the onslaught of information.

- Take learning vacations that immerse you in one subject. There is even a company now that will design a learning vacation for you—EduVacations, Inc.
- Make a point of reading the Bible all the way through once every five years.
- Resolve at least once a year to spend one week reading one book. Speed and field reading treat books as objects, not as subjects. Because I shudder to think of other authors reading my books as I read theirs, once a year I slow down my thirty-plus book intake a week to one book that I revel in and read every word of.
- Become a devotee of one literary magazine. Approach reading it as an intellectual devotion.
- We are living in a golden age of poetry, especially religious poetry. Become an acolyte and patron of at least one contemporary poet, and correspond with him or her. Most poets are starving for attention.

The Creativity Underclass

If the knowledge underclass is growing at an alarming rate—many of whom are CEOs and other top executives who don't know how to send e-mail much less understand electronic technology—how much more serious is the growing creativity underclass?

> We would rather be ruined than changed.
> —W. H. AUDEN

I just finished a live interview with a Dallas radio station. The liveliest topic of discussion for the evening was this: Why is there so little creativity in the church? Why is there a "crisis" of creative leadership in the church? How can people of faith, in a creative world designed by a Creator God and packed with creative people, do so little that is creative?

Creativity is not coming up with something new from scratch. Creativity is scratching something new out of the old. Only God creates *ex nihilo* (out of nothing). The rest of us create *ex complexio* (out of complex somethings). Oh, to be Adam and Eve, knowing that everything you said was being said for the first time and you weren't quoting anybody! Only our prime parents were blessed with original utterances. Everything said since then is a quote.

Walter Benjamin had a dream of writing a book that consisted entirely of quotations. In one way or another, every book ever written is Benjamin's dream come true: it consists entirely of things already said somewhere at sometime by someone. The creativity is in the assembling and disassembling, the twists and turns and odd juxtapositions that make something old become new and original.

Leonard Bernstein had a favorite story about Beethoven's creativity. The ending of the first movement of his Fifth Symphony was giving him trouble. He had a long ending, but he decided it was too long. He had a much shorter ending, but he decided it was too short. The mark of his creative genius was that he did not compromise between the long and the short endings; he opted for something even shorter. Creativity is in the unlikely, the unexpected, the startling choice.

One of our tradition's greatest antagonists lived in the second century. His name was Celsus. He based his whole attack on the charge that Jesus wasn't an original thinker but an audacious plagiarist. Jesus stole his best ideas from Plato, Celsus said, and then soiled and spoiled what he stole.

Celsus was partially right. Much of Jesus' teaching was not original. Want to talk about the originality of the Lord's Prayer? You can find almost exact parallels to each of its six petitions in some Jewish source. The originality of the Lord's Prayer is not in Jesus' choice of words but in the order, brevity, and synthesis of its design. The originality of Jesus was in the way the teachings of his ancestors lived and evolved in him. Jesus lived these teachings and reworked them for the first-century world.

To be sure, there is a thin line between robbery and reference, between burglary and shopping. The most famous metaphor in modern literature, the "waste land," T. S. Eliot stole from Madison Cawein, a Louisville, Kentucky, poet who used to walk around the vacant lots of the city. In January 1913 Cawein published in the Chicago magazine *Poetry* a poem called "Waste Land."

A friend of Mark Twain's pointed out to him that Twain's dedication to *The Innocents Abroad* was similar to the dedication in a book by Oliver Wendell Holmes. Twain realized he had read Holmes's book years earlier and that it had made a big, if subconscious, impression.

Years later he spoke at a dinner honoring Holmes's seventieth birthday. Twain recalled:

> Of course I wrote Dr. Holmes and told him I hadn't meant to steal, and he wrote back and said in the kindest way that it was all right and no harm done; and added that he believed we all unconsciously worked over ideas gathered in reading and hearing, imagining they were original with ourselves. He stated a truth, and did it in such a pleasant way ... that I was rather glad I had committed the crime.

As someone said long ago, the only thing original about each of us is original sin. It is that awareness that enables me to say with Thomas Jefferson, in my favorite quote about growing a soul from the learnings and leavings of others: "He who receives an idea from me, receives instruction himself without lessening mine; as he who lights his taper at mine, receives light without darkening me."

It was partly this notion of the mutuality of learning that prompted the tradition of the *havruta* in Jewish learning settings. Traditionally Jews do not study alone. They are assigned a study partner who functions as a sounding board, another voice of the tradition that checks and balances one's own inclinations, and who contributes both intellectual insight and spiritual formation to one learning journey.

A sign before a long bridge in Florida reads: "It is against the law to run out of gas on the bridge." It ought to be a law to run out of creativity and spiritual energy before making it to the other side.

It is better to seek shelter in the shadow of a big tree.

—*JAPANESE PROVERB*

1. Join the conversation on Meta at http://www.meta-list.org/. Meta is an edited and moderated listserver and news service dedicated to promoting the constructive engagement of science and religion. Subscriptions are free.

2. For inspiration, read a few of the "Autodidact Profiles" on the Web site of Autodidact Press (http://www.autodidactic.com/profiles.htm/). It will show you what self-taught men and women can accomplish.

3. Grab a Bible and start flipping through the Gospels to find different ways that Jesus taught those of his day. Make a list of as many different techniques as you can find. Here are some passages you might want to come to roost on for a while: Matthew 13:10–17; Mark 12:41–44; Luke 9:18–20; Luke 22:17–20.

4. Albert Einstein, after fleeing from Hitler and settling in the U.S., said that he had constantly "to guard against becoming superficial in thought and feeling: it lies in the air here." What are you doing to make sure you breathe different air?

5. What are the advantages of adopting a group model of Bible study? Why is it important for each of us to test our interpretation of Scripture against that of others?

6. Thomas Jefferson was right: "I cannot live without books." But the days are long gone when the oft-quoted remark (1869) of Sir Thomas Phillipps, "I wish to have one Copy of every Book in the World!!!!" could be greeted with anything but laughter. Nineteenth-century British prime minister William Gladstone built up a personal library of over eighty thousand volumes. At his death in 1833, Richard Heber had amassed a library estimated to contain between one hundred fifty thousand and two hundred thousand volumes.

   What is your personal library like? Where is it in your house? Do you separate your books from your tapes, CDs, etc.? Why?

To what sources of information (magazines, e-newsletters, etc.) do you subscribe?

How well do you know the services your public library provides?

7. Draw a diagram with you in the middle. Label arrows pointing toward you that represent sources of information. Label arrows pointing outward from you representing your outlets of creativity. How can you increase the inflow of ideas and the outflow of creativity?

8. At Virginia Tech, some professors have created "The Cave" where learners can walk around inside a molecule. What can your church do to make learning more auditory, visual, or kinesthetic?

> Everything has been said before, but since nobody listens, we have to keep going back and beginning all over again.
>
> —ANDRÉ GIDE

6

Do Dirt and Do the Dishes

SOUL ARTISTS KNOW WHEN TO GET INVOLVED IN THE
"DIRT" OF LIFE AND WHEN TO COME CLEAN.

Postmodern pilgrims like to get dirty.

In a world that puts the "dirty" out of sight—in sinks, in dishwashers, in disposals, in cans, in hampers, in nursing homes, in jails, in human landfills called urban ghettos—Jesus' followers turn this world upside down.

To be healthy is to do dirt. Germ-free, squeaky clean is not healthy; it's sickening. Germ-free environments are dangerous to your health. When we separate ourselves from whence we came—the dust of the ground—we debilitate ourselves.

Some attribute the rise in "friendly fire" diseases—such as asthma, rheumatoid arthritis, type I diabetes, and other autoimmune diseases—as due to our aversion to grime and germs. The "hygiene hypothesis" argues that we need microbes to develop our immune system. And where do microbes live? In the bacteria within us that keep us alive, and in the soils and streams all around us. To send our children out into those streams and soils and tell them to "get dirty" is preventive medicine.

Some of my most vivid memories from my growing-up years are of standing at our kitchen's "soil and stream." As soon as I could stand on a chair, my mother conscripted me for sink duty. This involved more than clearing the table and scraping, washing, drying, and putting away the dishes. It involved Mother's handling each dish, placing it carefully in my little hand, and telling me its story—who owned it, how it got chipped, how she inherited it, why Dad bought it. Mother didn't wash the dishes; she valued them. Mother didn't dust the furniture; she narrated it. Mother didn't sweep the porch; she surveyed it.

The Sweet kitchen was a laboratory of the spirit. Doing dishes was a spiritual exercise connecting us to our ancestors and transmitting to us our stories. We learned the feel of a dirty dish, the feel of a clean dish, the feel of a dish that was used by Grandmother. Doing dishes was doing relationships.

In Praise of Stuff

The Sweet household didn't have a lot of "stuff." I was born on a street known as Hungry Hill, named for the numbers of poor living there. There is an old saying: "If you have to be poor, have the good sense to be poor when everyone else is." We were the working poor—too proud to ask for welfare but dependent on the generosity of welfare recipients for government-surplus cheese, sugar, etc.

This is the problem with "plastics," the archetypal modern material: it has no social life. You don't develop relationships with plastics, partly because you don't clean plastics. You polish silver. You wax wood. You burnish brass. You wipe off wallpaper. You scour porcelain. You do nothing with plastics. You can't even repair plastics. Plastics repulse relationships.

Partly because plastics contain the new information (computers, medicines, TVs), postmoderns surround themselves with the old. The old is authentic and social; the new is pseudo and unfriendly. Ask anyone who has walked into our home on Orcas Island or my "hoffice" in Morristown, New Jersey. They will tell you they stepped into an 1890s time warp of high Victoriana. Those who have attended our island and mountain advances testify to having had an ancient-future experience.

After having denigrated material culture forever, scholars are now beginning to study it and discern its ways. It's time someone offered a good word on behalf of artifacts. There is a vast difference between being an accumulator and being a collector.

The difference is threefold.

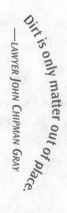

Dirt is only matter out of place.
—*Lawyer John Chipman Gray*

FIRST, A TRUE COLLECTOR
GATHERS STORIES, NOT STUFF

If something doesn't have a story, it's not worth having. How many homes have you entered that feel sterile, antiseptic, soulless? The ceilings and walls may be well furnished, but the space is empty.

The rule of the Sweet house is this: when you clean something, if you can't tell a story about what you're cleaning, get rid of it. Surround yourself with stories, not with stuff. A disciple should feel free to populate life with "things"—provided those "things" are hallowed with memories, packed with stories, and charged with mission.

SECOND, A TRUE COLLECTOR ACCUMULATES BY DESIGN AND THUS IS MORE INTERESTED IN QUALITY THAN QUANTITY OR NOVELTY

The J. B. Phillips translation of the Lord's Prayer says, "Give us each day the bread we need." This forces us to ask, "What do I really need?" and "How much do I really need?" The answer to those questions will be different for everyone, but they will be godly answered only when we die to self and live to mission.

How do you die to self in a self-obsessed, self-esteem culture? How do you never forget the Godness of God in a culture of "god games" *(Sim City 3000, Populous, Alpha Centauri)* where you preside as a god over your city, world, universe? Once a god-game generation has tasted power and comes to think that nothing is impossible for them, how do they believe that it is only with God that all things are possible?

"Know thyself" has been made into a mandate of self-recovery. It began as a mandate of self-discovery where we learned by such examination our need to be humble and eschew pride and never to forget the Godness of God. Every time I look into the mirror, I say to myself these words: "You're not it." To a culture that tells me "You're God. You're God," I need to look myself in the mirror and declare, "God is God. You're not it."

It is all too easy to slip into unholy living. What threatens to capsize us in life is less the big wave than a host of small swells—temptations, irritations, and distractions. So instead of a list of things to do, I have an S.O.S. list: a list of things not to do, a Surrender-Obey-Serve list. I am going through life with some small, humorous goals that keep my feet to the fire, my hands to the plow, and my heart in God's heart. When I die, I want to be able to say I

1. never bought a state lottery ticket (church "lotteries" of hand-made quilts are different)
2. never stole a hotel towel
3. never watched the program watched by one-fifth of the people in the world: *Baywatch*
4. never felt bound to answer every question
5. never gave in to the allure of owning a luxury automobile (I admit to Jaguar lust)
6. never used an ATM machine
7. never saw a slasher movie
8. never ate at Hooters

Do not make room for the devil.

—Paul (Ephesians 4:27 nrsv)

SoulSalsa

THIRD, A COLLECTOR USES "THINGS" AS RESOURCES, NOT AS ENDS IN THEMSELVES

What pitcher Jim Bouton said about baseball when he retired is what many people aren't saying about their relationship with material things: "For years you think you're gripping the ball when all along it's gripping you." Every person reading these words has ample evidence of what happens when being becomes owning, when loving becomes controlling, when knowing becomes showing, when means become ends, when gripping becomes being vice-gripped.

Postmoderns soothe the soul by shopping. The "retail therapy" of shopping when depressed actually works—for a night. But jadedness and judgment come in the morning. There are certain things we can do to make sure what we purchase is a resource for mission, not a therapy or an end in itself:

- Practice inconspicuous consumption. Don't buy things that will get a lot of notice.
- Go through catalogs, mark the things you want, then stack those catalogs in a pile and don't go back to them for a month.
- Take your name off holiday catalog mailing lists.

Christ alters the character of our dirt and how often we deal with our dirt. The story is told of a peripatetic rabbi who was walking with some of his disciples when one of them asked: "Rabbi, when should a man repent?"

The rabbi quickly replied: "On the last day of your life."

"But," protested several of his disciples, "we can never be sure which day will be the last day of our life."

The rabbi smiled and said, "The answer to that problem is very simple. Repent now."

The New Testament gives the same advice: "Let not the sun go down on your dirt" (see Eph. 4:26). When the writer of Hebrews reminds us to "lay aside every weight, and the sin which doth so easily beset us" (Hebrews 12:1 KJV), he is really saying, "Do the dishes." Paul offers the same advice: when testifying to the dirty dishes strewn all over the church at Philippi, he speaks of "forgetting those things which are behind" (Philippians 3:13 KJV).

Down and Dirty, Up and Clean

No disciple can claim to be free from dirt. There is not one who can boast: "I'm too neat to get dirty." And there is not one who can legitimately claim, "I'm too nice to have to deal with dirt."

> **Look in the mirror before you look out the window.**
> —CHRIS SEAY OF UNIVERSITY BAPTIST CHURCH IN WACO

Author Steve Smith tells of a man who lived a "safe" life. He decided not to love too much because love cost too much. He decided not to dream too much because dreaming only brought disappointment. He decided not to serve too much because serving got your hands filthy and got you in trouble.

When he died, he presented his life to God—undiminished, unmarred, and unsoiled by the messiness of a fallen world. He proudly said, "God, here is my life!"

And God said, "Life? What life?"

Dirt is a by-product of godly living. My study is dirty, littered with the debris of dashed ambitions and smashed projects. Jesus gave us a sacrament of failure when he told the disciples to shake the dust off their feet when leaving an unreceptive town. I've been shaking dust off my projects ever since I learned about this sacrament.

Dirt is generated not just by our lifestyles but by souls in mission. Even good intentions are begrimed. Our best foot forward has something in it to be forgiven.

Sometimes it takes a historical perspective for us to see what needs pardoning. In 1712 the Society for the Propagation of the Gospel (SPG) was bequeathed a plantation called the Codrington estates on the island of Barbados. It was known as one of the most progressively run plantations with respect to its treatment of slaves. The trustees gave the slaves Saturday afternoon and evening off to work in their own gardens so that they would be free on Sundays for religious instruction and worship. It became the prime worldwide model of how slaves should be treated.

One of the first things the SPG managers did was brand the name "Society" on the chests of the three hundred slaves who worked there. How does this "prime model" look now?

In the same way as arrangements must be made to take care of the dirt that accumulates in our home, so also in our spiritual life there must be periodic spring cleanings to dispose of dirt properly. Self-righteousness is the foulest of the spiritual odors.

Our nation's greatest "American," Abraham Lincoln, said that "in politics, every man must skin his own skunk." Not just in politics are we called to do dirty jobs. No one likes to do chores, but everyone has to do them. Like Peter, we'd rather build tabernacles than change diapers or wash feet or take out the garbage.

A lot of us think nothing of asking God to take out our garbage. A lot of us are asking God to do things *we* should be doing. How do we keep clean while getting dirty?

One could mention here the obvious spiritual practices—prayer, fasting, meditation, etc. But the greatest "cleansing stream" I have found in my life is the Eucharist. First John 1:9 is a daily mantra for me. If we sin—and of course we all do, daily, maybe hourly—we can be forgiven just by confessing to God. But there is something about having to wash one's hand before one comes to the table, having to wash one's soul before one sits down with Jesus and handles the food and wine of our Lord and Savior (1 Corinthians 11:28). This is why the greatest spiritual masters of our tradition could never take the Lord's Supper enough.

It keeps us clean and fresh and honest.

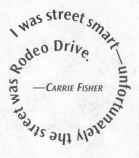

I was street smart—unfortunately the street was Rodeo Drive.

—CARRIE FISHER

> Everything in God's store is on the bottom shelf—you have to get on your knees to get it.
>
> —ROBERT COLLIER

1. Do you have an electric dishwasher? Just over half of all U.S. households do. Let yours sit for a week or a month and do your dishes by hand. Get to know each plate and cup and utensil. If you live with someone, share the task and use this time to talk. Or else use the time to listen to God tell you where your life is too dirty or too clean.

2. A missionary reported on an unusual service/pre-evangelism project: "Our group in Kumasi, Ghana, has been organizing cleanup projects. Before an evangelistic campaign, Christians ask government leaders if they can clean up the city. Then they go out in teams with makeshift straw-brooms and pails of soapy water to scrub the city before major outreaches."

   If all of us Jesus followers—right where we live—were to become more willing to deal with the dirt and muck of life, how might it change others' attitudes toward us and toward Jesus?

3. Raphael Carter got so disgusted with commercialization that he put tongue-in-cheek ads for a "Product Placement Bible" on his Web site (http:www.chaparraltree.com/oneshots/product.shtml/). See the revised stories of the three wise men, the feeding of the four thousand, and Psalm 23.

   What "dirt" caused by our hypercommercial days galls you the most?

4. In 1998 alone, more than 15 million WWJD (What Would Jesus Do?) bracelets were sold. Is this just the latest success story in selling what's known in the business as "Jesus junk"? Or is this a genuine outpouring of heartfelt piety that needed material expression?

5. Got young kids in your house? If so, instead of telling them a "once upon a time" bedtime story tonight, pick an interesting item in your house and tell your kids the true story that lies behind it.

6. Did you know there is such a thing as the Museum of Dirt? There is; it exists in "clean" cyberspace. Go to http://www.planet.com/dirtweb/dirt.html/. From there you can follow links that will let you see such things as the dirt in different celebrities' yards.

7. You've probably heard the camping motto "God made dirt, so dirt can't hurt!" Where does it apply beyond camping?

8. When did you feel the most spiritually "washed clean"? What would it take to get back that feeling now?

9. Career consultant Barbara Moses contends that "Never before has people's measure of worth and 'fitness' been so intimiately tied to their economic viability."* Do you agree? Is this reflected in the values of your friends and neighbors?

> Christians are not relevant in the mundane; how are we going to be relevant in the profound?
> —PASTOR ERWIN MCMANUS

cycle to church

SOUL ARTISTS LOOK OUT FOR THEIR PHYSICAL AND SPIRITUAL HEALTH.

We have two choices in life. We can look at the body, as the Upanishadic Hindu saint Maiatri did, as "an ill-smelling mess of skin, marrow, blood and mucus," a "bag filled with phlegm, feces, urine, wind and bile." Or we can look at our body as the "temple of the Holy Ghost" (1 Corinthians 6:19 KJV). Godly living makes the connection between body and spirit.

Each of the main words in the chapter title, "cycle" and "church," releases an Andromeda strain of radiant issues in the art of godly living. They remind us that postmodern disciples are concerned with both physical health and spiritual health—and aren't especially interested in separating the two.

I inherited from my grandfather a three-legged milking stool. Herbert Benson, president of the Mind/Body Medical Institute in Boston, recommends we think of health as just such a three-legged stool. One leg is pharmaceuticals. One is surgery. The third is self-care—nutrition, exercise, stress management, and faith.

My three-legged stool for health is a little different. One leg is God. The second leg is nature. And the third leg is medicine. The godly art of living soulfully puts all three legs of the stool on the ground.

I call these three stool legs of health the "pathways of the soul." If we would all cycle down these soul pathways, we'd be the healthier for it.

Soul Pathway 1 — God

It is now front-page news that those who go to church are healthier than those who don't. Weekly churchgoers have healthier immune systems than those who don't attend religious services. The curative and causative role of faith in healing is almost more accepted in medical circles than in theological ones. Georgetown University physician Dale Matthews, who wrote *The Faith Factor*, has personally brought to over thirty medical schools (one wonders how many divinity schools) the news that faith can lower your blood pressure, elevate your immune system, and help you live longer. Faith is an antibiotic for the spirit.

Years of sunbathing by my chief assistant, Lyn, led to a malignant melanoma that then entered her bones. She was given only a short time to live. Her sole hope was some experimental spinal treatments that could only be given in Europe.

At the same time I was praying with her about her decision to undertake such risky treatments, an eighteenth-century French prayer kneeler went up for auction at DuMarchelles in Detroit, Michigan. I put a ridiculously low bid on it and forgot about it. A month later they asked where I wanted it delivered.

I moved the *prie-dieu* into my office as a reminder of the key role that prayer and faith play in the healing enterprise. That kneeler still stands in my office as a witness to the healing power of prayer in Lyn's life. Of the first batch of six patients who received the experimental cancer treatment, Lyn is the only one still alive. She holds the world's record for the number of CAT scans performed on an individual within a five-year period. Although she has declined all invitations to appear on television with her doctors, she has agreed to be flown out to the Mayo Clinic and to London as a glass-case exhibit of this new treatment. But whenever she tells her story, she witnesses to the power of prayer in her healing.

Soul Pathway 2—Nature

The best brand name for medicine is Nature. God designed the human body to heal itself if it is properly taken care of. What comes from physicians and pharmaceutical companies are added bonuses to what nature provides.

Nature includes good fuel for the body (physically—food; mentally—thoughts; emotionally—feelings), good exercise, and daily swigs of vitamins and echinacea (downed with grapefruit juice) and coffee. That's right. Coffee.

Coffee is not a drug. Millions of dollars have been spent trying to discover the deleterious effects of coffee drinking. To no avail. If anything, the researchers are finding just the opposite. Drinking four cups of coffee a day reduces the risk of colorectal cancer by 24 percent. Coffee has more antioxidant activity than red wine, green or black tea, or orange juice. Simply smelling the aroma of coffee (which contains

Man eats too much. Thus he lives on only a quarter of what he consumes. The doctors, however, live on the remaining three-quarters.
—ANCIENT EGYPTIAN
PAPYRUS INSCRIPTION

about three hundred antioxidants) gives you the same health benefit as eating three oranges. I could go on and on. Besides, disciples of Jesus are protected by the "coffee verse" (Mark 16:18): if you live in the Spirit, you will be able to drink deadly poison and no harm will come to you.

In comparison with other religious traditions with their extensive food laws, a disciple of Jesus enjoys remarkable freedom about food. In the 107 New Testament references to "eat" or "eating," and the fifty-five references to "drink" or "drinking," a wide range of menus are on display. In fact, there is an Indian adage that anyone who eats everything must be a Christian.

This doesn't mean that eating, the most basic of human activities, isn't invested with soul significance. From a biblical perspective, what we eat and how we eat has more than social meaning; it also has spiritual meaning, as our signature dish of bread and wine reveals.

Both spiritually and physically, we are what we eat. In fact, the theme of John 6:51–58, where Jesus unpacks the meaning of his being the "bread of life," might be known as "You Are What You Eat."

If I heard this once from my mother, I heard it a thousand times. "Don't live to eat, eat to live." Stop eating as a hobby.

The ancient Greeks abhorred extremes. The two poles of life were what they called *enkrateia*, or self-control, and its opposite *akolasia*, excess. For the Greeks the key to life was living in the balance between them, summed up in the Delphic aphorism "Nothing too much."

My postmodern rule of thumb takes the Greeks one further: everything in moderation, including moderation. Practice everyday abstinence and self-control in one's eating habits. But every now and then, be "naughty" and eat what's bad for you. My mother called such naughty times "splurges." Mary Oliver speaks of our need to write into the poem of our lives a few "wild stanzas." Theodore Roszak calls these same periodic naughty episodes "sustainable extravagances."

The norm is moderation and fasting. The exception that proves the norm is periodic "naughtiness." Fasting is good for the body and soul. Clearly fasting relates to larger issues than meat and drink. "One does not live by bread alone, but by every word that comes from the mouth of God" (Matthew 4:4 NRSV). Fasting can connect us to those around the world who live with hunger every day. It is one thing to starve yourself (fasting); it is quite another to be starved by others or by forces beyond your control (famine). Both moderation and fasting can help us identify with those who have gone before us as well as what is going on around us, like the Irish grandfather of an anthropologist who told of a "famous Irish dish" named "potatoes and point." He described it this way: "One boiled up a pot of potatoes, then hung a bit of salt pork

SoulSalsa

on a string over the table. Then one stuck one's fork in the potato, pointed it at the salt pork, and ate the potato."

Daniel fasted not only from food and wine but from "lotions" as well (Daniel 10:3). We need a lot of different "fasts": image fasts, people fasts, sound fasts, etc. In fact, as Reinhold Niebuhr argued, if expressions of asceticism are absent, it is "proof of a lack of vitality in religion. A sun warm enough to ripen the fruits of the garden must make some fruits overripe."

But fasting is no way to go through life. Too many "spiritual people" live in constant fear of ecstasy. I myself suffer from "uplift anxiety." I can feel bad about feeling good and must continually remind myself that God created everything "good" and expects us to enjoy the goodness of creation.

The question becomes how to be "naughty" without endangering our soul or society or the planet. I haven't got it all figured out yet, but that doesn't stop me from every now and then vaccinating my soul with a "naughty night." I go out with friends or just with my wife and we're ostensibly, avowedly naughty. We pig out on barbecue or prime rib. We buy a bottle of wine. We spend too much money on a meal. We talk too much. We laugh too loud. We eat the dessert with the "devil" name prefixed to it.

When the "naughty night" is over, it's back on the wagon.

I have an annual ritual of my one ice cream cone. It's always the same flavor—the very worst-for-you flavor there is: coconut. But I get the biggest cone of coconut ice cream anyone will sell me and make myself sick on it. Once a year I have the biggest prime rib money can buy. I periodically overdose on fats and sugars. Then it's back on the wagon.

Everything in moderation, especially "naughtiness." Too many of us are too fat. It's not just Willard Scott who worships in "the church of Krispy Kreme." All those luncheon rendezvous at the "roach coach" and "yuck truck" food vehicles are taking their toll. For the first time in history, the number who are clinically overweight exceeds the number at or below normal weight.

What is more, the more religious the person, the more rotund the bodyscape. The most secular places in America are also the skinniest. Fitness physician Kenneth Cooper did a study of seventy-five different professionals—doctors, lawyers, accountants, etc. Guess which professionals were at the bottom of the list when it came to physical conditioning? Pastors. When a reporter asked Jerry Falwell about these findings, he replied, "I fit the mold. I don't think God gives a flip either way."

Not that I would know anything about these phenomena firsthand. At fifty, I have finally come to appreciate that clothes get smaller just from being in the closet. My hero is Thomas Aquinas (nicknamed "Ox" by his students), who weighed three hundred pounds.

But here's the clinker: religious fatties don't suffer the downside of their bad habits like nonreligious fatties. In other words, obesity among the spiritual doesn't have the debilitating physical downsides that obesity has among the nonspiritual.

Psychological factors like stress and depression have a greater impact on health-care costs than physical factors (smoking, obesity, blood pressure, etc.). The godly art of soulful living includes mastering nature's relaxation response: (1) repeat a beautiful thought for a period of time; (2) cleanse your mind and body, especially through "moodling" or exercise.

Living soulfully is a whole-body art. It matters little whether exercise is walking or wrestling, cycling or softball. The connections between the body and the soul, the physical and the imaginal are mysterious and deep.

The more sedentary one's lifestyle, the greater the risks of all sorts of diseases. Too many people expect some dippy *deux ex machina* to dive-bomb their lives and rescue them from the consequences of their laziness. As the human genome research is coming to a close, the rescuer-god is increasingly seen as science itself.

In spite of what health fascists insinuate, if we live long enough, we will get certain diseases. The oldest old males all have prostate cancer; the oldest old females all have osteoporosis; the oldest old males and females all have memory loss and heart disease. But exercise reduces our risk of disease and keeps us healthy and vital for as long as possible.

Soul Pathway 3 — Medicine

There are more than ten thousand known diseases, three thousand drugs to treat them, three thousand different radiology procedures, and eleven hundred available lab tests. Thank God for medicine. I am here today because of its healing presence in my life.

But the medicalization of everyday life has gotten to the point where basic human feelings and emotions, the by-products of everyday living, are being treated as "symptoms" of "illnesses" to be treated by feel-good pills and happiness-on-demand therapy. The rise in psychiatric services in the U.S. has been spectacular. In 1955 psychiatric services connected with only one percent of the USAmerican population; by 1980 it was 10 percent. By 1990 it was climbing toward 20 percent.

What is depression? Novelist William Styron, who knows firsthand the disease of depression, complains that the word *depression* has "slithered through the language like a slug, leaving little trace of its intrinsic malevolence and preventing by its very insipidity, a general awareness of the horrible intensity of the disease when out of control." Depression has become a medicalized name for problems of the human condition: common unhappiness, spiritual angst, "the winter doldrums," "a bad case of the blues." The reasons for our existential brooding, the cause of our lives being "out of joint" are too often finessed by Prozac, muffled with Valium, or stifled in lithium. Prozac sells at a million prescriptions a month, grossing $1.2 billion a year for Eli Lilly.

Let the example of depression serve as a cautionary tale for us. And yet medicine, properly prescribed and used, is an undeniable good. It's one reason survival rates for most kinds of cancer are climbing—in some cases, soaring. It's one reason why some diseases that used to strike fear into the hearts of our ancestors are barely remembered anymore. We can think Methusaleh in large part because of the achievements of the health-care industry. Along with the pathways of God and nature, medicine is a soul pathway that postmodern disciples should be prepared to cycle down.

Going to Church

Church is a word that used to convey the comforting image of little brown churches in the vale filled with box pews and holy smog. No more. Note the roads while you're driving to church some Sunday. Note how many people *don't* go to church. This doesn't include the numbers of people who still go but wish they didn't, or who go but not because they're drawn there by some mysterious fire. British novelist Barbara Pym, after a long, clichéd sermon that had fallen into mere formula, wrote in her diary that she wished she had the courage to give up church for Lent.

A few weeks before he took his life, former Methodist preacher Vincent van Gogh painted a picture of a church. It emanated a dimly eerie light from the inside, but it had no doors. There was no way in.

Van Gogh's *The Church at Auvers* gets my vote as the most haunting painting in the history of religious art. It is lobbed into our midst as a missile from the past to be a missal for the future. The disconnect between the language of devotion and liturgy and the way postmoderns perceive themselves and the world is alarming. Or as New Zealand theologian Michael Riddell puts it, "The church is inhuman in the dual sense of being cut off from the humanity of its own members, and being absent from the mass of humanity outside its doors." Will the church as we know it have a future?

Princeton sociologist Robert Wuthnow believes that the church of the twenty-first century will remain vital insofar as "it can provide people with a strong sense of community." But that is precisely what is at issue. The church increasingly is unable to sustain a sense of "community," at least a community "woven together in love" (see Colossians 2:2) with which postmoderns can connect.

M. Scott Peck, in his book *A World Waiting to Be Born* (1993), argues that most organizations aren't willing to take the steps to become communities and so remain "pseudocommunities." He's right. While the early church may have been a model of community, churches today are the hardest kinds of groups in which to build authentic community. Church is all too often a pretend community populated by pew-sitting toads.

This book is based on the conviction that God is releasing streams of living water on this planet. The floodgates of heaven are open and the latter rain is falling. God isn't so much creating a new church as a new world. What we are in the midst of now is more than a "reformation." It is more than an "awakening." We have no name for it because it is something totally strange and new.

In late springtime, high in the mountains, snows melt and form small threads of living waters that merge with others to create gushing streams that flow down to the flatlands. When they fill existing creek and river beds, it is called "renewal."

Sometimes the tributaries merge to form mighty rivers that over time cut wide swaths to the sea. When these waters run deep, it is called "revival."

On certain occasions and under special conditions, however, rivers overflow their banks. When there are heavy snowmelts and increased gushes, when rain has drenched the plains, floods occur. The riverbanks simply cannot contain the flow. In these extraordinary times, the course of the river will actually change. The flow of living waters cuts a new channel, leaving the old riverbed and moving across new ground, finding new paths to the sea.

This does not happen often. But it does happen. Because of the silts of self-centeredness and the dregs of despair, the old riverbanks simply cannot contain the outpourings, and new riverbeds are formed to channel the water. When God cuts a new channel for a new age, it is called "reformation."

What happens, however, when cataracts become cascades and downpours become deluges? What if the windows of heaven opened to shower the whole earth with "latter rain," a rain so heavy and unrelenting that it overflows all boundaries and covers the whole earth?

What does one call this new water world, this aquaculture, this soul-tsunami?

The church of the future, like Noah's ark of old, will be an outside-in church, not an inside-out church. It will be a part of what God is doing in the world, even when it doesn't understand what God is doing, and will help others to be a part of God's mission of creating this new world, this world with no name.

Unlike the church of those old riverbanks, this new entity will not do church for people. It will send them forth into these new waters to take responsibility for constructing their own spirituality in the biblical faith and unfurling the sails of their own souls. The church thus functions less as a guardian than a guide, less as port of entry than port of call. The aquachurch helps seafarers assemble and assimilate a vast range of resources (texts, images, commodities, rites, music) in the godly arts of living soulfully, rigging a Jesus sense of identity that can moor in multiple harbors, navigating a biblical course and spiritual direction that fits our wharves and world.

An aquachurch doesn't fit any prefabricated human mold but only God's mold.

A church like Steve Ayers's aquachurch, Hillvue Heights, in Bowling Green, Kentucky. A church that practices what I call "de-evangelism" (the churchly equivalent of Madison Avenue's demarketing). This is a church both condemned and celebrated as the last public space in the county where people can still smoke. Why? It's a church where people are trying to get their lives together—people who have smoked things a lot worse than cigarettes. It's a place where people who really need community can go and find help for rebuilding their lives and planting new ground for their souls to grow in.

This is a new world church.

This is a new world, church.

1. If you want to learn more about how to take care of your own health, check out the periodically updated health tips posted on the Web site of the Cooper Aerobics Center (http://cooper-center.com/). Kenneth Cooper is a Christian physician and the man who made aerobics a household word by writing a book with that as its title.

   For reliable public sources of health information, choose Healthfinder (http://www.healthfinder.gov/) or MEDLINEplus (http://www.nlm.nih.gov/medlineplus/).

2. Vincent Rossi says, "It is a law of creation that life must live on life. Consumption is that law in action in the natural world. Eucharist is sacred, sacramental, holy consumption: life feeding on Divine life for the sake of salvation and eternal life."

   Would you characterize your experience of Communion as living on the life of Jesus?

3. Tim Dearborn has suggested that the role of Christians is "as 'appetizers' for the world. We are to live in such a way that when the world bites into us, gets a taste of us, its appetite will be stimulated for more. We are to be hors d'oeuvres of the future kingdom banquet."

   In what ways have you been an appetizer for a spiritual seeker?

4. Julia Child, the TV chef, was asked by a journalist how she began her journey to becoming perhaps the world's favorite chef. Julia told how she and her husband, Paul, lived in France for seven years. "Early in the '50s," she said, "after one taste of French food—that unforgettable lunch—I was hooked. The wonderful attention paid to each detail of the meal was a whole new experience for me. But you don't just spring into good cooking full-fledged. It's like looking at a painting. You need background to know what you're looking at. I was thirty-two years old when I started cooking. Until then I just ate."

   One taste of life in Christ, and you can never be the same. Are you tasting the riches of the menu of discipleship? If not, you're not really living. You're only existing.

5. Be a visitor to a virtual art museum. Take a look at Van Gogh's *The Church at Auvers*, available at http://www.vangogh-gallery.com/painting/p_0789.htm/. How might your church seem doorless to the people in your community?

6. Why is church so unwilling to become community? M. Scott Peck outlines some stages that groups go through to reach community (although most do not). These stages he prefers to call:

   a. Pseudocommunity: a "stage of pretense" that pretends there are no differences that could cause conflict. Because this stage takes time and work, and is not easy or effortless, many never get beyond this stage.

   b. Chaos: this is when "profound individual differences" emerge, and chaos follows in the wake of trying to obliterate the differences. This stage can be self-destructive or a retreat to pseudocommunity. It means loss of control—giving up some control for sake of community.

   c. Emptiness: the "hard, hard work" when members work at getting rid of everything that is in the way of genuine community—"prejudices, snap judgments, fixed expectations, desire to convert, heal, or fix, the urge to win, the fear of looking like a fool, the need to control," or more personal "hidden griefs, hatreds, or terrors." It is a slow, painful process that requires open conflict and discussion—people must pass through the pain of intimacy; churches plaster over the pain rather than pass through it; we avoid pain at all costs.

   d. Community: often comes suddenly and dramatically, in a spirit of peace. "There is more silence, yet more of worth gets said. It is like music. The people work together with an exquisite sense of timing, as if they were a finely tuned orchestra under the direction of an invisible celestial conductor. Many actually sense the presence of God in the room." Community comes when people feel they can be "real"— they don't have to like one another but must care about each other.

   How does your church match up to the above considerations?

If God wanted me to touch my toes, He would have put them on my knees.

—T-SHIRT

7. Read Neil T. Anderson and Elmer L. Towns's *Rivers of Revival* (Ventura, Calif.: Regal, 1997).

8. To learn more about Steve Ayers's church, go to http://www.hillvue.com/. Or if you want links to this and several other aquachurches, go to the profiles page of my AquaChurch Web site, http://www.aquachurch.com/churches.htm/.

We go farther faster when we go together.
—Martin Luther King Jr.

SoulSalsa

8

Brush Your Tongue

SOUL ARTISTS TAKE CARE WITH INFORMATION.

There are some things doctors aren't going to tell you. Someone has to pass on this information. I'm just sorry it has to be me.

No one should use antiperspirants. If you must use something, supplement your deodorant with baking soda (Arm & Hammer) or sage (Weleda). Antiperspirants contain tetrachlorohydrex, which is like soaking your underarm lymph nodes in liquid aluminum siding.

No one should eat something from a kitchen surface without the surface having been cleaned with tea tree oil or citrus (both much safer than bleach and water or Microban). A microbiologist at the University of Arizona in Tucson demonstrated that people's toilet seats are one hundred times cleaner than their cutting boards.

No one should drink tap water. Drinking water is dangerous to your health without water filtration systems. Between 65 and 87 percent of all surface water in the U.S. contains the parasite cryptosporidium, and that's just to name one contaminant.

No one should wear light-colored, lightweight T-shirts in the sun. If you do, you might as well go bare-chested. There is no protection at all from the damaging effects of the sun.

Everyone should eat pizza. Pizza is health food, with or without the vegetables. Tomatoes are anticarcinogens, but only when the antioxidant lycopene is released, which happens only when tomatoes are cooked and laced with a little oil.

I could go on and on. But I think you get the picture.

There are two things no doctor told me, things I wish I had learned to do much earlier in life. The first is floss my teeth; the second, brush my tongue. Once you start flossing and brushing, you can't imagine how you lived life without them. Like strapping children in seat belts. How did parents manage all those years—and kids survive—without constraints?

Maybe if I had actually been told, it wouldn't have made a difference anyway. My preacher mom, Mabel Boggs Sweet, who continues to control my theological agenda from her grave, reared my brothers and me to save time, to monitor time, to resent time being taken away. All my life I've hated sleep. What an awful way to go through life—dead to the world! So I often sleep on the floor or in chairs. On the road, I don't go to bed, I go to sleep. Sleeping at attention, whether vertically or horizontally, reduces sleep time as dramatically as being cocooned in covers and pillows increases it.

My ears perk up when I hear that using a certain wrinkle cream can cut your shaving time by one-third. My hairs rise up at the unfairness of having twenty-three minutes of every waking day stolen from me by blinking. I fantasize about being able to reverse night and day schedules like Glenn Gould and Marcel Proust did. How much more could I get done?

But I have learned over time that the godly art of living involves taking the time necessary to take care of yourself and perform some rawly human acts. Like brushing your tongue. That little red rake may be the weirdest contraption you'll ever hold in your hand. But cleaning your tongue makes your mouth at least as clean as that of dogs. And it significantly reduces bad breath and the threat of heart infections that come from the buildup of bacteria in the mouth. That is what killed my favorite columnist/humorist with his coffin cough and tombstone teeth, Lewis Grizzard.

Since I have to invest the time to do it, I have made this physical exercise of brushing the tongue double as a spiritual exercise in information management.

Cat Got Your Tongue?

The tongue may just be the sharpest knife in the drawer. Every time I drag a brush across my tongue, I scour my soul with the words of the Miranda rule: "You have the right to remain silent, because what you say can and will be used against you." What do they mean?

The ancient wisdom is more true today than it was then: "If you can't find something nice to say about anyone, don't say it." My postmodern addition to this ancient version of the Miranda rule is this: "If you find out anything negative about anyone, think it and sink it." Do what Mary did when her world was rocked by some news: "Mary kept all these things, and pondered them in her heart" (Luke 2:19 KJV).

You can never be too busy, too tired, or too pressured not to always check the accuracy of the data that comes your way, and to greet every-

94

SoulSalsa

thing you hear with a healthy skepticism. If you don't "keep" and "ponder" before talking and proclaiming, you can inflict heavy pain and damages—whether to communities or careers or companies or yourself. I can make my lifespace full of inaccurate, inconsequential, inconsiderate garbage just like I can litter my front yard with garbage.

The World Wide Web is making it harder, not easier, to evaluate the quality of information. Which of the following do you believe? (1) Those studies that show the overall incidence of cancer increasing by 44 percent from 1950 to 1998? (2) Those studies showing that "cancer mortality rates have remained essentially flat for as long as they have been measured—all of the knowledge accumulated so far has not led to significant advances in treatment"?

And you wonder why I have a severe case of what John Betjeman called derisively "foot and note disease"? But even footnotes do not insure against being wrong-footed.

One of the most powerful weapons at our disposal, for good or ill, is the tongue. Honoré de Balzac once said that every day, in Paris, a paper with one hundred thousand subscribers was produced yet never printed—distributed by word of mouth.

One of my favorite medieval stories lets us listen in to a confessional. The sinner begins, "Father, I have sinned. I have spread a falsehood about someone. I need forgiveness."

The priest responds in traditional fashion: "On the basis of Christ's atoning work on your behalf and your repentance of sin, you are forgiven."

Then he continues, "But before you go, take this down pillow. As an atoning act of penance, cut it open and walk through the city spreading its feathers everywhere. Then return to me, and I will reveal your next penance."

The man faithfully follows the priest's instructions. He goes through the city, spreading feathers. Finally, he returns, asking what he is to do next.

"Now go," the priest responds, "and collect every one of those feathers."

The man protests, "It's impossible!"

At which the priest says, "You're so right. You are forgiven. But it is impossible to ever undo all the harm you've done with your gossip. Disaster follows upon disaster when information is not right. Read Ezekiel 7:26. And go and sin no more."

The New York Stock Exchange has recognized the power of bad information in its Rule 435. It is now illegal to spread rumors on the floor of the stock exchange, even when no overt fraud is intended. The perception in the business world is much more advanced than in the religious

I will condemn you out of your own mouth.
—Jesus (Luke 19:22 RSV)

world that nothing destroys community morale and group harmony faster, nothing rips apart the fabric of covenant more dangerously or drastically than bad information and rumor-mongering.

One of the biggest postmodern temptations is to use information as power. We live in a world where there are two major sources of power: economics and information. The less one has of one, the bigger one's need for the other. Hence our insatiable appetite for news—information about anything, anyone, anywhere—especially those noted for being noted, not the notables. The Nobel Prize-winning Mexican poet Octavio Paz died on the same day as Linda McCartney. Death notices and coverage were about ten to one. Not in Paz's favor.

Of course, we all need information, especially comparison information. Informal networks of information gathering are particularly powerful. But the impact of the mass media on traditional categories of information gathering has been enormous.

Gossip used to serve a communal function, drawing people together to reinforce shared values and norms. The word *gossip* derives from the Old English *godsibb*, which means "godparent" or, literally, "related in God." It came to refer to any friend or acquaintance of the parents of the baptized child or of the other godparents who had the privilege of talking with each other about the family to which they were mutually akin, and about its various members. The element of responsibility and accountability in this early understanding of gossip is what astonishes. The gossip performed critical functions of telling the stories of the family and passing on the stories of the tradition. Gossip aided in group problem solving. It was a coping mechanism for uncertainties and helped in anxiety and stress reduction. It provided structure for finding meaning in events. It was a means of showing interest in each member of the family. It showed a healthy mistrust of establishment versions and a probing for information beyond what was readily accessible.

And on top of all that, gossip had wonderful entertainment value. In other words, gossip was a primary resource in social exchange. This was the evangelism strategy of the early church. It was really a nonstrategy. They gossiped the gospel until the church spread like wildfire.

Or as Paul put it, they spoke truth in love.

The office "rumor mill" or church "grapevine" can still be useful in improving morale, productivity, job satisfaction. It all depends on whether these grapevines produce wine or vinegar, enhance communication or curdle it.

Mischief shall come upon mischief, and rumor shall be upon rumor; then shall they seek a vision of the prophet; but the law shall perish from the priest, and counsel from the ancients.

—THE SOVEREIGN LORD
(EZEKIEL 7:26 KJV)

Pander to Slander

Most gossip today is more vinegar than wine, less bridging gaps than widening them. Fascination with the number of Imelda Marcos's shoes or the amount of Michael Eisner's bonus or the size of Pamela Anderson's disimplants is not just the preserve of gross tabloids.

Vicious, malicious gossip is the postmodern equivalent of the persecution of witches. And Christians today can conduct as many witch-hunts as they did in the past. The amount of skulduggery in some churches and communities would make Salem proud.

Gossip is dictionary-defined as "idle chatter." In the best sense of the phrase, "idle chatter" is the same as "small talk." In the worst sense of the phrase, "idle chatter" is the same as "idol chatter." And the idol is oneself. The natural light of postmoderns is limelight.

Gossip has become a primary cultural device for forwarding one's self-interests. In this sense of "idol chatter," gossip is information that protects and promotes the godness of oneself. Boiled down to the bones, the most fundamental of human desires is not for sex; it is for control. Not surprisingly, Hitler had an almost Napoleonic obsession with detail. He was a total control freak. The advanced technologies of bioinformatics only increase our evil delusions that we're in control.

Gossip is the "idol chatter" of control.

If anyone ought to know the meaning of the commandment "Thou shalt not take the name of the LORD thy God in vain," (Exodus 20:7 KJV), it ought to be disciples of Jesus. We ought to know better than anyone that God cares about how we use names. By giving us his name, God put his reputation at risk.

Names have power. To attach someone's name to an idea or a cause or a report is to add or subtract power. Yet how loosely we use each other's names! To violate a trust by lifting the veil off that trust, to take anyone's name in vain in pursuit of our own gain, is to take God's name in vain. Your name, the reputation of who you are and for what you stand, is your most highly prized treasure. It is the hardest thing in the world to win. It is the easiest thing in the world to lose.

One of the classic lines in literature is Shakespeare's distinction between the theft of property and the theft of name:

Who steals my purse steals trash; 'tis something, nothing;
'Twas mine, 'tis his, and has been slave to thousands;

> **Gossip is a beast of prey that does not wait for the death of the creature it devours.**
> —DIANA WARWICK, HEROINE IN GEORGE MEREDITH'S NOVEL DIANA OF THE CROSSWAYS

But he that filches my good name
Robs me of that which not enriches him.
And makes me poor indeed. (*Othello*, Act III, Scene 3)

Satan is called "the prince of lies" for a reason. This is my spiritual ancestor's advice to a young disciple in 1772:

> Of all gossiping, religious gossiping is the worst: it adds hypocrisy to uncharitableness, and effectually does the work of the devil in the name of the Lord. The leaders in every Society may do much towards driving it out from among the Methodists. Let them, in the band or class, observe, (1) "Now we are to talk of *no absent persons*, but simply of God and our own souls." (2) "Let the rule of our conversation hereto be the rule of all our conversation. Let us observe it (unless in some necessarily exempt cases) at all times and in all places."

John Wesley recognized that the human inclination is to be more ready to share the scoop about others because we find it less threatening than sharing the inside scoop about ourselves. But Wesley also argued that disciples of Jesus are more likely to bare the truth about themselves than commit pious perjuries against each other.

Hearsay need not equal heresy. Gossip can be a way of building the body of Christ.

But only if we continually brush our tongue. Only if we're gossiping good news about each other, stories that enhance and benefit others, instead of juicing our conversations with squeezes of scandal.

False Accusations

What does a pilgrim do when he or she is falsely accused? Opposition and misunderstanding can come from within the Christian community even more than from the enemies of Jesus. Some people don't want to understand their spiritual brothers and sisters.

Let us keep brushing our tongue and trusting in God. Let us take care of ourselves and conduct ourselves with dignity. Even when the accusations knock us off course, let us remember that all detours are not only part of life's journey but can contribute to that journey.

We can be confident about two things in life. One is that in this world we will have trouble (John 16:33b). Trouble will come.

The second is that we can take heart. Christ has overcome the world (John 16:33c). Trouble will pass.

Both parts of John 16:33 are conveyed in the first double entendre I learned in the Bible: "It came to pass."

Trouble will come. We will touch the raw reality of being falsely accused or maligned. We may not get in as much trouble as Paul, with his eight floggings, three shipwrecks (124 hours in the water), one near-death experience (2 Corinthians 1:8), and at least four imprisonments. But we will be attacked and treated unfairly.

What is true in nature is true of human nature: 95 percent of the seed you plant is good, 5 percent is bad. You can trust 95 percent of the people; the other 5 percent of the people are crooks, cranks, cheaters, and crackpots. Do you live your life ruled by the 95 percent or the 5 percent?

The cottages at our Orcas Island Advance Center are filled with fine art, rare artifacts, one-of-a-kind relics, unusual antiques. Each cottage boasts its own theme library filled with rare books, first edition signed books, collector's copies. People can't believe we rent these out as "guest cottages" or host strangers in them. The most common question after a tour of one of the cottages is "How much of this gets stolen?"

The answer is "None of it." As far as we know, we have not had one thing stolen from any of our cottages in our mountain or island advance centers. We have had some things broken, including a signed Galle desk lamp emblazoned with an eagle. But this is the price one pays for living a life of trust. For 95 percent of the time, you will be blessed; 5 percent of the time you will be burned.

It came to pass. Or in some of the most comforting words of Scripture, "This too shall pass." Confidence is faith. You can be confident because you trust in God. And because you trust in God, you do not need to lie, seek revenge, or defend yourself. Because you trust, you can weave around your life a tapestry of trust that may be slit and stained, tattered and torn, but never pulled down.

One of the most difficult moments in my ministry came when I was falsely accused. The accusation came just before I was to leave my front seat and deliver an address. A tap on my shoulder summoned me to the back of the auditorium, where the organizer of the event sat me down and said: "Leonard, I need to hear from you that something is not true. Or if it is, I need to know right now."

I couldn't believe my ears, but I sat down and looked him in the eye. "What is it?"

"Someone just came up to me and informed me that you and your wife are separated, and that you are moving in with another woman."

The bigger they are, the harder they fall on you.

—PETER PORTER,
"MUTANT PROVERBS
REUNITED"

My heart discharged in my throat as fast as my soul tumbled to my soles. I asked him to repeat what he had just said. The words were hard for me to hear.

After he repeated it, I shook my head vigorously and said, "All I can say is that my marriage has never been stronger. My wife and I are bicoastal, so that may create some confusion in people's minds. I was divorced in 1984 after a disastrous elopement at nineteen and over a decade of trying to make it work. But Elizabeth and I are deeply in love, we are faithful to each other . . ."

Who knows what else I said? All I remember are the words of the event organizer when he said, "That's all I needed to know. You can go up there now and speak."

To this day I have no memory of how I got up there, much less of how I spoke during this fiery furnace of wrong. The only thing I remember is mentally clutching an image recommended to me by architect/sculptor James Hubbell that he got from a colleague. The author who recorded this story had a recurring dream that he was being led to the executioner's block. As he knelt and presented his neck, the sword came swooping down. Just before it sliced off his neck, it glided into slow motion, glanced off his neck, and touched his shoulder. "What had begun as an execution turned into a ceremony of knighting, marking not the end, but an initiation into a new life. The sword, the very thing that can destroy us, became a source of learning and blessing."

The sword that would take my head off I imagined to be the sword of the Spirit, mightier than any creature, including the tongue. And I wielded the sword of the Spirit that day, trusting God to turn untruth into anointing.

The second thing that saved me that day was a card I pulled out of my wallet as I walked behind the podium. I sat it down in front of me next to my notes. And I looked at it more frequently, from out of my salt-dripping eyes, than at my notes. The card has only two words on it and one grammatical marking. The card is black. The words are gold. Between the two words is a comma x-ed out. The words I keep in my wallet in front of my credit cards are these:

Please, God

One of my besetting sins is that I get mired in the need to be admired. I am a people pleaser. I like to be a crowd pleaser. I have a huge amount of the spaniel in me. I love being petted and stroked and told what a good boy I am. Scholars are usually not rewarded for straying, however circumspectly, outside their immediate parishes. And I stray uncircumspectly all the time. My hardest inner struggles have been over this sacrifice of scholarly praise and guild approval.

My prayer life now is dedicated to getting rid of one little comma, the comma that can transform the Mayday prayer of "Please, God" to the Good Friday prayer of "Please God." The removal of one little comma can change a prayer from "What can you do for me?" to "How can your purposes be fulfilled in my life?"

Who are you going to please? What's your governing goal in life? Jesus' was this: "I have come to do your will, O God" (Hebrews 10:7). Even Jesus did not please himself. "I seek not to please myself but him who sent me" (John 5:30).

Who do you want to please the most?

If it's God, then you can survive whatever is thrown at you.

If it's people, then you can count on betrayal, loneliness, mistrust, failure. Wait for applause, and you'll wait forever. Wait for consensus, and you'll wait forever. Wait for people's approval, and you'll wait forever.

We put the comma in the "Please God" prayer because we don't trust God. We don't really believe Jesus when he said, "It is your Father's good pleasure to give you the kingdom" (Luke 12:32 WORLD). We have trouble taking to heart the promise that God "richly furnishes us everything to enjoy" (1 Timothy 6:17 WORLD). Jonathan Edwards said that the pleasures of God are "an infinite ocean." Why can't we receive more? Our hands are so small. "We don't open [our] mouths wide enough," Edwards said. God doesn't have a giving problem. We have a receiving problem. Our hands are clutched around status, success, money, power. To receive all that God wants to give requires we release those things that we grip (and that are, remember, gripping us) and open our hands to receive what God wants to give.

I want to be a God pleaser, not a people pleaser. When someone asks me, "What's your greatest pleasure?" I want to be able to say—and mean it—"Pleasing God." When someone asks me, "What do you do for pleasure?" I want to be able to say—and mean it—"I do God for pleasure."

One day I will stand before God and hear one of two verses. One is the best word I can ever hear; the other is the worst word I can ever hear. The best word? It's the word Jesus heard at the Jordan: "You are my beloved son. You bring me great pleasure" (see Mark 1:11). The worst word? It's the word that goes to those who have lost their confidence, endurance, and faith: "Depart from me. Your life brings me no pleasure" (see Hebrews 10:38).

A life with this one focus—"Please God"—enables us to say over and over again, "This is a great day to live." A world where dreams are possible. A world where truth will win out over falsehood. A world where we can endure rejection, humiliation, failure, confusion. A world where brushing your tongue can cleanse the soul as well as the body.

> Gossip is a sort of smoke that comes from the dirty tobacco-pipes of those who diffuse it; it proves nothing but the bad taste of the smoker.
>
> —GEORGE ELIOT

Brush Your Tongue

1. Gossip is a prime research topic among anthropologists and sociologists. Max Gluckman, in a 1963 study, was the one who first drew attention to the value of gossip in the moral life of a community and the role of gossip as a force for group cohesiveness and social control. Studies have shown that where gossip is repressed or outlawed, community life is difficult.

   Can you give concrete examples from your own life where this may or may not be so?

2. Patricia Meyer Spacks argues that the origin of gossip is in the twin impulses of intimacy and aggression. "Gossip feels good, I am saying: a form of closeness, a mode of power. And gossip feels bad: a devious and treacherous kind of power, a potentially threatening attachment. In literature and in life, it signifies ambivalence."

   How does this help explain the tremendous emotional power of gossip?

3. Read the story of the prodigal son (Luke 15:11–32) and speculate for a moment. Did the elder brother simply conjecture how his younger brother spent his inheritance, thereby impugning his brother's character any way he could? Or did he have some information that he was saving to use against his brother whenever the opportunity arose? Was he passing on secondhand information?

4. The average person admits to telling two lies a day. We always have to tell the truth. We don't always have to tell "the whole truth." If you ask me whether or not you like the hairstyling you just spent $150 on, it may not be wise for me to tell "the whole truth." The test of whether to tell "the truth" or "the whole truth" is embodied in this question: "Does not telling the whole truth protect the other person or does it protect me?" So says Donald McCullough: "Real honesty is speaking the right truth to the right person at the right time in the right way for the right reason."

Lately, have you been telling "the whole truth" when you should have been telling "the truth"? How about the other way around?

5. Is lying to oneself as bad as lying to others? When did you last lie to yourself about something?

6. What do you think Paul meant when he said, "Evil communications corrupt good manners" (1 Corinthians 15:33 DV)? What proofs of this proverb could you offer?

7. Here is Martin Luther's hymn "Would That the Lord Would Grant Us Grace," published in 1523, based on Psalm 67. It has been called "the first missionary hymn of Protestantism." Commit to memory its words:

> Would that the Lord would grant us grace,
> And with clear shining let his face
> With blessings rich provide us,
> To life eternal light us;
> That we his gracious work may know,
> And what is his good pleasure,
> And also to the heathen show
> Christ's riches without measure
> And unto God convert them.

8. Do a word study of the twenty-one uses of the Greek euj-dokevw (yoo-dok-EH-oh), which means "be well pleased" or "take pleasure." They include Matthew 3:17; 12:18; 18:5; Mark 1:11; Luke 3:22; Romans 15:26–27; 1 Corinthians 1:21; 10:5; 2 Corinthians 5:9; 12:10; Colossians 1:19; 1 Thessalonians 2:8; 3:1; 2 Thessalonians 2:12; Hebrews 10:6, 8, 38; 2 Peter 1:17.

I can please only one person a day. Today is not your day. Tomorrow isn't looking good either.
—SIGN ON A SECRETARY'S DESK

Brush Your Tongue

cheer Rivals from the Bench

SOUL ARTISTS ARE HUMBLE AND WANT THE BEST FOR OTHERS.

O ne test of a healthy soul is whether or not it can cheer a rival from the bench. I first learned this sitting on the bench as a freshman in high school after being brought up to play varsity basketball. That year the Gloversville, N.Y., team made it to the state sectionals, where the person playing my position on the opposite team—Schenectady's 6'4" Pat Riley—blew us out of the water. At first I went through three of the five bench sitter's transgressions: (1) *Why doesn't Coach Kobuskie send me in there? I'd do better against Riley than Bob Miller is doing.* (2) *Maybe Miller will get tired or sprain an ankle and I'll get to go in.* (3) *Coach doesn't know how to coach.* I never got to the fourth and fifth transgressions: (4) *I hope we lose; then Coach will take another look at me.* (5) *I quit.* Before I got to them, something happened.

I found myself watching in admiration a true artist at work and cheering him silently from the bench. Pat Riley had the smoothest set shot and jumper I had ever seen. His movement down the floor was liquid. He was unflappable (a characteristic he did not always take with him to the NBA as its winningest coach in the 1980s or into the 1990s with the L.A. Lakers and Miami Heat). But when confronted with true greatness on the court, I lost myself in the wonder of a rival's gifts.

Seeing the Heavenly Host

A disciple of Jesus has an orientation to life that is one of celebration, not critique; oil on a wound, not sticks and stones.

The eighteenth-century poet/artist William Blake asked himself, "What do you see when the sun rises? A 'disk of fire'? A 'bright round disk of light'? O No, No, I see an innumerable company of heavenly host crying, Holy, Holy is the Lord God Almighty."

What do you see when the red ball rises? My "modern" education in the scientific method taught me to break down dusk and dawn into their component colors and to understand them critically. I'm only now learning to see and hear the heavenly hosts singing, "Holy, Holy," at the dawning of a new day and to understand the rising and setting of the sun spiritually.

The modern world has been keener on criticisms than conjectures and celebrations. That's why modern churches are all in a tizzy over praise choruses and celebration music. What good could come out of repetitious praises or monotonous chants?

Whenever I'm doubting the power of praise choruses, I remember Joshua. One simple phrase blasted on a trumpet, repeated over and over, brought down the walls of Jericho.

Whenever I'm doubting the power of chants, I remember LBJ. One chant did as much to convince President Johnson to bow out of the White House as anything political. It was this Vietnam protester chant: "Hey, hey, LBJ, / how many kids you kill today?"

My education taught me to major in criticism and minor in stand taking. Celebration wasn't even part of the curriculum. To understand how anything works, even the soul, we learned to take it apart, break it down, dissect it, and let someone else worry about fitting the pieces back together again. Any good "critic" worth his toolbox had a can that squirted more venom than Vaseline. "Experts" were expert at lifting up shortcomings in an artist rather than celebrating what is good in the artistry. The sound of axes being ground, sticks and stones being thrown, was deafening.

Before I could quote anyone, good scholarship required me to first put my authority before a critical firing squad and show off my mastery of their mind and material. Of course, I was only expected to affirm authorities with whom I was in agreement.

One person, having just finished reading my book *A Cup of Coffee at the SoulCafe,* exclaimed in amazement, "Sweet, you'll quote anyone!" Nothing could be closer to the truth. I relish the opportunity to glean insights and fresh truths from those with whom I most frequently and rabidly disagree. I have been known to quote Jerry Falwell approvingly. Not everything Falwell says is wrong. When he is right on about something, I delight in quoting him. I have been known to quote philosopher Georges Bataille. Not everything Bataille says is wrong, even though he got so sucked into the Marquis de Sade's erotic violence and was so enamored of Hitler and Stalin that he set in motion plans for human sacrifice.

In a world where we are prone to "die a little" when someone else succeeds, spunky critic/poet Ezra Pound marveled at novelist Ford Madox Ford, "the one man who is really happy when someone else

There are three kinds of people. Those who complain, "Too much! Too much!" Those who argue, "Not enough! Not enough!" And those who smile, "Ah! Just right!"
—OLD PHILOSOPHICAL SAYING

writes a good book." In a world where someone else's success diminishes my success, Anton Chekhov sneered: "Success? Write about my success? What's the criterion for success? You need to be God to distinguish success from failure unerringly."

Success hucksters would define a successful church as the world defines success. Francis Ford Coppola helped me unfreeze a few 1950s paradigms of what a successful church means with his response to an interviewer that success, like beauty, is in the eye of the beholder: "People are shocked to hear that I think of *The Godfather* series with sadness. I see those films almost as a personal failure. They changed my life detrimentally, even though the world treated them as big artistic and commercial successes. Their success led me to make big commercial films—when what I really wanted was to do original films, like those that Woody Allen is able to focus on."

Unattainable success to me is helping twelve true leaders "get it" and get turned around during the course of my ministry. I'd be content with half that. To save the world, just twelve was all the "success" Jesus needed. Of course, those twelve went on to turn around and transform twelve others, and those twelve exponentially twelve others, until a spiritual ocean of love connected planet Earth to itself and to God. But the real power is in the love.

It's not the numbers, big or small. It's the love—the love of Christ that constrains us and holds all things together. Nathan Cole was a carpenter and farmer from Connecticut. After hearing George Whitefield preach in 1740, his life was transformed. He could never be the same again, and his pet hatreds and feuds melted into thin air.

Now I had for some years a bitter prejudice against three scornfull men that had wronged me, but now all that was gone away Clear, and my Soul longed for them and loved them; there was nothing that was sinfull that could any wise abide the presence of God; and all the Air was love.

As we travel on this journey of life, we can enjoy the company of a love that never lets us go, a love that frees us from always having to be right or always having to fill in the silences left by Jesus. Or we can find our way around in this difficult world by dividing everyone up into the saved and the damned. There are other ways of making ways and waves in this world than shoving God off the judgment seat. As I heard a professor say my first year of seminary, at least 20 percent of my theology is wrong. I'm just not sure which 20 percent. Each of my steps is taken with a confession: I boast no immaculate perceptions, only a theology

SoulSalsa

of the dimly seen. The closer I get to God, the denser the mists until the fog of mystery becomes smoky-thick.

Believing by Candlelight

Part of the journey from modern to postmodern is coming out of a fluorescent consciousness back into a candlelight faith. The year 1877 is when Edison made the shadows flee with his invention of the electric light. When moderns took it further and installed overhead lighting, the artificial light banished every shadow from the room as ruthlessly as modernity drove mystery from faith. In the words of biologist Richard Dawkins, who is one of the world's leading Darwinists and is himself stuck in the modern paradigm, "The ultimate goal of science is to remove all mystery."

But there is a reason for the shadows. A candlelight consciousness reveres mystery, revels in marvels, avows awe, and is not afraid of measured hemmings and hawings. We can cheerlead the most uncheerable because we respect the shadows: we are aware of life's startlements; we find companionship in lilies of light and nimbus shadows; we never know what is lurking in the corners of someone else's life.

A deep spirituality is not afraid to let the mystery shine: the mystery of why a spotted animal can have a striped tail, while a striped animal cannot have a spotted tail; the mystery of why people with weak bladders prefer window seats on airplanes; the mystery of a "love, so amazing, so divine, [it] demands my soul, my life, my all."

Even when my beliefs are at their surest and strongest, I'm full of uncertainty, riddled with the mysterious, and crammed with weakness. Protestant Reformer Martin Luther wrote to his friend Justus Jonas, pointing to Paul as an exemplar: "I don't think [Paul] believed as firmly as he talks. I cannot believe as firmly either, as I can talk and write about."

That's why I try not to have convictions. The word *convict* is the root of that word *conviction*. Convictions can be prisons that keep you locked into cages and prevent others from getting to you.

I try to have confessions, not convictions. If it isn't anything outright gospel, I have confessions about it. I am more interested in relational prepositions than in doctrinal propositions. Relational prepositions are words that draw people into/within/among/between/amidst a divine connection. Doctrinal propositions separate people into categories and camps and positions. It's the difference between faith as a set of ideas about Christ to be believed or a relationship with Christ that is lived.

Rather than a dealer in dogmas, why not be a dealer in love? Every thought, every action is shadowed by the cross. Listen to people talk. The spiritual, other-centered person asks questions and enters into relationships. The self-centered person makes statements, especially ones intended not to open up subjects but to close them.

True humility is being ever willing to cast the first stone at oneself, and to "regard others as better than [ourselves]" (Philippians 2:3 NRSV). Protestant Reformer John Calvin loved the golden-tongued preacher named Chrysostom:

A saying of Chrysostom's has always pleased me very much, that the foundation of our philosophy is humility. But that of Augustine pleases me even more: "When a certain rhetorician was asked what was the chief rule in eloquence, he replied, 'Delivery'; what was the second rule, 'Delivery'; what was the third rule, 'Delivery'; so if you ask me concerning the precepts of the Christian religion, first, second, third, and always I would answer, 'Humility.'"

Not one of us has any basis for boasting—even about our attempts to be humble. Let me just say it: I can get angry because God doesn't do what I think God should do the way God should or when God should. As humble as I try to be, I still succumb to the pride of thinking I'd make a better God than God. That's when one of my favorite Welsh theologians, John Owen, kicks me in the posterior with his reminder that the gospel "keeps the heart always in deep humility, in abhorrence to sin, and in self-abasement.... It keeps the heart humble, lowly, sensible to sin, and broken on that account." God's word to Job also keeps my humility alive and kicking: "Where were you when I laid the foundation of the earth?" The world is God's to order, not ours.

Humility's Habits

There isn't just one human nature; there are many natures to any human being. Every person has many "sides" filled with good and bad qualities and quiddities. I can flip from sweet-talking to raising Cain in a nanosecond. Each one of us is a masterpiece of cognitive and emotional dissonance. Even at our best, as the apostle Paul put it, "The good that I would I do not: but the evil which I would not, that I do" (Romans 7:19 KJV).

In a moment of deep self-revelation, Leo Tolstoy wrote in a personal letter,

Nobody sees a flower—really—it is so small—we haven't time—and to see takes time like to have a friend takes time.

—PAINTER
GEORGIA O'KEEFE

SoulSalsa

Attack me, I do this myself, but attack *me* rather than the path I follow and which I point out to anyone who asks me where I think it lies. If I know the way home and am walking along it drunkenly, is it any less the right way because I am staggering from side to side!

You and I are where we are by the grace of God. It's *all* grace. It is grace alone and grace amazing and grace abounding.

Certain daily habits follow this. First, I have no right to critique anyone if I can't first celebrate him. Celebration comes before critique. There is a musician's motto: three strokes for each poke. If I can't say three positive things about someone and lift her up with prayer and thanksgiving to God, I have no warrant for complaint.

Second, I should not argue with anybody until I can state their position back to them in such a way that they approve. I never cease to be amazed at how many times this little habit forces my mouth shut.

My third habit is to listen to friends for confidence and courage but listen to enemies for wisdom and information. L. L. Bean uses this formula: there are twenty-five complaints for every one you hear. Multiply every criticism you hear by twenty-five. That's the reality you live under. Now, what can you learn from the criticism?

George Orwell, in a chronicle of his experiences during the Spanish Civil War, tells the following story:

> Early one morning another man and I had gone out to snipe at the Fascists in the trenches outside Huesca. . . . At this moment, a man . . . jumped out of the trench and ran along the top of the parapet in full view. He was half-dressed and was holding up his trousers with both hands as he ran. I refrained from shooting him. It is true that I am a poor shot and also that I was thinking chiefly about getting back to our trench. . . . Still, I did not shoot partly because of that detail about the trousers. I had come here to shoot at "Fascists"; but a man who is holding up his trousers isn't a "Fascist," he is visibly a fellow-creature, similar to yourself, and you don't feel like shooting at him.

Our enemies are people too, with ideas of their own that we can learn from.

Fourth, I recognize that it's my choice: will I spread kudos or kudzu? Kudos are compliments. Kudzu are complaints and criticisms that spread like . . . well, kudzu. Kudzu eventually covers everything and chokes the life out of whatever it touches. The tallest tree can be felled by this little vine that starts as a tuber in the ground.

I'm in training to earn a black belt in kudos. I am a compulsive kudoser and a chronic apologizer. But I haven't yet reached the level of Bishop Emerson Colaw. He is the church's foremost master in the spiritual art of kudos.

My favorite mail carries Emerson's return address. Whenever he hears a negative about someone, he brushes it off. But whenever he hears a positive, he passes on the compliment in the form of a short note like this one: "Just thought you'd like to know that I heard an alum say you were doing a great job at Drew. Nice knowing my alma mater is in such good hands. Keep up the good work and keep the faith."

Passing on a compliment is more than simply cheering people up. It's not an exaggeration to say that one simple letter can make all of my ministry here at Drew feel worthwhile.

There is a risk here. Compliments can be misread as come-ons, especially when most people are on starvation congratulation-diets. But Jesus took similar risks with the starving of his day. Whatever person you face has something that needs commending and something to teach you. Whatever book you are reading has something in it to help you on your way. No book can be all bad, and many are in fact mostly good. Sometimes the ore is hidden deep in the mine, and one labors at the coalface for unnecessary amounts of time. But there is no person, no book, no movie, no art that is so bereft of value that it is utterly worthless. In every act of creation God is present, waiting to be discovered. The essence of the spiritual journey is the discovery of the presence of the sacred in everyday things, in everyday people, in everyday life.

Finally, it's my habit to try to dechip my shoulders. Why do Christians have such a tremendous capacity to take offense? Most of what hurts and offends us are matters of the highest inconsequence. Why do some Christians have on their shoulder not a chip but the whole tree? I've known some Christians to be so angry and argumentative that they can't even take yes for an answer.

If you go looking for "offenses," there will be no end of them. Some people think I'm hard of hearing. My hearing is fine. I'm just hard of taking offense. I don't have to scold every inanity, confront every insanity, or rebuke every obscenity. Groucho Marx even gave me a way of not fighting every battle by making someone think I'm agreeing with him even when I'm not and while telling him I'm not. "I cannot say that I do not disagree with you," Groucho liked to say to contentious guests on his show.

The candle allows the darkness to keep its secrets.
—ANCIENT CELTIC SAYING

Soul Salsa

Keeping My Fingers Crossed

Everything I have said in this chapter gets incarnated in gestural form with everyone I meet. Some people notice. Most don't. Some think I have deformed fingers. But everyone I shake hands with gets a blessing.

The tradition of crossing fingers, in its origin, is unrelated to wishing or dissembling in distress. The crossing of the fingers began when some early Christians wanted to disclose their faith to one another without risking the death sentence imposed on those who made a public profession of faith. Crossed fingers was a secret hand signal and body ritual that kept early believers uncompromised while in the midst of compromising life situations. As a tradition, it was largely abandoned after Constantine stopped the persecution of Christians and established Christianity as the religion of the empire.

The earliest benediction and blessing was the elevation of the right hand and the lifting up of the thumb, index, and middle fingers. As the priest would wave these three fingers over the congregation, he would offer the trinitarian prayer: "God the Father [the thumb], God the Son [always the longest finger], and God the Holy Spirit [the index finger] bless, preserve, and keep you, now and forevermore. Amen."

No one knows when this first happened, but by the end of the fourth century some bishop resurrected the tradition of the crossed fingers and mixed it with the trinitarian benediction. After raising the three fingers and offering the benediction, the bishop crossed the Son and the Spirit fingers, harkened back to the faith of the martyrs, and spoke these words while waving his crossed fingers: *"Christus Victor, Christus Victor, Christus Victor."* It means "May Christ be victorious in your life."

Our communities, our families, our friends, we ourselves are severely underblessed. As my own way of cheerleading people whose paths cross mine, I have a secret body ritual that has become as second nature as the act of looking someone in the eye. When I reach out to shake hands or give a hug, I automatically cross my fingers and breathe the words of the ancestors, *"Christus Victor."* In a world that shoots the finger of hate, flip the world off with two crossed fingers.

The gates of my soul clang open and shut with a handclasp, a gesture that holds the weight of the past and the buoyancy of the future. Have the two of us ever shaken hands? Then you've been blessed. Whether you knew it or not or wanted it or not. From the moment our hands gripped, your life has been ridden with a God-hidden, Jesus-bidden, Spirit-driven blessing that turns temporal handshaking into spiritual arm wrestling: "May Christ be victorious in your life."

The *Christus Victor* blessing is this: in life, may you lose and God win.

1. Get a copy of the essay by Søren Kierkegaard called "Ultimatum: The Upbuilding That Lies in the Thought That in Relation to God We Are Always in the Wrong" and read it and ponder.

2. What might poet Emily Dickinson have meant when she wrote this prayer: "We thank thee, Father, for these strange minds that enamor us against thee"?

3. Whenever megachurch pastor Bill Hybels is questioned about how he reacts when his methods are attacked, he quotes something his mentor, Gil Bilezikian, told him years ago: "Bill, sometimes your critics are your best critics."

   Who are your critics? If you really listened to them, what might you learn from them?

4. Bring the flicker of mystery back into your home by turning off the lights at night and burning candles instead. Sure, you could buy candles, but it's more fun and meaningful to make them yourself, perhaps with your spouse and kids. For step-by-step instructions on how to make candles, go to http://www.learn2.com/04/0481/0481.html/.

5. Patricia Brown begins the day with ten coins in one pocket. Every time she compliments someone, she takes one out of that pocket and puts it in the other. If she slips up and criticizes someone, she moves a coin back to the first pocket. At the end of the day, the emptying of her pockets is a tallying up of her spread of kudos or kudzu.

   Try this exercise for at least one day.

6. Read the following Bible verses on humility and pick one to memorize: Matthew 18:4; Luke 18:10–13; Romans 12:3, 10, 16; 1 Corinthians 3:18–20; Galatians 5:26; Philippians 2:3–5.

7. University of Chicago historian Martin E. Marty keeps on his study wall an inscription given to him by a Lutheran bishop a long time ago:

   Life is short and we have not much time for gladdening the hearts of those who travel this way with us. Oh, be swift to love, make haste to be kind.

   Describe the wall-hangings and plaques that you surround yourself with that keep your soul focused spiritually.

10

Give History a Shove

SOUL ARTISTS MAKE A DIFFERENCE IN THE WORLD.

"You can't save the world." We've all heard that one. And it's true: you can't save the whole world. Only God can save the whole world. But we can help a Johnny here, a Jamile there, a Juan Carlos over yonder. It's only a drop in the bucket. But it's *your* drop in the bucket. It's *my* drop in the bucket. And like the steady drip of a leaky faucet, with everyone doing their part, the bucket will soon be full of the living water that never runs dry. With everyone doing their part, the beat of suffering love at the heart of the universe can go on to heal the whole world.

> "Scientists announced today that they have found a cure for apathy. However, they claim that no one has shown the slightest bit of interest in it."
> —GEORGE CARLIN

Look How They Love One Another

Sociologist Rodney Stark asks in his textbook *The Rise of Christianity,* how and why did the church grow so fast? For Christianity to have reached the size it did in the time it did, it must have grown 40 percent a decade for three centuries.

How? Stark sums it up this way: early disciples of Jesus were more compassionate than others around them. They outloved others. They outserved others.

Here are a couple examples. In A.D. 165 an epidemic (perhaps smallpox) spread like wildfire throughout the Roman Empire. Within fifteen years a quarter to a third of the entire population within the empire died. Ditto A.D. 251, when another epidemic (perhaps measles this time) emptied whole towns and left the wind whistling through uninhabited regions.

Unlike their pagan neighbors, Christians took care of each other and those outside the church during those plague times. A bishop named Dionysus writes of what happened:

> Most of our brother Christians showed unbounded love and loyalty, never sparing themselves and thinking only of one

another. Heedless of danger, they took charge of the sick, attending to their every need and ministering to them in Christ, and with them departed this life serenely happy; for they were infected by others with the disease, drawing on themselves the sickness of their neighbors and cheerfully accepting their pains.

Contrast that with Dionysus's description of the pagans:

At the first onset of the disease, they pushed the sufferers and fled from their dearest, throwing them into the roads before they were dead . . . hoping thereby to avert the spread and contagion of the fatal disease.

As a Christian himself and a church leader, Dionysus admittedly had a biased viewpoint. But a hundred years later the Roman emperor Julian essentially confirmed what Dionysus had claimed, touting the Christians for their "moral character," bashing the pagans for their selfishness, and inviting citizens to greater "benevolence toward strangers."

It was not only to the sick that the early Christians displayed a supernatural compassion. In Stark's words:

To cities filled with the homeless and impoverished, Christianity offered charity as well as hope. To cities filled with newcomers and strangers, Christianity offered an immediate basis for attachments. To cities filled with orphans and widows, Christianity provided a new and expanded sense of family. To cities torn by violent ethnic strife, Christianity offered a new basis of social solidarity. And to cities faced with epidemics, fires, and earthquakes, Christianity offered effective nursing services.

The compassion furnace burned brightly in Christianity's natal days. Souls forged and fired in the ovens of service went on to warm others with good deeds and good news. That's how the church exploded. Now our compassion furnace is going dark. Our sound and fury signify less and less in name and in fame. That's why we're shrinking. In another phrase postmodern culture has stolen from the church, those institutions that boast "dedicated servers" are esteemed and envied. While the church clings to the language of the "volunteerism," the culture lifts up "servant leadership" and "dedicated service."

Too much of postmodern spirituality equates sacred space with only that which lies between both ears. Sacred space in a biblical spirituality brings together the internal space of joy, peace, contentment, and meaning with the external space of justice, harmony, truth, and compassion. A self-focused soul is a contradiction in terms (Philippians 2:3–4). Unselfing is a godly turn of heart, a soul-way of being in the world.

No matter how cynical you get, it's impossible to keep up.

—LILY TOMLIN

Soul Salsa

The godly art of living soulfully erects a culture of service. The closest thing to Christmas on the children's cable channel Nickelodeon is "Big Help Day." For weeks leading up to this day, our kids are inundated with images and urges to get involved in doing something good for others. It's the biggest youth group project not connected with the church that's out there. It is now routine for corporations to offer employees paid release time to volunteer in community agencies. The number of schools making community service a requirement for graduation is skyrocketing. When schools, businesses, and cable channels are known more than churches for making community service a requirement and mark of membership, it is a wonder the baby Jesus isn't being thrown out more with the unholy bathwater.

Your Coronation

The last coronation of an English monarch took place on 2 June 1953 at Westminster Abbey. A kneeling Elizabeth II was given a sword, taken from the altar and handed over to her by the archbishop of Canterbury assisted by the archbishop of York and the bishops of London and Winchester. As she held it before the altar, she heard these words:

> Receive this kingly Sword, brought now from the Altar of God, and delivered to you by the hands of us, the Bishops and servants of God, though unworthy. With this sword do justice, stop the growth of iniquity, protect the holy Church of God, help and defend widows and orphans, restore the things that are gone to decay, maintain the things that are restored, punish and reform what is amiss, and confirm what is in good order: that doing these things you may be glorious in all virtue; and so faithfully serve our Lord Jesus Christ in this life, that you may reign for ever with him in the life which is to come.

It is the mission of the pilgrim to proclaim to the principalities and powers of this world the power from on high and what that power is. Higher power is service. In the computer game *Ultima*, the kingdom is ruled, not by the eight Britannic virtues (compassion, valor, honor, honesty, spirituality, sacrifice, justice, and humility), but by power, force, and conspicuous consumption. In a world where real and virtual kingdoms are ruled by power and greed, godly pilgrims call cosseted rulers to eat the hot peppers and do that for which they have been coronated: to engender a holy economy of long-serving, long-suffering sacrifice in the midst of a gross economy of money and power.

I don't care how high the saints jump, just so they keep walking when they hit the ground.
—OLD CAMP-
MEETING SAYING

Every soul needs a coronation service. When was your coronation into a life of service and sacrifice? It does not matter what it is you're doing or where you're doing it. Whatever your passion or predicament, you've been coronated. If you're flipping burgers at McDonalds, you've been coronated to bring your soul's passion for truth, beauty, and goodness into that kitchen and into the lives of those around you.

Way of Life

"We are what he has made us, created in Christ Jesus for *good works*, which God prepared beforehand to be our *way of life*" (Ephesians 2:10 NRSV, emphasis added). If your heart is in the right place, it's not enough. The most frightful thing anyone can say at my funeral is "Sweet meant well." That gets my vote for the most damning epitaph of all time. Our feet and hands must be in the same places as our heart. Godly living is a "way of life" or it is nothing.

We aren't all called to be Mother Teresas. But we are all called to be Jesus. "God has chosen us *all* in Christ," Karl Barth wrote in my favorite quote from all his writings: "at the deepest level we are all called Jesus in the eyes of the Father." The essence of "in his steps" and "in his spirit" is to do whatever you are doing as if Jesus were the one doing it. A Jesus pilgrim performs life as Jesus performed life. To be a follower of Jesus is to have Jesus' spirit living and growing in us.

Praxeology is the study of human actions and conduct. Jesus invited the world to judge his followers by their *praxis,* their actual practice in life of his commands and example. He extended this invitation by his list of Beatitudes, which is riddled, according to Christopher Levan, with "performative language." Jesus used the Greek word *makarios,* which we translate as "blessed." But a "blessed" life, in Jesus' sense of the word, means a life of service dedicated to extending God's promises and protection to those who need them the most. To be faithful to God means being faithful to those at the bottom of the social scale. To be "blessed" by God means one is a blessing to those least blessed. The Beatitudes, then, are not "a throwaway list of bedtime benedictions," Levan insists, "but the marching orders for a new world."

The paradox of history is that where the light is brightest the shadows are darkest. The tragedy of this moment in history is that there aren't more bright lights walking out of our hermetic churches. Something is terribly wrong when the strongest moral voice out there is Oprah Winfrey and Laura Schlessinger. The world is in danger of losing its soul because the church's moral autism and shrinking domain of moral responsibility blunts and stunts its ability to strip evil of its generative power.

He who sees a need and waits to be asked for help is as unkind as if he had refused it.

—DANTE

116

SoulSalsa

My soul gets hung with cement when it ponders all those things done in Christ's name over the past two millennia. How can sin (or call it "human nature" if you must) not be a fundamental category of sociological and psychological analysis as we leave this "never again" century to the doleful tunes of ethnic cleansing in Kosovo, the genocides of Bosnia and Rwanda, the outrages of East Timor, and so on. Christians ought to shiver with an unshakable sense of self-disgust when we look back on our own history and see the prominence of sin everywhere.

There is an old air force saying: "If you can keep your head when all about you are losing theirs, then maybe you just haven't grasped the situation."

If we, the Lord's disciples, keep silence when a billion people (229 million of them Christians) live in absolute poverty . . . the very rocks will cry out.

If we, the Lord's disciples, keep silence when developing countries are being paved under by the information superhighway . . . the very rocks will cry out.

If we, the Lord's disciples, keep silence while millions are struggling to emerge from the thick capitalist undergrowth . . . the very rocks will cry out.

If we, the Lord's disciples, keep silence as the world's population soars past 6 billion . . . the very rocks will cry out.

If we, the Lord's disciples, keep silence as people are more concerned about accumulating physical assets than spiritual ones . . . the very rocks will cry out.

If we, the Lord's disciples, keep silence as the combination of overpopulation and overconsumption impacts global warming, resource shortages, ocean and freshwater pollution, air quality, traffic congestion, the unequal distribution of wealth . . . the very rocks will cry out.

If we, the Lord's disciples, keep silence when to say that something is "wicked" now means that something is "cool" . . . the very rocks will cry out.

If we, the Lord's disciples, keep silence when there is no one to bridge the ridges that divide one generation from another . . . the very rocks will cry out.

If we, the Lord's disciples, keep silence in a world that feels like an unmade bed . . . the very rocks will cry out.

> O Lord, open my lips,
> and my mouth will declare your praise. (Psalm 51:15)

If there is one teaching of Jesus that makes more scientific sense today than on the day it was uttered, it is this one: "Inasmuch as ye have done it unto one of the least of these my brethren, ye have done it unto me" (Matthew 25:40 KJV). Jesus taught that we live in a world where what goes on in one corner affects every corner, where what happens to one child in Turkey affects every Manhattan. How can this be?

Now we know. Locality is dead. Distance is dead. The deterministic worldview of classical science is dead. The Newtonian stance of "local realism"—to study a phenomenon here you didn't need to worry about phenomenon elsewhere—has been repudiated. Quantum nonlocality now rules the day.

What killed locality was what physicist Henry Stapp calls "the greatest discovery of all science." Quantum mechanics first posited nonlocality in the 1920s but couldn't prove it. Then in 1964 a proof emerged from John Bell, who forced physicists to choose between local realism and quantum nonlocality. Finally in 1982 Alain Aspect at the University of Paris proved nonlocality the law of the universe when particles a few meters apart had a "communication" time that was twenty times faster than the "unbreakable" speed limit of light. Particles communicate with each other instantaneously. They know what is happening to each other without signaling each other. They even dance together. The more quantum you get, the more everything seems to be dancing all the time. Dancing atoms. Dancing cells. Dancing DNA. Dancing to the same music.

We are now living in a time when scientists are patting theologians for resisting the seductions of reduction, even to the point of saying—and I quote—"The structure of the universe is sympathetic to the ideas of many spiritual traditions, including those of Christianity. The holism, the interrelatedness of everything.... The spooky nonlocal correlations-at-a-distance might evidence a Holy Ghost at work." Even the high priests of agnosticism are losing faith.

Whether or not nonlocality turns out to be "the greatest discovery of all science" remains to be seen. But one of the greatest discoveries of the soul, Jesus said, is the awareness that there is no separation between anything. Touch one thing and you touch everything. Touch earth and you touch heaven. Help one life and you help every life. Show one person love and you show love to the universe.

Never before has it been so possible for one person to make the world different. Smallness is a strength, not a liability (as the "small" Michael Jordan proved to the giants of the game). Just as the figure skater spins faster the smaller he or she becomes, so the smallest units can amass the greatest amounts of energy and generate the greatest amounts of change. Never before has the world been so instantaneously

SoulSalsa

reachable by one person, one touch, one helping hand. If this doesn't fire up the salsa in our souls to live lives of significance, what will?

Inasmuch as you did it to the least, Jesus said, you did it to me.

It is said that after Mother Teresa received the Nobel Peace Prize she was approached by some reporters. They asked her if such acclaim and recognition might not go to her head. In response, she asked them if they remembered the story of Christ's entering Jerusalem on a donkey and the road being strewn with garments and palm branches by the adoring crowd. They said they did. She replied, "And do you think the donkey thought it was in his honor?"

The whole earth is shifted from its orbit by one wren lighting on a branch.
—LEONARDO DAVINCI, NOTEBOOKS

1. Former Secretary of the Treasury under two U.S. Presidents, William E. Simon, when asked the question that forms the title of a recent magazine article—"How Can I Find God?"— answered in this way:

> On one occasion, I was visiting a young man who was dying of AIDS. His body was pitifully thin, racked with pain. As we prayed together, I looked down on this poor soul and remembered Christ's words—"Whatsoever you do to the least of my brethren, you have done for me."

> I've thought about that moment several times since. And I realize that I was not just looking into the face of that young man—I was looking directly into the eyes of Christ.

When you come in contact with the needy—the child living in a shack with an abusive parent, the scruffy Vietnam vet holding a cardboard sign on the street corner—do you see Jesus? If not, what's keeping you from seeing them that way?

2. New Zealand novelist and theologian Michael Riddell argues,

> We have succeeded in separating Christ from people, so that they imagine he is the icon of good and respectable people, and has little relevance to their own sordid and tangled lives. Jesus who lived and died as a "friend of sinners" has been blasphemously translated into the enemy and judge of sinners. The grace and forgiveness which he offered has been swallowed up by self-righteous and prudish moral cru-sading. The healing love of God is once more locked up in sanctuaries and ceremonies.

What keys will open that lock?

3. When is the last time you got your "helper's high," the rush that comes from helping others in need? What would it take to addict yourself to that high?

SoulSalsa

4. Read the World Hunger Education Service's recommendations to help reduce hunger (http://www.worldhunger.org/reduce.htm/). Are any of these steps ones that you are willing to take?

5. When I asked someone recently how things were going, she replied, "I feel like a rented mule." How do you keep from getting "weary in well doing" (Galatians 6:9 KJV) in your own life of service and sacrifice?

6. Read the full text of the English monarch's coronation ceremony at http://www.oremus.org/liturgy/coronation/ cor1953b.html/. Let it inspire you to write your own coronation ceremony for the servant role God has called you to.

7. Jacob Burckhardt (1818–97) contends, "Even times of decay and decline have a sacred right to our compassion." Some people (such as Roger Scruton, a prominent philosopher who has announced that he is now a Christian) consider postmodernity to be a time of decay and corruption.

   Is a Jesuslike servanthood needed more, less, or the same in postmodernity as in modernity? How are the types of servanthood needed now different than in the modern past?

8. Discuss this quote from Goethe: "In the realm of ideas everything depends on enthusiasm. . . . In the real world all rests on perseverance."

   From your life experiences, is he right?

9. Soujourners community/magazine founder Jim Wallis splits Washington, D.C., into two cities—one Washington, one D.C.—and argues that "Washington, D.C., is a microcosm of the dynamics that now govern the world order."

   If Washington is the most powerful city in the nation, D.C. is the most powerless, without control even over its own affairs and destiny. As the "Last Colony," D.C. symbolizes the relationship many other parts of the world have with official Washington. The revealing paradoxes exist on almost every level of life in Washington, D.C.. Housing costs are among the highest in the country, as are the rates of the

Give History a Shove

homeless. Infant mortality is at Third-World levels in a city that contains more lawyers and real estate developers than any other. Black youth unemployment is above sixty percent, while white professional couples with two incomes search for investments. Scholastic Aptitude Test scores for students in D.C.'s public schools are one hundred points below the national average, while students in the city's private schools score one hundred points above it.

Do you think he's right? If so, do we live accepting these realities or do we live changing these realities? If the latter, what might you do from where you are to change this?

10. You can donate every day 1.5 cups of rice, wheat, maize, or other staple food. Visit www.thehungersite.com. Click the "Donate free food" button, and a contribution to the U.N. World Food Program will be made. Every day if you click the button every day. One hundred tons of food are now being donated weekly in this way.

11

Kill Two Birds With One Stone

SOUL ARTISTS MULTITASK THEIR WAY TO PRODUCTIVITY.

Some people see the "stacking" phenomenon of doing several things at once, or as my Appalachian ancestors put it, of "killing two birds with one stone," as evidence of a conspiracy to increase consumption. In the words of one critic, "vaunting such skill makes good corporate advertising sense; people use up more stuff that way. No one seems impressed by the fact that Mozart didn't chew gum or watch TV while he was writing piano concertos."

But the truth is that we all live in multiple worlds simultaneously, and the godly art of living soulfully involves learning to multiply and complexify life *before* we simplify it.

Savage Swiftness

The ultimate stacking, theologically speaking, is the doctrine of the Trinity. Too many believers have sunk into "serial monotheism"— practicing one member of the Trinity at a time—rather than synchronous monotheism, where all members of the Trinity are working in, out, and through one's life at the same time.

This book is based on the premise that biblical faith contains multitudes and stacks multiples. There is *chronos* time (your basic clock time) and there is *kairos* time (the "right time" for something). There is priestly time and there is prophetic time. There is one Hebrew people but twelve tribes. There is one Yahweh but many names for the name not spoken (*El Shaddai, Adonai, Elohim*).

The Great Commission is at base a Great Excitement to stack the gospel—to see the gospel contextualized in every cultural group. In Matthew 28:19 the word we translate as "nation" is in Greek *ethne,* from which we derive the word *ethnic. Ethne* means "an ethnic or cultural group of people." There are thoughts pilgrims can't think and insights into God blocked to us when the gospel isn't indigenized into the world's six thousand or so languages. Cultural diversity is as important to Christianity's health as biological diversity is to the planet's health.

The passion to see God made manifest everywhere and in everyone is the heart of the Great Commission. There are multiple Christianities (Jerusalem, Rome, Philippi, Ephesus; African, Chinese, Hispanic, Korean; Roman, Orthodox, Protestant, Pentecostal; apostolic, patristic, medieval, modern) that have flowed from the life of Jesus. From the standpoint of Western Christianity, there's the "West" and there's the "rest." Except the "West" was known as the "North" to the Spanish, who explored it from the "South" of Central America. It all depends on where you start. Current Western Christianity is only one possible version of biblical faith, and from a postmodern perspective, not the best one at that.

Let's forget godly living for a moment and just talk about living. You can't live anymore without the artistry of stacking. Postmoderns need help keeping all the spaghetti on their forks. Random House CEO Alberto Vitale has said that in the economic world, "Now everyone has two jobs," referring to the need to both carry out one's current duties and retool for the future. I tell pastors that every one of them has two jobs: one is as pastor of the church in which they are working; the other is in new church development. I tell churches the same thing: every church is in the church planting business.

We live in a world of savage swiftness. But we don't know the causes or the reasons for what happens until years later. Stacking is second nature to high-speed-living postmoderns, partly of necessity and partly because grazers have such low monotony thresholds. Television viewers in the U.S. allegedly switch channels every three minutes. Call it "short attention span" or societal "attention deficit disorder." ABC's Ted Koppel notes that over the past several decades sound bites have gone down from an average of twenty-two seconds to eight seconds in length.

My wife does backgrounding really well. While she's talking to me on the phone, she's cooking in the kitchen, giving directions to the kids, and working at her business (and that's just what I know about). In other words, she's not giving me her full attention (she does refuse to take call waiting while we're talking); she's multitasking.

My favorite way of conjuring titles for books or articles is while I'm playing baseball with my son. In other words, I'm not giving *him* my full attention. My favorite way to go online and answer e-mail is while I'm watching TV. In other words, I'm not giving friends my full attention. If truth be told, "full attention" moments are few and far between. When they do occur, it's called "worship."

Even our architecture is killing two birds with one stone. There are now five hundred churches nationwide with steeples that double as antennae. Washington D.C.'s National Cathedral is paid $100,000 per year by Motorola for its 234-foot antenna on the west tower. Postmodern steeples are now high-bandwith links to God that double as profit centers for the church.

The postmodern challenge of "killing two birds with one stone" is that one bird now is a buzzard and the other is a chickadee. Historian Eric Hobsbawn calls this an *Age of Extremes* (1994). Walk the candy aisles of Kmart, Wal-Mart, or Target. Gone are the Tootsie Pops of my youth. In their place is extreme candy: candies you experience and interact with through extreme flavors (super sour, super sweet), extreme pleasure, extreme pain. Candies like Big Bang, Skull Suckers, Monster Mouths, Shock Tarts, Nestle's Armageddon Asteroid and Nuclear Chocolate, Tongue Splashers and Mega Warheads that come with warnings like "Eating multiple pieces within a short time period may cause a temporary irritation to sensitive tongues and mouths."

Postmodernity does multiples to the point where generations almost constitute parallel universes to each other. The lightning-fast speed of change is creating distinctive generational cultures with their own vocabulary, customs, behavior, and outlooks. In one decade there is now more change than occurred in an entire century in times past. As self-identification according to class, region, and denomination is diminishing, self-identification according to generation has become stronger. Aren't generations at least as different from one another as are races or sexes?

In postmodern culture opposite things happen at the same time that aren't contradictory. Postmoderns can have their cake, eat it, and throw it too. This is the secret of the World Wide Web: its simultaneous anonymity and intimacy. One-third of all USAmericans use e-mail to send 2.2 billion messages a day (compared with 293 million pieces of first-class mail) partly because the immediacy of "You've got mail" conveys both privacy and friendliness.

The word *respect* means to look again. To re-spect life is to look at it multiple times and in multiple ways. Or in the words of Blackfoot Indian Jamake Hightower, "You must learn to look at the world twice if you wish to see all there is to see."

Reading the Bible is an exercise in seeing double. Humans are at the same time worm food and stardust. One part of you is a Holy Roller; the other part, a hellion. There is nothing new under the sun, but you can't step into the same river twice. Jesus is fully divine and fully human. The first shall be last. The least shall be greatest. God reigns

The crocodile is swift to dive but slow to surface.
—INDONESIAN PROVERB

from a cross. The best revenge is to forgive. The meek shall inherit the earth. You can love your neighbor and hate his guts at the same time. Less can yield more. Dream dreams and get real: "As it is in heaven," so may God's kingdom come on earth. Put your head in the clouds and your feet on the earth. And on and on.

A Doubling of Double Worlds

I spend my life in two worlds times two. The first two worlds I live in at once have all of me based in a chronological calendar and the other all of me based in a liturgical calendar. Instead of Day-Timer schedules competing with the divine schedule, we can live both at the same time. How? These are some methods that work for me. Some might work for you too:

- Driving has become war by other means. Why not spiritual warfare? Other people talk on their cell phones to other people while driving; I talk to God. I know people think I'm crazy: sometimes I'm crying, sometimes laughing, sometimes talking out loud, sometimes lavishing impassioned outbursts into empty space. In spite of the double takes, make drive time devotion time.
- Engage in intercessory prayer while watching the evening news. Indeed, how can a pilgrim *not* pray while watching the evening news?
- Bring a child along on a business-related trip. Combine pleasure and profession. Mix family vacations with business trips.
- When you're jogging or riding the stationary bike or doing that funny duckfoot fast-walking, wear a Discman loaded with whatever praise music carries you along. Worship as you sweat, sweat as you worship.
- I joined the "singing impaired" when I got my tonsils out. But I can sing hymns or praise songs in the shower that are broadcast quality. Where do you sing to God?

The second two worlds I live in all at once are the worlds of real space and cyberspace. In the medieval world, life was split into two spatial dimensions: physical space and spiritual space. In the modern world, those two worlds collapsed into one. In the postmodern world, we are now back in two spatial worlds: the real world of physical space and an electronic world of cyberspace that didn't exist fifteen years ago. Both the real world and the cyber world need spiritual care and nurturing.

What is going to kill reading in our time is writing.

—POET/ANTHOLOGIST/
TRAVELER/IRONIST
D. J. ENRIGHT

Soul salsa

I am searching for rituals that can bridge both worlds. Here are a few that I am now using:

- The music that swells stereophonically when I open Windows is my awakening anthem to the original music of creation still sounding forth today. I use "the Microsoft sound" as a call to prayer, dedicating my creativity to continuing God's creativity and harnessing my energies to those of the Spirit.

- I cruise the Net by scented candlelight to the aroma of antique leather bindings. Very soon, as I saunter through cyberspace, I'll be able to check in at Martin Luther's home and pick up the inkwell that he threw at the devil—an inkwell, indistinguishable from the original, that I will be able to touch and squeeze and weigh in my hand. As for now, I reach for the mouse more like I used to reach for the phone book. By placing my laptop on an old leather-bound book, and by engulfing my browser in the glow of beeswax candles, I get a peak ancient-future rush that roots my soul in the real world even while I'm exploring an emerging virtual world that is already so real it sucks me into its vortex.

- I have taken David Gelernter's advice and replaced in my mind the "desktop" imagery displayed on the computer screen with "Lifestream" images and information. "Desktop" is the application of print categories to electronic media. "Lifestream" is Gelernter's suggestion for a parallel electronic category that conveys more accurately and relevantly exactly what the computer is doing and can do to help us live our lives.

- "You don't find the words of an e-mail smudged by tears." So writes the Peruvian novelist Alfredo Bryce Echenique. I'm proving Bryce Echenique wrong every day in my printouts of e-mail over which I pray.

- In Indian mythology avatars were deities brought to life in human form. In postmodern culture avatars are your human form brought to life in cyberspace—your digital self, your online identity, your virtual representative. Avatars may be to our cyber-world lives what Social Security numbers are to our real-world lives. These digital characters and the new social reality they create will raise new questions of individuation, integration, status, and reputation. Avatars are how others will come to see and know you, and how you will come to see and know yourself in the cyber world. My avatar will have a reputation as significant as my real-world reputation. I have already been developing ways for my avatar to do "e-vangelism" in this cyber world.

> **The real voyage of discovery lies not in seeking new lands but in seeing with new eyes.**
> —MARCEL PROUST

Killing Two Birds with One Necktie

Michael Christiansen is a young Drew scholar, author, and administrator. He yokes prophetic and priestly time in his service as an usher at the seaside religious resort of Ocean Grove, New Jersey.

There is no more vintage moment steeped in the Ocean Grove tradition than to watch as a couple dozen ushers fan out across the vast amphitheater in their white pants and blue blazers to collect the offering in old-fashioned wicker baskets. When the offertory anthem is finished, they emerge from everywhere and nowhere to waltz back to the front and line up for the offertory prayer while Gordon Turk plays on the great organ the tune of "The Ushers March." It's quaint. It's campy. It's the signature of Ocean Grove. There's only one problem. All the ushers have been, from the opening day of Ocean Grove, male. (There are a couple of services each year when women usher. But these are the exceptions that prove the rule.) And the seniority system of ushering still rules.

What is a young postmodern evangelical and feminist who loves Ocean Grove to do? "Selected" for the honor of ushering, Michael decided to give in to his nostalgia for lost customs but not without combining priestly and prophetic time. He agreed to serve this high priestly role at Ocean Grove but vowed never to usher without prophesying the day when women and men would usher together. His "prophesying" role is fulfilled by wearing a tie with some woman on the front of it (my favorite is his Princess Diana tie) whenever he is ushering.

Dedication Bible

My own favorite stacking exercise of "killing two birds with one stone" is something I do with my Bible. My growing a soul and growing a family have done a fandango for years. Here's how it goes:

I take my study Bible everywhere. I write in it, mark it up, underline passages, and generally make it beautiful with rain, tear, and coffee stains and dog-eared edges. It's been rebound in leather twice, and the gold lettering on the brown binding is almost invisible. It's almost ready for me to turn it over to my son Thane.

On the day Thane was born, I dedicated this Bible to him. For the past nine years, I've been underlining passages for him, writing notes to him in the margins, and inserting prayers for him in various places throughout the text. I will give this Bible to him after I have him read this chapter you are now reading. He won't fully understand its significance, or what I've inscribed to him, until he's much older. But it's perhaps the best gift I'll ever give him. I have already ordered a new study Bible, which will be dedicated to another of my kids.

It is one of the favorite things I do in life: make my kids a part of my devotional life. Through stacking, I fold them into my daily adventuring with God, and in the form of a beat-up, used-up, beautiful Bible, it becomes a lasting bond between us.

He who has eyes sees something in everything.

—ROY LICHTENBERG

Kill Two Birds with One Stone

1. The ancient-future methodology for living in the world is conveyed by this quote from the first-century A.D. Roman poet/epigrammatist Martial: "To know how to relive the past with pleasure is to live twice." That's why I put a Web TV in an old Sinclair gas pump in Sweet's Body & Soul Cafe and Mountain Store in Thomas, West Virginia. Can you think of other ways to "relive the past with pleasure"?

2. What would it mean to live aesthetically on three levels: high culture, folk culture, and popular culture?

3. Is it truly "balance" that you need between work and home? Or do you need both fully? How can you pull it off?

4. Brennan Manning said, "St. Paul looked so unflinchingly at himself, others, and the world through the eyes of Jesus that Christ became the ego of the apostle"—"I live now not with my own life but with the life of Christ who lives in me" (Galatians 2:20). Didymus of Alexandria said that "Paul was full of Christ."

   How can it be possible that the more we are full of Christ, the more uniquely ourselves and original we become?

5. Is the world norm bilingual, multilingual, or monolingual? (Hint: it's not the latter.) Do you think it is important for English-speaking followers of Jesus to learn and use and teach their children another language?

6. Barbara Moses, in her book Career Intelligence, presents as rule 10: "Decide, Are You More of a Specialist or a Generalist?" How can you kill these two birds with one stone?

7. The online Jargon Dictionary cross-references the terms multitask and thrash. Look up those two definitions (http://www.netmeg.net/jargon/terms/m/multitask.html/ and http://www.netmeg.net/jargon/terms/t/thrash.html/) and think about how you can multitask without thrashing.

8. Reread the story of Jacob wrestling the angel (Genesis 32:22–32). If this is a metaphor for our relationship with God and each other, what does it mean that we are left wounded and blessed at the same time?

12

Build a Compost Heap

SOUL ARTISTS TRANSFORM AND REUSE ALL KINDS OF "WASTE."

The godly art of living soulfully requires the ritual of composting or recycling almost everything: cabbage leaves, orange peels, plum pits, glass, aluminum, paper, whatever. And in the spiritual world as well as in the natural world, waste equals food. What seems useless can be converted into something desperately needed.

Kilian McDonnel, a monk at St. John's Abbey in Collegeville, Minnesota, wonderfully categorizes the spiritual life as a combination of three things: treasures, baggage, and garbage. Treasures are those strengths and riches, he says, that give life spiritual identity and integrity. Baggage is all those things, more external than internal, that we choose to carry with us but that aren't essential to the journey. Garbage is the stuff that accumulates and should be thrown out, even those good intentions gone astray.

I love the idea of it all being that simple but haven't found life so obliging. How can I vulgarize what might as well be the symbol for my life—the garbage can?

Wasteland

Like the world around me, my life has become one vast wasteland. I am in a solid waste crisis, both physically and spiritually. I consume most of my own body weight in basic materials each day. I create my own body weight in greenhouse gases every day (approximately twenty-six tons per person per year). I discard six pounds of trash a day. I live in an affluent culture where most of what I use I throw away. I throw away more when I've finished than most people have when they begin. In my throwaway world 70 percent of all the metal I use is used only once. Some municipal dumps have higher percentages of copper than some mines that are operated profitably right now in the Rockies.

It is not just this "Waste Land" (T. S. Eliot) that is junked to the hilt on the spiritual junketings of a junk-food, junk-bond, junk-mail, junk-values waste-society. Bloated dumps, overflowing landfills, over-crowded prisons, homeless dopesters, drifters, and dropouts attest to the toxic contamination of our outer and inner environments.

If our souls are not to waste away, we must develop a waste aesthetic, even to the point of seeing our churches as a waste culture. We must develop a spiritual equivalent of waste management.

The Chinese have a saying: "All waste is treasure." Instead of throwing away garbage, it is time we, like some twenty-first-century prospectors mining landfills for profit, mine our garbage. Nothing is ever lost. Everything goes from here to eternity. How do postmoderns put it—the best definition of "feedback" ever devised? "What goes around comes around."

Try to burn it, bury it, ban it; try to dump it, drown it: you can't get rid of it. Sweep it under the rug, and it comes out the air vents. Burn it, and it goes into the air in the form of industrial pollutants like hydrochloric acid; organic pollutants like benzene, butane, furan, and toluene; cancer-causing metals like lead, cadmium, and mercury; or a toxic ash residue. Even "degradable plastics" and other biodegradable products degrade into things like heavy metals and toxins that leach into the ground and aquafers. Wastes wash up on our beaches, leak from landfills into the water and soil, and spew from incinerators into the air.

The postmodern world lives between the need to throw things away and the realization that nothing ever really goes away, that there is no "away" to which things can go. How does one live between the hell of a world in which nothing is ever thrown away and the hell of a throw-away world? How does one take out the garbage in this postmodern world?

The Composting Solution

The waste in our lives is best managed by multiple methods of composting. Of course, to some people composting makes about as much sense as collecting garbage. But that's precisely it: I have come to see that one of my prime jobs in life is as a garbage collector.

In composting, one season's refuse becomes fertilizer for next season's growth. That is why compost is the densest fertilizer imaginable. One day human, animal, and industrial wastes will replace all fertilizers.

A compost heap—this stewing, shredding, steaming, smelly cauldron of leaves, garbage, earthworms, insects, sawbugs, fungi, and bacteria—is a thing of beauty. Its importance was recognized by Jesus when he described savorless salt as not even fit to season a manure pile (Luke 14:35). There are some habits, some attitudes, some waste not worthy of a compost pile.

In the remote hollows of West Virginia I noticed something as a small child: grass grows greenest on graves. Later I learned what the green grass meant: humans are some of the most biodegradable products ever made. Everything God made is biodegradable. Rottedness and rootedness go together: a tree is fertilized by its dead branches. The soil is nothing more than planet Earth's compost heap. Old disintegrating habits and patterns fertilize cultural change; dung stimulates the true and the good and the beautiful; out of the chaos of the old, the new bloom is created.

The most seemingly godforsaken, unspeakable places may be precisely where God is to be found.

In fact, God has this habit of choosing the little, abused, maligned things to do his greatest work. Like planet Earth. Nothing special, this planet called Earth. The more we know about where Earth fits in the Milky Way galaxy, the less special it seems. It's a planet that goes around an ordinary star in an ordinary galaxy in an ordinary supercluster. Yet in this ordinary place God found an ordinary town, and some ordinary parents, to smuggle into the cosmos the very being of God.

That is the message of the gospel. In the least likely of times and places, God does God's greatest work. Wholeness is not the absence of disease but the creative combination of affliction and health, independence and dependency.

A boat-full of suffering and pain can be either a casket or a cradle.

The links between creativity and pain, creativity and suffering are symbolized in the story of Kopi Luwak coffee, the most expensive, exquisite, exotic, flavorful coffee in the world. The story of what makes Kopi Luwak worth $300 per pound is the gospel in a coffee bean.

The Luwak is a rare kind of civet cat native to Java and Sumatra. In Africa the civet cat (or more precisely its sex glands) is the source of musk, the chief ingredient in men's perfume. In Indonesia the civet cat is the source of the world's best coffee beans. A lot rides on the health of these fox-size creatures.

The Luwak has a very picky appetite. You might call it the Juan Valdez of the animal kingdom. It eats only the choicest, most perfectly matured coffee cherries, which it partially digests. The coffee beans then travel through the animal's intestinal tract and are evacuated.

The hard bean is then collected, roasted, and brewed. Stay in an East Java plantation, and this is the coffee they might serve you for breakfast.

Where in the waste is the wisdom?

—JAMES JOYCE

Build a Compost Heap

133

For the rest of the world, there are only about five thousand pounds of it available per year to people outside Bahasa, Indonesia—at $300 per pound. The most expensive coffee in the world carries the name "Dung Coffee."

Nature is filled with "dung coffees." What is honey? What do truffles grow in?

The message of the gospel is this: God can take the worst and turn it into the best. In the most wasted places, God does the greatest work. God can turn any Sheol into a Shiloh.

Where was Jesus born? What goes on in a stable? What were baby Jesus' first smells on earth?

Where was Jesus crucified? What were Jesus' last smells on earth?

The classic image for Ash Wednesday is burned garbage. Ashes are more than recycled palm fronds. They are a powerful reminder of that defoliated tree planted in the midst of Jerusalem's garbage dump, a place called Golgotha, a symbol of cruelty and ugliness and death that at the same time became the "fount of every blessing."

We coo about the dove, the symbol of the Holy Spirit. Artists paint doves sitting on the head of the Virgin Mary. But what is a dove? A dove is a pigeon, a trash bird. Pigeons become "doves" only on paper and out of the pens of poets.

The gospel of grace is a waste aesthetic: there are treasure chests buried in trash cans. Grace moves us from buried trash to buried treasure.

Take the story of how rugby began. A boy by the name of William Webb Ellis was playing soccer for a British school by the name of Rugby one day in 1832. Due to a lapse of concentration, Ellis caught the ball and ran to the goal with it instead of kicking it. The inevitable laughter and ridicule ensued. But instead of laughing along with everyone else and profiting from his mistake, Ellis was psychologically damaged. He felt brutalized and was painfully sensitive about his "mistake."

Someone who saw Ellis's "mistake" let it spark his imagination about a new sport in which the ball would be caught instead of kicked. A blunder became a boost to creativity, and a new sport was born, a sport that was never envisioned by the person who inspired it: rugby, the parent of football, the national sport of New Zealand. The Rugby World Cup has a worldwide viewing audience that, for a sporting event, is exceeded only by the Soccer World Cup. The trophy awarded every four years is named, ironically, after the person who "invented" the sport but who never claimed or envisioned the sport he invented: the William Webb Ellis Cup.

In every batch of garbage there is something to be composted, something to be transformed into a usable product.

SoulSalsa

The Recycling Solution

What can't be composted can be recycled. In recycling one takes worn-out, used-up, valueless objects and places them in a new context—giving them new identity and purpose. Our ancestors were recyclers. They used everything. For them, Reuse and Repair were first cousins. Even dog excrement used to be collected and sold to tanneries for the softening of skins. It is time to transition from modernity's planned obsolescence to a premodern/postmodern ethic of recycling.

The most efficient, safe, and beneficial way to dispose of uncomposted garbage is to recycle. There are a billion people who call themselves Christian. If each one of us would recycle, don't you think this world would be changed for the better?

My wife nails her recycling colors to the mast . . . and to my spine. I like the idea of recycling, but if it gets inconvenient or I get hurried, I make excuses and exceptions. My wife recycles. I want the glory of the winning tape without running the race. My wife runs. All the time.

She looks for goods made from recycled materials. She takes only paper at the checkout line. She disdains packaging, since half of all paper production and nearly a quarter of all plastics sold go to packaging. She practices the segregation of waste according to its content: organic or inorganic, wet or dry. She color-codes paper before recycling it at the dump (mixed paper brings San Juan County Solid Waste $7 per ton; sorted white paper brings $160 per ton). Such attention to detail is a big pain to me but a pleasure to my recycling wife. I tell her she's working harder than Cracker Barrel's full-time environmentalist (have you noticed their menus are printed with soy ink on recycled paper?). She tells me that the extra time for recycling this way is only about sixteen minutes per American household per week.

One of the best sources of fuel in life is recycled waste. So let's bring our garbage to God in humble repentance. Salvage what we can from past mistakes. Recycle the recyclable. Put the sins and missteps of the past to work for us in the present to transform our future. Recycle our mistakes so that they work for us, building us up rather than tearing us down. "It's not waste until it is wasted," says Dan Knapp, founder of Urban Ore, a recycling station in Berkeley, California.

Robert Frost put a fundamental spiritual principle poetically: "You have to live by shedding." The difference is that Christ changes not only the quantity of what we shed but its quality as well. Jesus' disciples are always shedding to the compost heap or the recycling bin things that others retain—hate, resentment, bitterness, jealousy, pride. We are

God moves mountains on rivers of tears.
—James Hisey II

always saving things that others discard—forgiveness, gentleness, vulnerability, sufferance, stillness, humility.

Everyone has met someone who is a walking bitterness bomb. Look at the Scriptures. Everyone knows someone who could have shed like Joseph. But instead of using his powers to make the sun stand still, he makes moonshine. Everyone knows someone who could have shed like Aaron. But instead of picking up heaven's manna and eating it as daily bread, he puts it in the freezer and saves it for a day that never comes. Everyone knows someone who could have shed like Lydia. But instead of the fire of the holy firing her up, she tries to put out the Spirit's fire. Everyone knows someone who could have shed like Rahab. But instead of letting her light shine, she turns out the lights.

It is now possible to recycle up to 95 percent of our waste. But recycling actually only treats symptoms of the problem, and may even exacerbate the disease unless recycling more is coupled with producing less. Waste reduction without source reduction (don't create the waste in the first place) is like trying to balance a family's clothing budget by making existing clothes last longer instead of spending less money on new clothes.

If putting on the mind of Christ does not stop the flow of garbage spewing forth from our lives, it does alter our garbage in three ways: what we throw away, how we throw it away, and how often we throw it away. Christians should generate less garbage than others. We will never shut down the waste industry, but we do need a source reduction mentality in our lives. It is time we stopped playing the package-to-garbage game in which our homes and hearts become revolving doors for things that look good in the shopping cart but are fit only for the garbage can.

There is one more biblical image that demonstrates just how powerfully Jesus turns trash cans into treasure chests. Along with the cross, spittle is the biblical image that conveys most forcefully how God can use the most unpromising parts of our past, the very worst and ugliest and most shameful parts of our lives, to be the greatest channels of blessing—to ourselves and others.

Ever notice how the body's fluids, when they leave the boundary of the body, become filthy and foul? Spit in the mouth is natural, even when it is shared between two people ("sucking face," in the colorful expression of our kids). Spit in the hand or air is nasty. Columnist/southern humorist Lewis Grizzard noted, "On New York City trains you get heavily fined if you spit. On the other hand, you're allowed to throw up for nothing."

The symbolism of spittle is an important one in the biblical witness. Spit expressed enmity and was itself considered to cause uncleanness

(Numbers 12:14). As the "suffering servant," Jesus suffered the indignity of spitting (Isaiah 50:6; Matthew 26:67). The affront of spitting was so severe that the Essenes punished spitting by a thirty-day penance. Today, spitting on someone is one of the most insulting things we can do to anyone. Spitting on someone is the closest we come to cursing someone.

Thelma was a black girl who, in the sixties, desegregated her eighth-grade Mississippi classroom. On her first day of school her teacher made her stand until everybody else had been seated. As Thelma stood there in her neatly starched dress, the other youngsters walked, one at a time, past her place and spit on her chair. The teacher then made Thelma sit down in that puddle of saliva, pretty dress and all.

What had been a symbol of enmity and derision became with Christ a symbol of grace and healing (Mark 7:33; John 9:6). When Jesus spat on someone, it became a healing ritual. It is for this reason that the ancient baptismal rites in Rome and Milan used spittle as part of the liturgy of water.

Jesus turned cursing into curing, belittling into blessing. The curse of being hanged on a tree was transformed into a symbol of forgiveness and salvation. This is the scandal of the gospel: that what in your life is most cursed and hateful, the trash of your soul, can become your greatest instrument for redemption and healing and blessing.

God is, if not happy about your errors, at least prepared to make almost anything you do grist for the divine mills. The Pentecostal ability of the Spirit to transfigure reality, no matter how harsh or horrific, continues unabated. Parched ground is some of the best soil in which to root a healthy soul.

Moses, a murderer, recycled his rage and hatred and became the greatest leader in Israel's history.

Jacob, a thief and a rogue, recycled his cunning and became the father of the nation.

David, an adulterer, recycled his passion and became the greatest of Israel's kings.

Simon Peter, a boastful, swearing fisherman, recycled his pride and became the rock on which Christ built his church.

Mary Magdalene, a mysterious woman, recycled her love and became a saint.

Zacchaeus, a quisling and a tax collector, recycled his miserly disciplines and became a disciple of Christ.

Saul of Tarsus, the leading persecutor of the Christian church, recycled his anger and assertiveness and became the greatest of the apostles, missionaries, and theologians.

Esther, a harem girl, recycled her sex appeal and saved the Jewish people from what would have been history's first Jewish holocaust.

"Paper or plastic?" is a moral choice, not a lifestyle preference.

—ERIC ZENCEY

Build a Compost Heap

137

Ruth, an idol worshiper and alien, recycled her foreignness and became a progenitor of Jesus the Christ.

Me . . . The very best in me is composted and recycled out of the very worst in me.

You . . . The very best in you is composted and recycled out of the very worst in you.

What treasures are we leaving buried in trash cans?

We have seen
The moon in lonely alleys make
A grail of laughter of an empty
    ash-can
And through all sounds of gaiety
    and quest
Have heard a kitten in the
    wilderness.
—Hart Crane

1. Discover the ritual of composting and share what you learn with at least one other person. If you need help getting started, go to the library and check out (recycle) one of the many excellent books on composting, such as Malcolm Beck's The Secret Life of Compost (1997).

2. Judith M. Myers-Walls, a professor of child development at Purdue, suggests this experiment to help children learn about the environmental impact of the polystyrene that encloses their hamburgers and fries and "find some green lessons in fast food." As she puts it:

   Layer a glass jar with gravel and moistened dirt and add some typical trash, including paper and polystyrene. Cover this with more dirt and add more layers as desired. Keep the material for a week or two. The contrast in the nature of the remains can help children focus on the problems created by the packaging of their favorite treats.

   Is there a kid in your life whom you'd like to try this with?

3. One of the most startling descriptions of God ever given was offered by Professor Albert T. Mollegen of Virginia Theological Seminary many years ago. God, he said, is a "celestial garbage collector. We live in the midst of our sin and it piles up until we are on a garbage heap with its stench in our nostrils. It is God who keeps our life livable and the atmosphere breathable."

   How do you bring your garbage to God? In what ways does God change what we throw away, how we throw it away, and how often?

4. Roy Dickens is a new kind of urban archaeologist. This professor from Georgia State University is dredging up history in the heart of the city by going on archaeological digs of old garbage dumps. Like other garbologists, he is poking through our garbage and finding that we are what we throw out. "People's garbage never lies," he says. "It tells the truth if you know how

to read it." Our lives, our values are reflected in our garbage. The only thing more personal than your garbage is your signature.

With your family gathered around, dump all the trash from the wastebaskets in your house onto a tarp (the easier to pick it up with later). What does your trash tell about you? What could you have kept out of the trash by shopping differently?

Follow up with field trips to a local landfill and recycling center.

5. Eric Zencey makes the case for both ecology and Christianity being "proselytizing, activist belief systems" that require "evangelists" who can preach "conversionism." He says,

> If I alone among two hundred and fifty million Americans recycle, I will still drown under mountains of trash and suffer the environmental consequences of our rapacious use of resources. My ethic requires me to try to change the behavior of others. If recycling does not become a public ethos, I fail in my ethical and practical purposes.

Do you think he's right? Do you know people who are more "evangelistic" about recycling junk in their homes than receiving Jesus into their hearts? Is Zencey being a bit severe or right on target in arguing that "recycling has become the primary ritual activity by which we affirm our moral value against the difficult and unforgiving commandments of ecology. It's how we prove ourselves worthy of ecological grace, it's how we redeem ourselves, it's how we assuage our environmental guilt"?

6. To what extent is retirement a throwaway culture's answer to dealing with its elderly? How would retirement change if we thought less of retiring and more of re-tiring, re-cycling, and re-treading lives?

7. If you can afford it and you've got the stomach for it, order some Kopi Luwak coffee online at http://www.thecoffeecritic.com/.

8. Instead of recycling, we are now being encouraged in "precycling," which means to cut down the amount of trash at its source. Or put simply, use less "stuff." Some companies who have experimented successfully with "precycling" are Procter & Gamble, whose use of flexible packaging (e.g., for Tide) seems

Not many of you were wise by human standards, not many were powerful, not many were of noble birth. But God chose what is foolish in the world to shame the wise; God chose what is weak in the world to shame the strong; God chose what is low and despised in the world, things that are not, to reduce to nothing things that are.

—PAUL
(1 CORINTHIANS 1:26–28 NRSV)

SoulSalsa

to be working. So too did Ocean Spray, which proved that cutting down on the initial packaging can mean greater profits.

For a free copy of the precycling resource Use Less Stuff Report, contact Partners for Environmental Progress, P.O. Box 130116, Ann Arbor, MI 48113. Or call them at 313-668-1690. Or access their Web site: http://cygnus group.com/PEP/About_PEP.html/.

Many of the insights of the saint stem from his experience as a sinner.

—LONGSHOREMAN/PHILOSOPHER
ERIC HOFFER

Build a Compost Heap

13

Declare a Sabbatical

One of the local characters on Orcas Island, where I live, is named Applegate. His friends call him App. For App, life holds nothing more precious than sailing. His passion is unending as he builds by hand his eighty-foot dream boat out of native Northwest timber. Locals trek up the mountain to cheer on this newest "Noah" as he builds his ark under a mountaintop's cover of cedars and Douglas firs.

For ten years now App has been hammering and sawing hour by hour, day after day, week upon week. The construction has been running a few years slower than he figured, App admits, but he's confident the yacht will be finished in the next few years.

App is in his eighties.

I look at App with Janus-faced irony. He's my hero: someone not afraid to commit to a project that takes him into his eighties and nineties. But in my about-face, he's my antihero: someone whose passion for a life experience has lifted that very experience out of his life.

One day a friend asked App to explain his obsession. "I love sailing," he disclosed.

"Been sailing recently?" my friend wondered. App's hesitant admission of "been too busy" seemed to shock him into momentary awareness. But he returned to his nails.

The harder we hammer nails, the more unfurled our sails. The faster the lanes get in life, the more fatal our inability to slow down. The hotter the culture gets, the cooler the soul's core becomes. The more culture accelerates, the more axiomatic the soul's decelerations.

Catch Your Breath

This art of godly living involves how you choose to spend your time. Since time has replaced money as the prime scarcity of this new world, this chapter may be one of the most difficult in the book for you to read, as it certainly has been the most difficult chapter for me to write.

The pilgrim's problem is not one of working too hard. When you're on a mission, there's no such thing as "getting ahead." You're always "behind" and "working too hard." The pilgrim's problem is not having spaces to recuperate in so that his soul can catch up, so that she doesn't leave her soul behind.

I suspect one reason why Jesus chose such a high percentage of fishermen to be his disciples was because who would better know how to adjust to fluctuating currents and weather conditions? For fishermen, life is a rhythm of sunshine and rain, of heavy lifting and light chatting, of work and play, of letting go and pulling in, of rumination and conversation, of speech and silence, of bending and bearing.

Tell me, what is it you plan to do with your one wild and precious life?
—POET MARY OLIVER

The word *spirituality* comes from the Latin *spiritus,* which means "breath of life." In Hebrew it is *ruah;* in Greek, *pneuma;* in English, *wind* or *breath*. A "spiritual" life is one that breathes in and out the "breath of life." The body is God-breathed. It cannot help but breathe with regularity. The soul must will itself to breathe and live. It gasps for air until it finds its breath.

Hence the Sabbath. The root of *Sabbath* means "to catch one's breath." The faster and fuller you exhale, the more you need to inhale. The Bible is designed to transform your life. One of the biggest transformations is the formation of multilingual souls: souls that have learned the languages of exhaling and inhaling, of speech and silence, the interior rhythms of space and time.

But a twenty-four-hour breath catching is one deep-breathing exercise that is too labored, too forced for postmoderns. Postmoderns can't hold their breath for one day and then exhale for six. They need multiple inhalations to breathe more deeply. Besides, for pastors that seventh day allows no rest.

In other words, to breathe new being into the soul, we need to decentralize our Sabbath keeping. Sabbath does not come just once a week. Every day needs a holy hiatus. Every week needs to be well ventilated with sabbaticals.

In many ways this used to be the function of the *Sanctus*. The *Sanctus* is sung or spoken at most Christian communion services. But the *Sanctus* (also called the *qedushah**) was originally chanted by Jewish congregants at dawn and dusk services as a coronation rite. In

---

*qedushah—The *qedushah* is recited by Sephardic Jews in the *Mussaf* service on Sabbaths, New Moons, and Festivals in this form: "A crown they give unto You, YHWH our God, angels enthroned above and Your people Israel gathered below. All of them together thrice proclaim Your holiness, as has been spoken by Your prophet's word: 'They call out to one another, saying: Holy, holy, holy is the Lord of hosts! The whole earth is filled with His glory!'"

early synagogue worship the *qedushah* was a daily enthronement of God as ruler of the universe and as Lord of one's life.

A weekly or daily Sabbath is a ritual crowning of God's reign and governance. It is life leaning into the sway and swag of the Spirit. But all of life can be a coronation rite. To acquiesce in the software language of "take time" to grow a soul, or "brick into your schedule" a firewall for divine downtimes, is to pander to today's instant everything (gratification, credit, communication) mindset and to fail to translate back and forth the languages of the spirit and of the body.

You can't download a soul or the software package for godly living. Growing a soul is a 24x7x365 deep-breathing lifestyle of soulful practices. The soul is forged over time through a patient and painful process in which everything that happens contributes to the soul's identity. There is no such thing as "unproductive time." All time is producing something. It takes all of life to fashion a soul.

I have stopped saying to people, "Have a good day." Good days don't just happen. Good days are created. I now say, "*Create* a good day." It is my way of saying to a pre-Christian culture, "Clothe yourself with Christ" (see Galatians 3:27).

One of the best ways to create good days is to open up on a daily basis macaroni spaces for Sabbath inhalations. Not manicotti spaces, which are more like the traditional twenty-four-hour Sabbath shutdowns. But rigatoni or ravioli spaces where life's sweetness is constantly being Sabbath-wrapped for savoring and sheltering. Macaroni spaces are not spent spaces but the most pregnant spaces of the soul.

SPACE 1: "WASTED" SPACE

In the art of soulful living, nothing is "waste."

In a culture where the less time you have to yourself, the more prestige and power you appear to have, one of the most revolutionary of acts is to "waste time" and to defend "wasted time" as a best use of time. To go through life never "wasting time" is to ride your gift-horse too hard and to overwork your gifts.

Waste space is most particularly God's space—the space God enters first. Look at all that empty, wasted space in Gothic cathedrals. That was God's space. Look at all the empty, wasted space in one's life going to concerts and plays and baseball games. That is God's space.

Time off, wasted time, useless time is often God's time. Even God wasted time. "On the seventh day God rested and drew breath," the Bible says (see Genesis 2:2).

SPACE 2: SIESTA

Jesus took naps. The "Lord of the Sabbath" (Mark 2:28) wasn't shy about taking minisabbaticals. One of the least celebrated of the soul arts is knowing the "times" and knowing what to do about them—not the outer "times" à la the descendants of the tribe of Issachar (1 Chronicles 12:32), but the inner "times" à la the descendants of the tribes of Aaron and Levi, who provided priestly services to their nation.

There is a time to get a grip, and a time to loosen your grip. There is a time to press the flesh, and a time to press the pillow.

But siesta Sabbaths involve more than nap taking or midmorning breaks and midafternoon "delights." For Jewish theologian Abraham Joshua Heschel, Sabbath was a "sanctuary in time," an enchanted island of space and time in which the Sabbath keeper explored fresh reserves of energy and courage and creativity. This can happen communally and individually in a variety of ways. A church picnic can be soul manna for one, a soul meat grinder for another. Just as there is no one life plan for every life span, so there is no one blueprint for building "sanctuaries" in time and space.

I should tell you that I am writing here against the grain of my own preferences and habits. If God had ever consulted me, reduced sleep and an absence of siestas would have been my preference. A personal hero of mine is Randy Gardner. At my exact age in 1965 he set the world record for staying awake: 264 hours, or eleven days. I've done almost everything imaginable within the legal limits to cut down my sleep time. I've even experimented with my own versions of Aristotle's technique of studying while holding in his hand a metal ball. If he fell asleep, the ball would fall into a metal basin below. The noise was an alarm clock that awakened him so he could begin reading again.

To be given the rarest of all gifts—the gift of life—and to have the price of that gift be spending one-third of one's life "dead to the world" ... well, it all seems so unproductive to my overproductive mind.

But that's because some of us are better at unpacking than packing. It is trickier to know how to pack than unpack. But unless one spends a sufficient amount of time packing, the unpacking marathon of lectures and exhibitions and presentations will show the slight and suffer.

I still try to "stack" my packing and unpacking. A lot of this book was typed into my computer while listening on my computer to Internet radio stations featuring southern gospel artists like the Martins or the McKameys or the Gold City Quartet. Another favorite stacking siesta is my visits to sacred sites—both sites sacred to the Christian faith and sites sacred to my spiritual stock, places where my ancestors'

> Holy, holy, holy is the Lord of hosts! The whole earth is filled with His glory.
> —SANCTUS

torches of faith first flamed out and were then handed down to me. A travel sabbatical is less about sight-seeing than a spiritual quest that helps you find out things about who you are and where you've come from so that you can come back with a deeper perspective on life in the Spirit.

But I am learning (too often the hard way) that sometimes I need to completely focus on packing, with no thought of unpacking. So I physically "crash" in bed. Or I spiritually "crash" with my stash of Bill and Gloria Gaither "Homecoming" videos. I sink in my chair and let the Happy Goodman family, the Speers, Jesse Dixon, Russ Taff help me cry the toxins out of my system. Or I become a "kidult" (an adult acting like a kid) and roll in the grass or jump off a wall or hang out with buddies in a hot tub.

SPACE 3: SLOWING THE FLOW

There is a time to stack, changing the flow of change by making time do double, treble duty. And there is a time to slow the flow of change, to put life in slow motion and indulge the "MEGO" syndrome ("My Eyes Glaze Over"). You can leave a room without leaving the room by kicking in the MEGO syndrome.

Once again, I'm bad at this myself. I'm learning to slow the flow and let MEGO. But I don't allow myself enough MEGO moments, and too often I don't allow others sufficient MEGO moments. Any member of the Sweet family can declare a spontaneous sabbatical that stops everyone in their tracks and brings the family to a common halt of inhaling God's holiness. The master of spontaneity in our Sabbath-keeping household? The person who declares the most sabbaticals for the Sweet family is a four-year-old: Soren Coventry Sweet.

Two Dallas couples and I were on a ten-seat Harbor Airlines evening shuttle from Seattle to Friday Harbor in the San Juan Islands. We were flying over one of the most exquisite seascapes in the world, especially at dusk—the shimmering waters of the San Juans teeming with orca and minke whales, sea lions, otters, dolphins, not to mention the eagles and ospreys and legions of shorebirds.

One passenger read a business magazine the whole way, looking up only to smile at her husband. Another did not open his eyes once. Not because he was resting but because he was white-knuckling the whole thirty-minute flight with head down and lips in lock grip. Another didn't like the setting sun streaming in on her face, so she held up a flight magazine to cover the window and tried to doze off, leaning her head against the handmade blind. When the dozing didn't come, she began blowing bubbles of saliva to stave off boredom.

Only one passenger, the husband of the wife with head buried in business, basked in the beauty of the San Juans, his body perched on the edge of the seat so as to better take in as many of the 777 islands and countless spectacular scenes as the short flight afforded.

I saw myself in these passengers. Not in the one with the smiling face when we disembarked, but in the other three. In some ways I was worse off than all three put together. I was so busy watching them miss everything that I too missed out on the cosmos's symphony. Forget Kodak moments. How often am I in the midst of a God moment and can't receive it because I can't slow the flow of my own agenda and look up from my laptop, even if it is this book I am working on?

Every spiritual master has stressed the theological imperatives of slowing the flow sufficiently to savor the silent mysteries of divine design. Why else did Jesus "come apart" so often and instruct his disciples to protect his apartness?

The quickest way to slow the flow is to take a hike. Literally. Walk. Stroll. Saunter. Ride a bike. The scientific evidence is overwhelming. The best way to change your mood? Take a ten-minute walk. Get rid of that treadmill tension by getting on that treadmill in the basement. Feeling tense and anxious? Take a long walk, hot bath, hard massage, or quick sauna.

Part of Sabbath keeping is slowing the flow enough to become a drifter: drift through the woods, drift through your downtown, drift through your PalmPilot, drift through a park. Some people just need to get out more.

A favorite sabbatical that slows the flow of my soul is a day spent in creation's anthem of autumn in one of two places. Either wandering the back roads of New York State's Finger Lakes region, with a grape pie and jug of cider to take home at the end of the day. Or nibbling apples from the nippled hills of West Virginia after a day negotiating hairpin turns that slow you down upon penalty of death and forcibly twist your head to imbibe the russet colors of autumn.

I predict a renaissance for baseball in the next century. In a world that rewards speed and split-second decision making, baseball is so agonizingly slow that it's an almost out-of-this-world experience. Besides, like its midspeed competitor football (basketball and soccer are the fast sports), it gets us semi-outdoors and slows us down enough to relish in creation. The Seattle Mariners just built a $550-million stadium so they could play outside again.

There are even ways to slow the flow in the midst of cyborgian technology. Postmoderns don't give a second thought to technology. It's like an extension of their arms and legs because it *is* an extension of their arms and legs. I have fixed my computer so that every time I log in I must pass through a word that slows me down spiritually. My first password was "Shalom," but when too many people were accessing my accounts, I changed it to "Peace." For four years I have been slowed down when I signed my letters "Still in One Peace" and been slowed down before entering cyberspace under the portal of "Peace"—that is, until one of those six hundred thousand porn sites on the Internet stole my screen name and used it to assail a couple thousand unsuspecting friends and colleagues with porno pictures before AOL caught them.

SPACE 4: STOPPING THE FLOW

Connectedness mandates disconnectedness. Sometimes the soul requires a sabbatical that involves more than just "adjusting the dials" and giving it a soulful spin. Sometimes the soul needs the flow to stop completely.

Sometimes, to find yourself, you have to be able and willing to lose track of yourself. Can you take yourself off the track? When was the last time you got off the track?

The typical corporate employee receives 177 messages a day in e-mail, phone, faxes, letters, etc. To achieve spiritual mastery of your life, you need to know when to turn off the beeper, to leave the phone off the hook, to pace yourself, to join the Lead Pencil Club.

The Lead Pencil Club is a real club that exists to oppose this "godless age of speed and technology." Proud of being a "pothole in the Information Superhighway," members protest the way we have "raced at incredible speed on the Information Superhighway to reach our final destination—nothing." The club motto is "Not so Fast."

To join the Lead Pencil Club does not require us to become like novelist/musician Paul Bowles, who in his eighties lived in the desert without a telephone. But it does require us to sometimes turn off the phone and shut down the beeper. I don't wear a watch for the same reason I don't answer every question that someone may ask me or the same reason I don't answer the phone every time it rings and never at supper.

A healthy Lead Pencil Club ritual is not to answer the phone at supper time. This may cause a few toes to curl in and a few lips to curl up. But what better way of confessing that God is God and that you and I are not? Our illusions of omnipotence leave us in a state of impotence. God is in control. God is God. W. H. Auden's poem "Epistle to a Godson" includes this line: *"Be glad your being is unnecessary."* The axis of the world doesn't turn on whether you get through that list, accomplish that task, pick up that phone, or answer that question.

SoulSalsa

In fact, asking questions can be a form of control. A true answer doesn't solve anything. It opens up new problems. Theologian Paul Tillich was famous for never knowing a dumb question. He was wrong. There are some wrong, dumb questions. And there are some questions my life doesn't have to answer.

The greatest stop-the-flow experiences of them all, however, are the ones that occur in our communal religious life. Singing, praying, celebrating the sacraments: the congregation at worship is the intravenous feeding of the soul. You didn't give birth to yourself. You can't give birth to your soul yourself. To be connected to Christ means to be connected to other members of his body. In the words of "The Servant Song":

> We are travelers on a journey
> Fellow pilgrims on the road;
> We are here to help each other
> Walk the mile and bear the load.

The community of faith is where our lives are bound. To be sure, living sacramentally means one worships all the time, not just one or two hours per week. But an organic relationship of connectedness to the body is what ushers us into the truth.

And what is the truth? Truly, God is with us. When God seems most hidden, God is often most near.

It is only through the church's intravenous feeding of the soul that we gain the courage and confidence for the living of these spiritually daring and dangerous days. In times of hiddenness and despair, the simple prayer of one righteous person can set the whole ship of Zion to singing.

The big ferryboats, both the oldest and the newest, that carry cars and passengers back and forth across Puget Sound in the Seattle area are all plagued by a similar problem. As the big engines turn, they vibrate and send off a harmonic hum. But the frequency and pitch of this hum will inevitably be picked up by the steel girders of the ship's skeleton. As a result, these giant beams begin to sing like huge tuning forks. This "song" can be so loud that it alarms unknowing passengers and forces the bridge crew to wait for the humming to stop before they can hear each other speak again.

The sound of one voice praying, the peace of one soul breathing, the resonance of one soul vibrating with the divine is enough to release the full sound of the church's witness.

Nikolay Ivanovich Bukharin, communist propagandist and revolutionary leader, was sent to Kiev in the early 1920s to address a vast rally organized by the state. For an hour he harangued people about their

No one can be a Christian alone.

—JOHN WESLEY

Declare a Sabbatical

149

belief in God. He used mockery, satire, ridicule, argument. When he stepped down, there was silence. Questions were invited. There was silence.

Finally a priest of the Russian Orthodox Church asked to speak and was given permission. He marched up to where Bukharin was standing, faced the vast assembly, and greeted them with the ancient liturgical Easter greeting: "Christ is risen." Immediately the whole assembly rose to its feet, and the reply came back like thunder from the heavens: "He is risen indeed."

SPACE 5: RADICAL SABBATICALS

Sabbath was not designed to be a day to do what you please, Isaiah warned (58:13), but to do what pleases God.

Sometimes what pleases God is serious self-examination. The Hebrew term for the verb "to pray" is *le hitpalel,* which means "to judge oneself" or even "to struggle with oneself." Once in a while a sabbatical involves a season of prayer that puts one's life on God's plumb line. Every so often a sabbatical requires a pilgrim to become a theologian-in-residence on the road to who *you* are and to where *you* are headed in life's journey. Now and then life mandates an extreme season of study—"thinking is the dialogue of the soul with itself," contends Hans-Georg Gadamer—to discern the will of God and to decide what paths to take next.

Radical sabbaticals are transformative, especially when it comes to one's work life. The new economic order is a time of polyemployment, not unemployment, a time when one will have less a "career" than a "careen," as philosopher Dallas Willard puts it (although in the nineteenth century *career* meant "racing course" or "rapid and unrestrained activity").

This makes radical self-scrutiny all the more requisite. Periodically we need to ask the most basic questions: Am I doing what God is calling me to do? Is my life pleasing to God? Am I a change-the-world person? Or in more biblical phrasings, am I being "created in Christ Jesus for good works, which God prepared beforehand to be our way of life" (Ephesians 2:10 NRSV)? Though imperfect, does my "career" keep my soul sputtering and sparking into life?

People are feeling more pressed for time when they actually have more free time than ever. Why? Are we trying to keep ever more balls in the air?

During the last century, over 40 percent of a lifetime was devoted to leisure. In the next fifteen years that figure will be over 50 percent. How will we spend our "leisure time"? The original Latin word for school—

skhole—meant leisure in the pursuit of knowledge. Our "leisure time" will be occupied how? On carrying out spiritual pursuits? On doing good? On reinventing ourselves for new missions and ministries? On being creative parents? On balancing our soul's core identity with the need for perpetual makeovers?

Or on entertaining ourselves until our life becomes a grotesque monument to irrelevance?

Or on deluding ourselves with the notion that we can keep all our options open?

A radical sabbatical ruthlessly closes some options. If there is one thing postmoderns resent, it is having to close options. With literally thousands of options to choose from, we think we can keep them all open. We think we can be whatever we want to be.

You can't marry all the pretty girls you meet. You can't work for every company in town. You have to close some options. You either turn away from the worship of gods created by human hands or you pay the consequences. In a culture where we have choices for this and that and the other thing, there are some no-choice choices.

No choice. You're going to die.

No choice. You have to eat to live.

No choice. You have to sleep.

No choice. You are designed for the divine.

SPACE 6: SPIRIT-SOAKING

I can get stressed out trying to relieve stress. I can get unhinged trying to unwind. Sabbaticals can be provoking more than thought-provoking.

No wonder some 32 percent of Christians describe themselves as stressed out. That is similar to the percentage for non-Christians and the same as that of atheists (35 percent). For Christians as well as for non-Christians, the least stressful day of the week is not Sunday but Thursday.

What's needed is something I call Spirit-soaking. David Steindl-Rast, a Benedictine monk, calls it "God bathing." Whatever you call it, this form of sabbatical majors in "minor," mindless activities: "moodling," doodling, letting your mind "go blank," listening to repetitious sounds or drumbeats. All these things can calm the brain and body and usher the soul into the power, mystery, and sublime presence of the sacred.

One Spirit-soaking mantra I speak or whisper; the other I chant. My spoken mantra is an abbreviation of the prayer "Not my will, but thine." I've distilled it down to three words: "Not mine, thine." My

A true artist always puts something of his time in his art, and also his soul.
— FRENCH SCULPTOR AUGUSTE RODIN

chanted mantra is the Christian's equivalent of "Om." Its source is in the African American tradition: "A-men. A-men. A-men. A-men. A-men." Sometimes I'll chant these five "A-mens" a hundred times under my breath.

Sometimes I Spirit-soak in the surround sound of sacred music from the artistry of Paul Hillier's Theatre of Voices or Arvo Pärt or "Trane" (John Coltrane) or Gregorian chant. What Coltrane said about his masterpiece, *A Love Supreme,* can be said about all sacred music: 90 percent of his playing was actually prayer.

Jazz and chants deserve special note. Jazz has been called "America's classical music." Listening to America's true classical musicians perform has become one of my richest soul-soaks in the topsy-turvy, upside-down, wrongside-up, inside-out gospel of Jesus the Christ. Here is this nation's most distinctive music, created by a portion of the population that was denied by that nation its most basic benefits and rights.

The legend is that Gregorian chant was invented when the Holy Spirit, in the form of a dove, first whispered chants that quiet and soften the soul into the ear of Pope Gregory I (c. A.D. 600). Chants are what Dwight Ozard calls "living room records," musical collections "so intimate and telling that it's hard to imagine them being performed as much as being *shared.*"

The chants of the church are the spiritual law of gravity in musical form: Your soul is calibrated for the divine. You are designed to live in a temple of the Spirit. Live in a temple of the flesh and you die. Live in a temple of the Spirit and you dance.

God's people deserve to dance.

And God deserves dancing people.

You are a gift to life, and life is a gift to you. Rejoice and be glad in it.

How seldom is it that the soul keeps itself silent enough for God to speak.
—WILLIAM BUCKHOUSE
AND JAMES JANSON

1. Have you noticed how more and more businesses are allowing and even encouraging their employees to take naps and sabbaticals? Charles Schwab & Co., named one of the top ten companies to work for, has a fully paid sabbatical after just five years.

   What is the sabbatical policy for your church staff? If you don't have one, what should it be? Is "napping" on the job encouraged?

2. University of Chicago psychologist and creativity researcher Mihaly Csikszentmihalyi shows statistically that people are three times more likely to record positive experiences at work than at leisure. Why do you think this is so? Is it so in your own life?

3. Why does it seem that two hours in an airplane go on for two days, while two hours in a restaurant with friends fly by in two seconds?

4. In a culture that is time-conscious and cost-consuming, the church is time-consuming and cost-conscious. Is this where the church should be? Or do you see the church somewhere else?

5. Listen to John Coltrane's A Love Supreme (Impulse! 1964), which was recorded with his quartet of 1961–65. As you do so, explore the Web site of St. John Coltrane African Orthodox Church, located in San Francisco's Western Addition district (http://www.saintjohncoltrane.org/).

6. Theodore Zeldin, renowned French scholar and author of An Intimate History of Humanity, argues that sabbaticals, more than a career management idea, will be a human right demanded in the twenty-first century. Believable?

7. If you haven't already seen it, rent the video of The Karate Kid. Note how the young karate student learns the basic self-defense techniques not through exciting sparring matches but by completing a series of exhausting tasks his learned master assigns him. He learns to make a mantra, a meditative alpha-wave exercise of rubbing "wax-on/wax-off" an old car or painting "brush up/brush down" an old fence.

What can you do to be more intentional about finding ways to create alpha-wave moments in the midst of daily chores?

8. Can you keep up the pace you are living now for the next fifty years? What needs to change for the sake of long-term endurance?

9. Canadian postmodern theorist and culture critic Arthur Kroker, professor of Political Theory at Concordia University in Montreal, calls this time we live in "the recline of Western Civilization." Not "decline," but "recline."

What are some symptoms of our "recline"?

Isn't our inability to "recline" itself a symptom of our decline?

10. Management guru Tom Peters talks about "The Big R," which he contrasts with the "the 3 R's" (reading, attending seminars, taking three-week vacations). Some of his examples of "The Big R" are these:
- spending a year working in the inner city or Third World
- taking two hours off in the middle of the day, at least three days a week, to do whatever
- quitting a job with nothing particular in mind for a next step (drifting for six months to a year)
- grabbing a three-year assignment/demotion to a location or division totally foreign to one's expertise and training.

Have you known people to take "The Big R"? What "Big R" would you be willing to take?

I know, it was useless, of course, her dancing.
I know. But God above it was beautiful!
Beautiful! God!

—POET LAUREATE ANDREW MOTION

SoulSalsa

14

Play at Life

SOUL ARTISTS APPROACH LIVING NOT AS WORK BUT AS ADVENTURE.

In the grammar of my life, the word *play* has replaced the words *plan* and *work*. If life's journey is to be more than a chronological slog from cradle to grave, life must do more than "work."

I don't want my life to "work." I want my life to sing. And for that to happen, I must learn to count on one thing: life never turns out as you expect it will. In other words, I must learn how to play. Life is all about playing.

Play is more an approach to life than an activity in life. Play is already the number one learning experience of postmodern culture. Postmodern learning is shaped by "educational playthings."

It is not just children who play "war games." It is not just children whose toybox is a toolbox.

"Fun" is one of the official values of the publicly traded PeopleSoft, which sells ERP (enterprise resource planning) software. According to linguistic theorists, there is now more wordplay than at any previous period of history.

In the modern world, the Protestant ethic sanctified work. In the postmodern world, the Christian ethic sanctifies play. That word *work* was made sacred, as work itself was made sacred, by the Protestant ethic. But in the Bible, work is not sacred. Play is more sacred than work.

Find some work you can play.

Find some relationship you can play.

Clouds and Clocks

"Of Clouds and Clocks" was the title of one of Sir Karl Popper's most famous lectures. It was given in honor of Arthur Holly Compton, one of the first physicists to embrace Heisenberg's uncertainty principle and other concepts relating to physical indeterminism. Clouds symbolize physical systems that are highly erratic and unpredictable.

At the other extreme are physical systems that are uniform, orderly, and highly predictable, that is, clocks.

Popper's thesis was simple: life is more like clouds than clocks. In making this claim he was declaring his independence from some mighty big names. If clockwork precision was on the right and fickle cloudiness on the left, Sir Isaac Newton taught that everything belonged on the right. In fact, for Newton, clouds were clocks. It was the Newtonian view of the clockwork universe that dominated the modern world.

Only a few spoke for the clouds. The American philosopher Charles Sanders Peirce was the first to break ranks with the Newtonians and dared the dissent that, to some degree, all clocks are clouds. In fact, for Peirce "only clouds exist, though clouds of very different cloudiness."

The clock regulates our offices and homes. We hang it like a cross in some of the most prominent places in our homes, and we wear it on our bodies. Yet it is futile to expect a day to go "like clockwork," Popper claimed, since any day's horizons are as variable as the clouds in the sky. We are at the mercy of the unknown.

Popper did realize (as did Compton before him) that it is not enough to replace determinism with indeterminism without factoring in intentions, spirit, dreams (and divine providence). Popper illustrated it with this passage from Compton's Terry Lectures:

> It was some time ago when I wrote to the secretary of Yale University agreeing to give a lecture on November 10 at 5 p.m. He had such faith in me that it was announced publicly that I should be there, and the audience had such confidence in his word that they came to the hall at the specified time. But consider the great physical improbability that their confidence was justified. In the meanwhile my work called me to the Rocky Mountains and across the ocean to sunny Italy. A phototropic organism [such as I happen to be, would not easily] ... tear himself away from there to go to chilly New Haven. The possibilities of my being elsewhere at this moment were infinite in number. Considered as a physical event, the probability of meeting my engagement would have been fantastically small. Why then was the audience's belief justified? ... They knew my purpose, and it was my purpose [which] determined that I should be there.

Can you surrender to life's surprises? Can you entertain epiphanies that come out of the clouds? Or will you attempt to wrest control out of chaos and make clocks out of clouds?

If you follow only one recommendation from this book, follow the one suggested to sociologist Sherry Turkle by the thirteen-year-old she observed playing SimLife: "Just play."

—LAST SENTENCE IN LARRY DOWNES AND CHUNKA MUI'S BOOK, UNLEASHING THE KILLER APP

Life does not go according to plan. Long-range plans, even short-range plans, are exercises in turning clouds into clocks. If we cannot know what one day may bring forth, how can we lock in plans for a week, a month, or a year?

A whole-soul existence is not an "in control" life; it's an out-of-control life. Disciples of Jesus don't want the upper hand. God gets the upper hand. All of life is placed within God's control. Too much of the simplicity movement is less about simplifying your life than about bringing life under your control. Finding peace is not getting control of life. Finding peace is trusting God even when life is out of control.

And where is life more out of control than in our relationships, and especially in marriage, that tricky dance of two people who sometimes seem so much alike, sometimes utterly different?

Playing at Marriage

A marriage that isn't "working" is a marriage that isn't playing. Elizabeth and I are learning how to play at marriage, not work at it. To "make our relationship work" would be for us to grind away at it and grind it down. To "make our relationship play" is to orbit our lives around a mission—creating advance centers in the three landscapes Jesus picked to root and reboot his own spirit: the mountains, the water, and the desert. (We've got the desert center still to go.)

The Protestant reformer Martin Luther spoke some "real" words that have become more "real" with every passing anniversary. He said, "Some marriages are motivated by mere lust, but mere lust is felt even by fleas and lice. Love begins when we wish to serve others."

Marriage is a sign of our baptism, a part of our greater covenant relationship to God. What makes matrimony "holy"? One of the first things I remember hearing about holy matrimony is that "marriage is hard work." To have a happy marriage, a marriage where two people are "as happy as two owls in a hole," as poet Elizabeth Barrett said of her marriage to Robert Browning, both parties must be willing to "work at it."

Work at understanding. Work at listening. Work at praying together.

It is all too much work.

Some people are scandalized that my wife and I haven't "worked out" a more routine prayer life together. My wife is Episcopalian. Some of my intimacies with the divine leave her uneasy. My love of southern gospel music (the more nasal the better) leaves her completely mystified. Between her more formal style of spirituality and my tumultuous

> When two people love each other, they don't look at each other. They look in the same direction.
> —DANCER/ACTRESS GINGER ROGERS

schedule, we have decided that it is more important that both of us constantly pray and keep growing spiritually than that we consistently pray together. The two of us are not always on the same spiritual track. But we're always moving in the same spiritual direction.

Some people are scandalized that my wife and I don't work harder at "listening to each other." Studies have shown that "active listening" ("So what I hear you saying is . . .") doesn't work. Why? It is too much work.

Your average run-of-the-mill, run-at-the-mouth marriage runs on the work paradigm. The happiest marriages go with the flow—each giving in to the other, each letting the other "have their own way," each willing to be influenced by the other, each more playing than working at their relationship. For a marriage to sing and dance, for two people to make beautiful music together, they need to play, not work, at their marriage.

You learn to "play," not "work," a musical instrument, a character in a play, any art form. You don't "work" a bassoon; you "play" a bassoon.

Marriages are more complex and chaotic than ever. Dual-career marriages won't "work" on the work paradigm. Ditto commuter marriages and blended families. Especially intimate marriages.

It is hard for us to appreciate the fact that the Boomer generation is the first in history to attempt to base a marriage on something other than duty or obligation. It wasn't too long ago, in historical terms, that marriages were arranged by parents for economic or political reasons, or were at least orchestrated under parental supervision. The Puritans had a saying: "First you chose your love; then you love your choice." By the nineteenth century, a romance ethic came into play, but the love one falls into is the love one quickly can fall out of.

What kept marriages going for as long as they did (the average marriage in the 1890s lasted only twelve years) was the work ethic of duty and responsibility. These duty-based marriages issued in such sayings as "Marriage is a proposition ending in a sentence" and "Marriage is three weeks of curiosity, three months of love, and thirty years of tolerance." These duty-based marriages also issued in parents with separate beds, separate bedrooms, and shared lives that could sometimes be a sham. How many of my generation saw parents who could sit beside each other without any acknowledgment of each other's existence? How many of my generation vowed to ourselves in silence, *I'll die first*?

Some have argued that the recent emergence of intimacy-based marriages constitutes an epochal development in history. Whether or not that is overstated, the very concept of a "couple consciousness" or a "soul mate" makes a work-ethic marriage problematic. For soul mates

If A is a success in life, then A equals x plus y plus z. Work is x; y is play; and z is keeping your mouth shut.
—ALBERT EINSTEIN

SoulSalsa

marriage is not a work in progress but an art form in process where each person "plays" his or her strengths and covers the other's weaknesses.

We are at our most amateurish when we "work" anything. We are at our most accomplished when we "play" something. Amateur athletes don't "play" sports; they "work" sports. Michael Jordan didn't "work" basketball; he "played" basketball.

Fort Lauderdale pastor Dick Wills has a principle that goes like this: "The greater the relationship, the fewer the rules."

> When Eileen and I were first married, I was surprised to find out there were so many rules. There were rules about where to squeeze the toothpaste tube; rules about picking up one's dirty clothes; rules about how you wash dishes; rules about taking out the trash; and on and on. Now after thirty-three years of marriage we have only one rule in our family. The rule is to always tell the truth. Everything else is based on relationship. The greater the relationship, the fewer the rules.

Where relationship rules, there is little need for rules. Or as Augustine put it about the greatest relationship of all, "Love God and do what you will."

Get to Work Playing

Not only in marriage must we overcome the gravity of the modern tradition that would suck us into the black hole of work, work, work. The same is true in all our activities and relationships from alarm clock to hit-the-hay. It's time to put more life in our livelihood. It's time to play with God.

To live life as adventure over life as plan, to hardwire surprise into your life, here are some things you might do differently:

- When you take a trip, plan only a small percentage of it. Leave the rest open and make it up as you go along. Be free!
- Let the rhythms of your life reign supreme. Expect the world to keep time with the rhythms of your life, not always the other way around. Don't be dictated to by someone else's schedule or calendar.
- Go on watch fasts: don't wear your watch for extended periods of time. You don't need to go as far as I have and resolve to go through life without wearing a watch—my protest against the tyranny of a clockwork life. But next time you manacle your wrist with time-chains, think about how wearing a watch can be

May your wife's armpits be full of felt lice.
—*MONGOLIAN CURSE*

P l a y   a t   L i f e

159

the final capitulation. Many people are wearing their god on their wrists.

- If you continue to wear time-cuffs, every time you look down, look within. Where might your life be stuck in stockades not of your own making?

- The richer you are in spirit, the less need you have to carry either watches or money. I've negotiated up to three days on the road without a wallet (I put my license in my pocket), and I'm trying to set a personal record of seven days, which so far I've only been able to do because other people have made purchases for me. It's not easy living like this, but new mercies of grace and charity await the discovery of those who experiment with living by faith and not by sight, might, or MasterCard.

- Get rid of your desk. Or turn it into a display table. Any space can be transformed into your desk—a mountain cliff, a recliner in the living room, a mossy log in the woods, a hot tub, etc. Mobile phones, laptop computers, faxes, e-mail, pagers blur all boundaries between office/home/vacation anyway.

- Don't "read" the Bible. Let the Bible "read" you. Just as we end Scripture readings with "Amen," try to begin every Scripture reading with this refrain: "This text is being fulfilled today even while you are listening" (Luke 4:21 NJB). Hear and see how the words of these texts are coming true in your life.

- Let the Scriptures play themselves out in your life. Marinate your mind in sacred Scriptures so that you become an instrument of the Scriptures rather than using the Scriptures as an instrument.

- Live a trial-and-success life. Let your motto be "If you do it, they will let you." Or as the postmodern adage puts it, "It's easier to ask forgiveness than seek permission." The kingdom of Hollywood—where directors who lose hundreds of millions on a film that flops are "rewarded" with another contract—is not the only place where failures fall upward. Try the kingdom of heaven.

- Loosen your collar. Even boycott ties. There are twenty-three layers of cloth around my neck when I'm in a suit and tie.

- Live your life as story. You have no idea what the next page will bring. Better yet, live your life as God's story. Soak your soul in the Scriptures to the point where you can even anticipate what the next pages and chapters might bring forth.

- Prophesy your way forward. Instead of looking before you leap, leap before you look—trusting God's promises to be true.

Did you have a good time?

—*GOD AT JUDGMENT DAY*

SoulSalsa

- Start each day with these words: "Today, in every action I take, in every word I say, I am going to love God with everything in my soul."

If I make that an honest prayer and honest intent (sometimes that's a big "if"), the transformation of my day is indescribably delicious. Then I know I'm really playing.

Do you know what the best thing you can do for this world is? Have a good time.

—KEN CAREY

At the judgment seat, God will ask you to account for all the allowable pleasures that you did not indulge in.
—THE KABBALAH

1. Johann Sebastian Bach was once asked how he could play so beautifully. He replied that he didn't play the music; it played him. Where is the music playing you in your life and in your relationships?

2. There is an old saying that if you love what you do, you don't have to "work" a day in your life. Does this saying "play" in your life?

3. Go to the page in the PeopleSoft Web site where they describe their value for fun (http://www.peoplesoft.com/en/ why_-peoplesoft/why_fun_en.html/). Use it to focus your thoughts about how you can "play" rather than "work" at your job.

4. What are some of the "stockades" you find yourself trapped in?

5. Bishop Bevel Jones tells the story about a man who was complaining about the sorry state of his home life. The man confessed that "it's gotten so bad that the other night our faithful little dog came barking up to me and led me to the front door. I opened it to let him out, but he didn't want to go out. He wanted me to leave."

   Have you ever felt like that in your own home? What do you do, where do you go, when you feel like that?

6. Those who go to church regularly are 2.5 times less likely to have been divorced than those who did not attend. Why do you think this is so?

7. Listen to the Twila Paris song "God Is in Control." You can find the lyrics and downloadable music at the Twila Paris Fanpage (http://member.aol.com/Mazie20/twila.html/).

8. To what degree is the secret of a happy marriage found in such simple things as listening to your spouse, spending time together and with people you love, not marrying for looks or money. What else would you add?

9. Rent and watch the movie Big, starring Tom Hanks.

15

Make Love Like Tobias and Sarah

SOUL ARTISTS DARE TO BE BOTH SPIRITUAL AND SEXUAL.

In a sexually confused culture, the church is the only place you can go that doesn't talk about sex. it is time for the church to say a positive word about sex. It is long overdue for disciples to mature their sexuality and stop hoarding their precious erotic allowance. Strong faith and a strong sex drive are not incompatible.

For too long disciples of Jesus have witnessed to a faith that was "dead from the waist down." At least in public. In private we relished *National Geographic*'s ethnoporn, or we filled up every closet with sex drives that drove us as often as we drove them. Country songwriter Butch Hancock tells of growing up in Lubbock, Texas, where he learned "two main things": that "God loves you, and He's gonna send you to hell; and that sex is bad and dirty and nasty and awful, and you should save it for the one you love. You wonder why we're all crazy."

One wonders why more of us aren't crazier than we are. According to two Ohio State University psychologists, sex is one of the most important of the fifteen universal fundamental motives that drive human behavior. To take something so basic to our humanity and try to stuff it away somewhere is bound to make us a little bonkers.

Evidences of our crazed sexuality are everywhere. Just look at one of the greatest philosophers in Christian history: Immanuel Kant (1724–1804). It was not Kant's best moment when he defined marriage as a contract between a man and a woman that allows each the use of the other's genital organs for life. Or go back earlier in church history. In the twelfth century the register kept for Archbishop Eudes of Rigaud suggests an average of two to three pregnancies per nunnery per year. John XII (955–64) was elected pope at eighteen . . . and died at twenty-seven *in flagrante delicto.* More recently, Princess Diana died en route to a lovers' rendezvous. Yet Pope John Paul II assured Queen Elizabeth that he was praying, "summoning Diana to our Heavenly Father's eternal love."

If music be the food of love, play on.
—SHAKESPEARE

163

That's why I love the second century B.C. book of Tobit. It offers us a glimpse of sexual sanity.

Sex Instruction from Tobias and Sarah

From the early years of the church, the book of Tobit was in common use among Christians. In Jewish households it held much the same position, according to some scholars, as Bunyan's *Pilgrim's Progress* did in Christian homes. I know it's not in the official sixty-six-book canon but in the Apocrypha, those fifteen books that the Roman Catholic, Orthodox, and Eastern churches include as canonical Scripture but that Protestants and Jews do not. But I think this decision was a mistake. The Protestant Reformation didn't get everything right. And besides, find me an official decision declaring Tobit to be noncanonical. In my library I have lots of Protestant Bibles from the seventeenth, eighteenth, and even nineteenth century with Tobit in them. Tobit is the sixty-seventh book of my Bible. It's in my personal canon for a couple of reasons.

First, it's the only book of the Bible that says nice things about a dog. It doesn't say much ("the young man's dog went with him"), but enough for Verrocchio's most gifted pupil, Leonardo da Vinci, to paint the dog (a Bolognese terrier) on his mentor's masterpiece, *Tobias and the Angel,* one of my favorite paintings in the National Gallery of London.

Second, Tobit seems almost postmodern in style. What has been called "one of the dullest books in the Bible" I find one of the most postmodern: filled with hidden humor, irony, multiple voices, juxtaposed perspectives, edutainment, romance, elevation of family values. It even has the most sensuous passage in all of the Scriptures. Song of Songs 7 pales in comparison to Tobit 8.

Tobit 8 tells of the wedding night of Sarah and Tobias, two parallel figures, each carrying lots of baggage. Tobias is burdened for his father, Tobit, who is old, blind, and poor. Sarah is beautiful and brave but is oppressed by a demon and has buried seven previous husbands. They listen to God, fall in love, and get married.

On the night when Tobias makes the marriage contract, Sarah's parents escort the young couple to their bedroom. Tobias and Sarah get ready for their first night together. After burning special incense, the aroma of which banishes the demon that could have destroyed their relationship, they shut the door and jump into bed. Suddenly Tobias straightens up and says, "Oops. We forgot something." The two climb out and stand together by the side of the bed. They then offer the following dedicatory prayer basing their relationship on friendship and love.

Blessed are you, O God of our ancestors,
and blessed is your name in all generations forever.
Let the heavens and the whole creation bless you forever.
You made Adam, and for him you made his wife Eve
as a helper and support.
From the two of them the human race has sprung.
You said, "It is not good that the man should be alone;
let us make a helper for him like himself."
I am now taking this kinswoman of mine,
not because of lust, but in sincerity.
Grant that she and I may find mercy,
And that we may grow old together.
And they both said, "Amen, amen." (Tobit 8:5–8 NRSV)

Then they jump back into bed, make passionate love, and sleep soundly through the rest of the night.

From this story we learn at least four things about sex.

First, sex is a gift from God. In fact, *eros* (sexual love) is how we get here.

God created a whole range of sexual pleasures for us to enjoy, only some of which have anything to do with or lead up to sexual intercourse. Affection doesn't always have to end in sex. In fact, in most cases it doesn't. Could this be why a third of newlyweds admit to not having sex on their wedding night?

A little boy returning home from his first day at school said to his mother: "Mom, what's sex?"

His mother, who was waiting for this question and had trained herself to answer it competently, gave him a detailed explanation while putting everything in a biblical context.

When she had finished, the lad produced an enrollment form, which he had brought home from school, and said, "Yes, but how am I going to get all that into this one little square?"

God put a lot of joy into this one little exercise.

Second, sexual activity is good for you, especially good for your heart. The pleasures of sex have positive health benefits.

Some epidemiologists from the University of Bristol (George Davey Smith) and the University of Belfast (Stephen Frankel) have studied 918 males in a town in South Wales and discovered a direct relationship between the frequency of orgasm and mortality. Those men who had the most sex had a 50 percent lower mortality risk than those who didn't.

Would you expect that a gift from God would be other than good for us?

Nothing is free but love.
—LAST LINE IN NADYA AISENBERG'S POEM "THE HOME MUSEUM"

165

Third, the soul is the major sexual organ. Eroticism is less synonymous with love than with spirituality.

Postmodern culture is one of the most unloving cultures imaginable. Yet it is as rife with sex as it is rife with rage, hate, and bitterness. And I'm not talking merely about the proliferation of the wet T-shirt look, first pioneered by the Greek sculptor Polygnotus. Does it seem to anyone else that more and more we are living in one big, global nudist colony? Am I the only one finding it difficult to watch or read dialogue without sexual innuendo rampant? Am I the only one embarrassed to live in a culture where more kids can define "oral sex" than can define "chastity" and "fidelity"?

Disciples of Jesus don't mistake the crotch for the brain or the crotch for the soul. And yet they're happy to have one of each. It is for this reason that one poll finds married Christian women enjoy a vibrant and vigorous sex life that registers higher levels of satisfaction than among non-Christians.

Fourth, our sexuality relates directly to our physical, emotional, intellectual, and spiritual components, each of which is complicated by gender differentiation. In an increasingly desexualized world (unisex bathrooms, for example), let's face the facts: men and women are different. They may not be from different planets, but they are from different biological systems. There are at least 150 men's magazines. There is only one *Playgirl*.

The postmodern malady par excellence is for men or women to make sex into a category separate from marriage, commitment, and even love. If we come down with that malady, that's why and when we engage in inappropriate sexual conduct. We use sex to "fix things," especially "fix" other broken parts of our lives. Next to money and power, sex is postmodern culture's favorite ego booster and fixer-upper.

The healing postmoderns need comes only from our Maker. If *eros* got us here, *theos* (God) will get us home.

Sensuous Spirituality

While listening to Johnny Mathis make-out music, I committed my share of sexual mistakes, and I will pay for them emotionally, physically, spiritually for the rest of my life. One of the hardest things to do is to give yourself sexual amnesty. That's much harder than giving others sexual amnesty. But the gospel teaches that the pit of grace is as bottomless for sexual misbehavior as for any other sin.

The good news is that 58 percent of college freshmen are flatly opposed to sex without love. The mushrooming virginity movement among younger postmoderns may bemuse their Boomer ancestors, but it will only get stronger, including a definition of "virginity" that embraces those with previous sexual experience. The "sexual amnesty movement" makes it possible for people to forgive themselves for their sexual past and to declare, "I'm now a virgin, and will be until . . . death/marriage/betrothal/etc."

The bad news is that 42 percent of college freshmen have no problem uncoupling sex and love, not to mention sex and marriage. The worst news of all is that more than half of Christian teens engage in illicit sex. We've got a problem—a problem that Tobias and Sarah can help us solve.

Tobias and Sarah instruct us in a sensuous spirituality in which sex plays a leading but not exclusive role in a covenant relationship. Life is more than orgasms and embryos. The "white ecstasy of frictional satisfaction" (as D. H. Lawrence called sex) is a poor way for individuals or couples to eke out an emotional existence. Life is negotiating small triumphs and small disasters—blown diapers, fuses, and tempers—as well as the larger challenges of faithfulness, failure, disappointment, dailiness, cruelty, forgiveness, relatedness, committedness, and so on.

The most invigorating statistic to come down the pike as we turn the corner on the second millennium is one that no one yet has commented on. USAmericans pray more often than they have sex.

Like Tobias and Sarah, postmodern disciples make the two one.

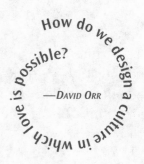

How do we design a culture in which love is possible?

—*David Orr*

1. Read the book of Tobit. If you're married, snuggle up with your honey and take turns reading its chapters aloud to each other. Then together discuss: Are you as comfortable combining sex and spirituality as Tobias and Sarah seemed to be? Why or why not?

2. Enjoy Verrocchio's Tobias and the Angel at http://easyweb.easynet.co.uk/giorgio.vasari/verrocc/pic12.htm /. That bit of gray fluff in the lower left-hand corner is the dog.

3. If you're interested in the facts and not the hype about sexual behavior and its outcomes (pregnancies, abortions, sexually transmitted diseases, etc.), check out the latest statistics provided by the Alan Guttmacher Institute (http://www.agi-usa.org/).

4. What parent didn't have to alter his or her children's sex education after the Clinton-Lewinsky scandal broke? Living in a post-Christian, sex-saturated culture means having to answer questions about sex with your kids at an earlier age than you would like.

   When and how do good postmodern parents explain sex to their kids?

5. What do we do about Paul's assertion that "it is good for a man not to touch a woman" (1 Corinthians 7:1 KJV)?

6. The sexual amnesty movement calls on people to clean out their sexual closets and come clean with moral integrity. In the words of one member, "I cleaned out my sexual closet, threw out all those self-destructive outfits and replaced them with moral fibers that covered me with honesty and self-respect. Once I faced my self-sabotaging sex life, the rest of my life was so easy to start fixing."

   For Jesus disciples, who believe in the reality of human sin and the need for divine forgiveness, what role could granting oneself "sexual amnesty" play?

Let virtue
and integrity
throughout your life
the mentors be.
—WOLFGANG AMADEUS MOZART,
THE MAGIC FLUTE

SoulSalsa

7. Help your marriage out by reading a Christian sex manual: The Gift of Sex: A Guide to Sexual Fulfillment by Clifford and Joyce Penner (Waco: Word, 1981).

8. For the Society for the Recapture of Virginity, check out http://www.thebluedot.com/srv/. Sure, it's for laughs, but what genuine longing might underlie the laughter?

9. Learn how to tie a "Love Knot." The tradition goes like this: a lovesick sailor would send his flame a length of fishline loosely tied in a true-lover's knot. If the knot was sent back as it came, the relationship was not going anywhere. If the knot returned snugly drawn up, the feelings were mutual. If the knot was capsized—time to ship out.

   Make a "love knot" and give it to the love of your life.

10. Sanskrit-based languages have ninety-six words for love; Persian has eighty; Greek has three; English has one.

    Do you think that the paucity of words for love in English reflects this culture's difficulty in coming to terms with the phenomenon of love itself? How can we get around this limitation of the language to express ourselves clearly?

11. A University of Nebraska freshman, when asked by the chaplain if his church had any influence in his view of sexuality, responded: "Are you kidding? People in my church don't believe in sex."

    What would the youth of your church say about the church's views on sex?

16

Don't Fall Out of the Family Bed

We live in a two-bedroom house—with three kids, two dogs, one bunk bed, and one double bed. No matter where everyone gets tucked in for nightly "sleep tights," the next morning everyone is thrashing about in the same place: the double bed. The 2:00 A.M. onward challenge is for two precariously perched parents not to fall off either edge while being kicked by a six-legged octopus.

Not falling out of the family bed may turn out to be the number one soul design issue of the twenty-first century. How does your soul embrace a life mission that doesn't cheat either family or career?

The family/career issue is more than achieving "balance" between work and family. It is more than combining a successful career with a happy home life. It is more than reconciling family obligations and job expectations that involve global travel and time away from home. It is a matter of achieving harmony between how you obtain your living, how you live a mission lifestyle, and how you make your family a mission team. The biblical model is clear: you are raising up children to serve.

Ancient-Future Families

Everything is changing in society, one way or another. And changing fast. Chris Rock quipped on an MTV music video awards show: "It used to be that music was here today and gone tomorrow. Now it's here today and gone today." How does one provide the stability of family life in this ever-changing world?

In the late 1990s a TV commercial portrayed in sixty seconds the average postmodern's self-image (at least in the U.S.). A stereotypic tow-truck driver (Joe America) is helping out some stranded motorists. He obviously loves what he's doing, relishes that mission. But Joe America keeps on his visor a picture of an island he owns. Joe America is fabulously wealthy. If he wanted to, he could live more like Joe Montana than Joe Bazooka. But he loves helping people in distress and carries on as if it's no big deal.

In this new world a global neural network of information technologies is creating a common epidermis for planet Earth. Global brands are turning their vast economic power into political power, functioning much like nation-states did in the modern world. In Thomas L. Friedman's wonderful book on globalization, *The Lexus and the Olive Tree*, the Lexus symbolizes speed, technology, and world markets; the olive tree stands for ancient values.

If the Lexus and the olive tree, the ancient and the future, find ways of working together, it could spell a whole new global awakening. But if the Lexus runs over the olive tree, the dangers of globalization are real: unfettered markets could despoil the environment worldwide; fast-paced economies could widen the income gap between rich and poor; galloping globalization could threaten to homogenize ancient cultures. And that's just the beginning.

The life-or-death issue of globalization is not whether it can revive local economies or repair local environments, important as they are. The life-or-death issue is whether postmoderns can use speed, technology, and a common epidermis to preserve and promote the ancient values of the family. True, more and more telecommuters are integrating their work and home life. But for every telecommuter who is returning to a premodern home/work life, there are more who are struggling, in the words of Elizabeth M. Hoekstra, to keep their family close when frequent travel pulls them apart.

The early returns are in, and the results do not look good.

Neither here nor there, and therefore home.

—*BERNARD O'DONOGHUE*

The Good News

The good news is that the *ideal* of family is stronger than ever. There's a huge revival of parenting and a rebirth of interest in family values and family-life issues, including a renaissance of courses in "family and consumer sciences," or what used to be called home economics.

Some evidence suggests that the fastest-growing household unit in the U.S. is the one-paycheck family. Two-paycheck families are increasingly problematic, as the cost of child care, the gridlock of commutes, and the popularity of home-schooling are increasing the number of parents who are deciding to manage the home themselves. The growing consensus that a newborn needs a minimum of two years of intensive parenting also is eroding the two-paycheck household, especially when corporations are stingy about long-term paid care or job-protected unpaid leaves to either parent. The figure of 75 percent of American women aged twenty-five to forty-four who were employed in 1990 may be a peak.

When the pollsters ask us, "What is going to change the world? What is going to improve social values?" and the choices we are given are government, schools, religious institutions, and families, we pick families. The consistency of this hard-boiled wisdom is heartening.

The Bad News

> For Jesus, the greatest sin one could commit was to cause children to stumble.
> —BISHOP MELVIN TALBERT

But the reality of our tending of the family farm is worse than ever. When our models have gone from *Father Knows Best* to *The Simpsons*, it's a wonder there aren't more fouled-up families than there are. The negatives felt among our kids—eating disorders, depression, suicides, alcohol and drug abuse, poverty, violence—are the aftershocks of an overturned culture. I call my generation's children, not the "busters" or the "X" generation but the "d" generation. The first generation of post-moderns was shaped largely by five d's: (1) divorce, (2) day care, (3) debt, (4) diversity, and (5) digimatics.

Is the family stable or declining? If by a "stable" family one means the family is a "stable," or a womb, there is not much stability, especially coming from fathers.

A man's place is in the home. But the absence of fathers from children's lives is getting more severe, not less. Four U.S. children out of ten live in homes where there is no father. The statistical studies are already overstuffed with one finding: the more time a parent hangs out with a kid, and the more parents there are who hang out with that kid, the less likely that kid will develop problems. Any problems and all problems. You name the problem.

One of the best fathers I know is Jesse B. Caldwell III, a senior resident judge of the North Carolina Superior Court. He is also an actor, writer, preacher, and athlete. While keynoting a 1999 awards banquet, he told a story on himself that reveals just how difficult it is for even the best of parents to "be there" for their kids.

Judge Caldwell's three older children played soccer. He was a good father. He came to the games. He cheered them on. True, sometimes he had a cellular phone at his ear. Sometimes he was scanning legal briefs. Sometimes he was jotting notes while the games were in progress. But at least he was there, right? After all, a judge has lots of responsibilities. Lots of people depend on him. He didn't shirk his responsibility as a father to meet his other responsibilities.

At his six-year-old son's soccer banquet, which celebrated twelve teams of all ages, Caldwell walked into the Family Life Center and saw a fellow he knew carrying a net and several soccer balls. The judge kidded, "Hi, Bob. What are those balls for? Door prizes?"

"No," he replied. "I was a coach, and I'm bringing this stuff back for storage."

"Really?" Judge Caldwell asked. "What age-group did you coach?"

Bob stopped, looking incredulous, and said, "Jesse, I was your son's coach."

Like my friend, I want to be the perfect father. I want a "normal" family life. I want to be home with the kids, tuck them in at night, and have set family routines of prayer, reading, and Bible study. I want to attend every soccer game, every play, every concert.

It ain't happening. And it ain't gonna happen.

The difficulties in not falling out of the family bed are not to be fobbed off with shreddable mosquito-net theology.

First, it's important not to romanticize the "family," and especially the father's (or mother's) role in it. For much of the church's history, Jesus' foster father was virtually missing from the gospel story. Teresa of Avila was the first person in the history of Christianity to make much of Joseph. Before the Reformation, one has trouble even finding feast days for St. Joseph. I collect reproductions of images of Jesus and Joseph together. There are only a score of them in the history of religious art.

There are plenty of biblical precedents and patterns for this world of increasing singles and mingles. Indeed, there is no such thing as "the" biblical family. There are many biblical models of the family. In fact, the basic social unit for the disciples, as taught by Jesus, was not the family but the community of believers.

Second, look at the history of families in the Bible. It's not the story of one perfect family after another but of one problem family after another. There are more nut-cake families and fruit-cake families than there are angel-food-cake families.

You think you've got a dysfunctional family? Try being a member of the Adam-Eve family. Or the Isaac-Rebekah family. Or the Zebedee family. My New Testament contains the story of nary a single couple who had a normal marriage or a perfect family life. Can you list me the names of the perfect families in the Bible? A typical biblical family looks more and more like a typical love affair, full of rapture one day, fury and disgust the next.

The First Family

A soul design that doesn't "fall out" must be built on a theological understanding of family. It used to be that scholars dismissed the "nuclear" family as more a product of modern industrial and capitalist societies than innate anthropological or scriptural principles. It was said to be not very ancient; it was only one small component of a vast kinship system; as a modern innovation it was fast becoming obsolete in a new and different setting.

Contemporary social anthropologists are now more prone to argue the universal need of families to make for themselves nuclear nests, which may be cultural more than biological. Adam Kuper's *The Chosen Primate* demonstrates that in one fashion or another what we mean by "nuclear family"—two adults, whether legally married or not, who raise and look after children—characterized the distant past from as diverse cultures as the Algonquian Indians, the Congo Pygmies, the Kalahari Bushmen, and the native peoples of Australia, the Amazon, and the Arctic.

While less stable now than in the past, and with wide variability as to its importance in individual lives, the Adam and Eve family structure turns out to be the traditional family form not just in Christendom but everywhere. In fact, the emerging popularity of marriage or its equivalent, with fewer lifetime singles than in the past ("confirmed bachelors" and "spinsters" we used to call them), partially explains the marked increase in the incidence of divorce. If the mission of the true first family was to embody in their relationship the triune image of God, the fact that even they did not succeed perfectly should give us pause. Even they could not escape issues of sex, violence, and philosophical differences.

Pilgrims can "be fruitful and multiply" in other ways than having children. Not every "family bed" need contain kicking and screaming mutants. When someone tried to get Dorothy Sayers to write for children, she replied rather characteristically, "I can't abide children, have never taught them Scripture, and shouldn't like to try." Perhaps the most influential religious writer of the twentieth century (author of, among other things, children's books), C. S. Lewis, confessed that he didn't particularly like to be around little children either. Children should not be brought into this world unless they're wanted and planned for.

In fact, even marriages with children should be more couple-centered than kid-centered. The more a marriage is spirited and sporting, the better off the kids. It's almost impossible to have a healthy family without a healthy marriage. One of the best gifts parents can bequeath to children is the example of two people in love bound together in a vibrant covenant relationship.

But it matters how we treat children: it matters theologically; it matters socially; it matters politically. Parenting is an exercise in hospitality to strangers: welcoming a child, educating and entraining a child, and freeing a child. Our kids are strangers first, and if we can't be hospitable to their sojourn under our roof, how can we move out into hospitality to community, country, world? Children "as tough as the troubles of '32" do not emerge without huge investments of spiritual, psychological, and financial resources. The virtues of hospitality are tested most severely not on strangers and enemies but on family and friends.

So, what can help our soul to not fall out of the family bed?

Act Family

We can do things a family does. Actually taking the time to act like a family is the first step to lifelong family bedhood. This means the family doesn't get the leftovers but the firstfruits of time and energy.

I'm parentally challenged and need help in doing things a family does. So I read resources like the book *How to Win Grins and Influence Little People,* which offers all sorts of helpful suggestions like:

- Out of the blue, mail your child an invitation to ice cream and bowling, or popcorn and a video. Kids love mail, and it shows them you think they are special all the time.
- Leave an outgoing message on your answering machine that callers have reached the home of [your name] and their incredibly talented son/daughter [your child's name].
- Out of the blue, say, "I'm so fortunate to be your dad/mom!"
- Put a note of praise in a bottle and float it in your child's bathwater.
- Snuggle in bed together and listen to an old-time radio mystery or comedy in the dark.
- Use notes, funny postcards, and letters as opportunities to put your pride in writing.
- Catch your child's eye across a crowded room or on the playing field and give him or her a wink and the thumbs-up sign.
- Leave a note on the bathroom mirror: "Good morning, Soren. What a fine smile you have!"

On-Mission Families

One of the surprises of living in a postmodern world is that one can increasingly do things a family does from anywhere on the planet. Distance no longer has much meaning. Anyplace becomes everyplace, and postmoderns are everyplace.

There is a need for new definitions of how to build stronger parent-child relationships. Much writing about the family makes it sound as if family had a transcendent, timeless role in human affairs. Much of our language gushes about always being there for our kids, which turns to mush when one bites down and chews it.

But there are a lot of ways now of "being there," even sometimes without really being there.

Ruth Bell Graham basically raised five children on her own. She spent many nights sleeping with husband Billy's tweed jacket. But in her words, "I'd rather have a little of Bill than a lot of any other man." (My wife has a different way of putting it: "A little of Leonard goes a long way.")

But Ruth Bell Graham found ways of helping her husband "be there" even when he couldn't physically be there. The key was building a family life around a shared ministry. The entire family was on mission with the Billy Graham Evangelistic Association and a part of and partners with the "Graham team." The whole Graham family was on a mission.

Why are you here? You're here for a mission. Or as my parents put it, "God has a purpose for your life." God is not impressed by the consumption lifestyles of the rich and famous. God is pleased by the mission lifestyles of the repentant and faithful. Especially family mission lifestyles.

Every family can compose together an agreed-upon family mission statement. One of my favorites is elegant in its simplicity: "Our family will work, play, pray, and study God's Word together with the goal of becoming Christlike and sharing the love of Jesus with all of those around us." This one act alone can help a whole family "sleep tight" and not "let the bedbugs bite."

The real coil in the bedsprings is prayer. The peace that passes all understanding does not keep itself. Peace requires constant vigilance and prayer. The most important thing a family can do is inculcate the faith effusions that can only come from a healthy family prayer life.

This doesn't need to be regimented in military fashion like my parents did it. Growing up in the 1950s, my three brothers and I sat and knelt through family prayer twice a day. At one time—when my mother felt especially "burdened" by my unrepentance—everyone came home for lunch (Dad included) for a third session of family prayer.

But every family needs their own prayer rituals—ones that fit their rhythms and schedules. Sometimes I crawl into either the upper or lower bunk with the kids and ask them how they would have me pray for them. Other times we let one of the kids lead in a more formal family prayer. You end up praying for interesting things. Just last night three-year-old Soren thanked God for her movies *Snow White* and *Cinderella*, and prayed for the conversion of the wicked witch.

Spare and Spoil

The biblical warning not to "spare the rod and spoil the child" sounds like an invitation to child abuse. We think of a "rod" as a paddle, a leather strap, or soap and Lysol. But guidance counselor Lex Rivers once reminded me that the "rod" in Psalm 23 is guidance, counsel, mentoring. "Thy rod and thy staff, they comfort me" is literally true. If we spare the mentoring, the guidance, the counsel, we spoil the child.

An "unspared rod" may take many forms. It may mean whole families doing mission trips together each summer. Or fashioning family vacations into faith journeys. Or home-schooling your kids—it was the norm for early Americans. Or getting the whole family involved in ministry projects: let the kids pick out the items to funnel to those less fortunate. Or setting the alarm variously for evening, midnight, cock-crow, or morning so you can discover and explore the four worlds of night with your kids.

Or an "unspared rod" may simply mean a parent's transparency to God's love and forgiveness through embracing acts or exquisite silences.

The "unspared rod" needs to be administered by the church family as well as by the biological family. For followers of Jesus, it doesn't take a village to raise a child so much as it takes a church to raise a child. The spiritual rewards of family life are being rediscovered by entire faith communities, which are increasingly stepping into the breach to assume the familial role. Baptismal waters should be thicker than blood. Congregations must get more involved in marriage and family training as well as counseling—not to mention the need for creative scheduling to fit the needs of postmodern families.

The ancient church's custom of godparenting is a living symbol of the fact that it takes more than a mother and father to raise and guide a child toward adulthood. It used to be an extended family that raised children. It still can be if a church calls forth singles, childless couples, and others to become part of parents' extended family.

Futurist Tom Sine is calling for churches to help parents learn new parenting styles that prepare kids for a wild twenty-second-century future, not a wishful nineteenth-century past. Too many parenting styles are "hovering" and dependency-producing. One Seattle

You will act like a Christian, or I will slap the snot out of you.
—*Vera Carp of Tuna, Texas*

Don't Fall Out of the Family Bed

177

Mennonite congregation has instituted a mentoring program for elementary school kids so that when they become teenagers they will be ready for the high-pressure world they will actually face. Every youth in this church is being mentored by an older adult. The lessons of a few days can last a lifetime.

Cohousing

Some postmodern pilgrims like Tom and Christine Sine are experimenting with changes in housing arrangements to inaugurate more harmonious ways of living. The cohousing movement originated in Denmark in the late 1960s and is now spreading throughout the U.S. It presents new architectural designs that protect families' need for private space and ownership while at the same time celebrating interconnectedness and interdependence on a day-to-day basis through some shared facilities, a commons area, shared expenses, shared rituals, volume buying, etc.

Virtual cohousing features a community life that doesn't require new building arrangements or a single residential cluster. Already going in Boulder, Colorado (TIMEWEAVE), virtual cohousing brings together private ownership and cooperative households through a variety of up-close and faraway methods that make relationships paramount.

Family Emporiatrics

Emporiatrics is a new word that will achieve wider currency. It refers to a new specialty in the health field called "travel medicine." Emporiatric physicians keep busy people well while they're living out their globe-trotting lifestyles.

Postmoderns are people on the move. They are not the first. The gospel is an "on the road again" story. Jesus was born "on the road"; the wise men traveled for upwards of two years "on the road"; the disciples spent their life with Jesus "on the road again."

Postmodern pilgrims are on-mission people on the move. The path of discipleship is a "walk" and a "way." Jesus' earliest followers, as recorded in Acts, called themselves "followers of the Way." "The Way" was the first name for the church (Acts 9:2). To follow Jesus in "the Way" was to follow in the footsteps of a Master on a mission.

"The Way" today is global. Postmoderns enjoy the freedom of being anywhere anytime. That's what it means to be "global"—even to live everywhere and somewhere at the same time. Talk to airline pilots

SoulSalsa

> Always have your bags packed; you never know where life's journey is going to take you.
>
> —OLD APPALACHIAN SAYING

and flight attendants. They live one place and work another. That's the new world.

A key to godly living in this new world is to learn how to be at home in both places. The more it's possible to live everywhere, the more important it is that we live somewhere—that we have a sense of "place" and know our "place." Know its trees, its insects, its colors, its smells, its poisons. The best travelers are those who have the best "homes," the best sense of place. Homeness enables roamness—a strong "home" gives us the freedom to roam in strange places with the security and safety of a home-base.

Canopy Bed

Technology is the netting that increasingly keeps the whole family in bed together. A joke is circulating that families synchronize the next day's schedules on their Palm Pilots before going to bed. It is technology that enables us to bring the helter-skelter parts of our 24x7x365 lives together: family, work, community, and so forth. In fact, 70 percent of high school students already carry pagers. It's just a matter of time until as many carry cell phones.

Thanks to electronic technology, which first extended our ears and now our eyes to encircle the globe, even us road warriors can "be there" with our kids in a variety of ways. We can make our mission a family affair in both physical and virtual ways.

PHONE

Don't call home when you're tired at the end of the day. Call when you're at your best or when your family most needs you. My wife and I rotate being each other's alarm clocks. Try to call just after the kids get home from school, or just before they go to bed so you can say prayers with them.

Elizabeth and I have an agreement: we will never show each other our phone bills. There are times to pinch pennies and there are times to throw pennies to the winds. Maintaining open lines of communication with the family is the penny-throwing kind.

SCREEN

Thanks to video-conferencing technology like CU-SeeMe, it is now possible for our kids to see us and for us to see them from anywhere we can access a modem: from a phone at an airline terminal, from a pay phone at a gas station, or even from your car while driving. To set up these connections takes only minutes. The variations on this theme are innumerable: watch TV shows together via the screen or phone; read the *Couples Bible* together while away; etc. There are more families having prayer time together via cyberspace than anyone has yet written about.

A Classic

It is unfairly easy to complain about intergenerational warmongering when everyone is pumping more blasts of hot air into the already inflated generational model of tracking social change. As self-identification according to class, region, and denomination is diminishing, self-identification according to generation has become stronger.

Ironically, the generational features of postmodern culture bring us closer to biblical modes of thinking than the modern congregational one. The Bible does not think congregationally or chronologically but generationally. The Lord's mercy and truth endureth from ... what? From decade to decade? From century to century? From millennium to millennium? No, "[the Lord's] mercy endureth for ever, and his truth to generation and generation" (Psalm 100:5 DV).

What's the difference? One difference is that "generational justice" is at the heart of the biblical witness. What is it one generation owes the next? What one generation passes on to the next is understood biblically as either a blessing or a curse for generations to follow (see Deuteronomy 4:9; 6:1–2; 29:12–15; Acts 2:39; Galatians 3:16–17).

What elder owe younger generations is mentoring in the arc of life. What younger owe elder generations is openness to the wisdom of the aged, smitten, and dying. It is good for the young to experience the monarchical privileges of a sick older relative. It is good for the seniors to remember that roller coaster of disappointments and humiliations that comes with growing up. For all generations, the grace of defeat is more soul-nurturing than is the gleam of victory.

The most neglected and richest niche of the postmodern church is one yet to be discovered: true multigenerational faith communities. Without multigenerational worship, learning, and other interactions, there can be no "Christian classics."

Another difference is that generations overlap. Centuries don't. The phrase "children's children" occurs fourteen hundred times in the Scriptures. In age-specific, generational thinking, the old is not discarded but made new. The form of rabbinic teaching called *halachah* was geared to being revised and/or confirmed from one generation to another—as new developments arose, or conditions changed, these principles of living were open to change.

"It takes three generations to make a gentleman" was the rule of thumb until the Industrial Revolution. It takes more generations than that to make a postmodern pilgrim.

1. What has survived your childhood? Here's my list:
   • some marbles
   • parts of an erector set
   • a stuffed animal
   • some report cards and pictures

   Most of your childhood is gone forever. Do you see in your childhood remnants any foretastes of who you are or faint rumblings of who you might yet become?

2. Best-selling author John Bradshaw estimates that 96 percent of all USAmericans are products of dysfunctional homes. Does that figure sound too high to you or about right?

3. To what extent does our culture's high divorce rate make security in God more fundamental than ever before?

4. How few children have a church or neighborhood behind them, much less a village! In fact, according to the 1990 census, every state in the nation except Idaho has distressed neighborhoods, defined as census tracts with four of the following five characteristics: a 1989 poverty rate of 28 percent or higher; a 40 percent or more rate of female-headed families; a 23 percent or higher rate of high school dropouts; a 47 percent or more share of men unattached to the labor force; and more than 17 percent of families receiving public assistance. This means that there are more than 4 million American kids who are growing up in danger (the ten worst states in descending order: Mississippi, Louisiana, New Mexico, Alabama, Arizona, South Carolina, Tennessee, Arkansas, Georgia, Kentucky).

   In what ways can your church give parents the support they are not getting elsewhere?

5. Do you think Hollywood is getting the message? In the mid to late 1980s, only 2 family films came out of Hollywood. In 1992 there were 6; in 1994, 75; in 1998, there were 107 family films.

   What are you and your church doing to promote family films, now and in the future?

6. Get family-friendly reviews of current movies from Ted Baehr's Movie Guide at http://crosswalk.com/.

7. Aaron, Eli, and Samuel were great leaders who did great things for their people at the expense of their own children. The Bible says wonderful things about all three of these men, but all three had kids who turned out to be rotten eggs and whom God punished severely for their disobedience (Leviticus 10:1–3; 1 Samuel 2:12–17, 22–25; 4:11; 8:1–3).

   To what degree were these men—or any parents of rotten-egg children—responsible for how their kids turned out?

8. Is Susan Hill right when she says, "The moment you have children yourself, you forgive your parents everything"? Have you forgiven your parents "everything"?

9. Try your hand at writing a mission statement for your family. What changes would have to happen for everyone in your family to get on board with your mission?

10. Do you remember the exchange in Zorba the Greek between the Englishman and Zorba in the storm-tossed boat? Both are baring their life stories to the other when the Englishman asks, "Do you have a family?" Zorba begins ticking off his "family"—his dependents, his debts, his chickens, his goat— "the whole catastrophe," he says.

    In what way is every family "the whole catastrophe"?

11. If cohousing arrangements intrigue you, learn more from the Cohousing Network (http://www.cohousing.org/).

12. The Jewish high holy days Prayerbook includes this rebuke/exhortation:

    Each second we live is a new and unique moment of the universe, a moment that never was before and will never be again—and what do we teach our children? We teach them that two and two is four, and that Paris is the capital of France. When will we also teach them what they are? We should say to each of them, "Do you know what you are? You are a marvel! You are unique. In all of the world there is no other child exactly like you. In the millions of years that have passed there has never been another child like you. . . . And when you grow up, can you then harm another who is like you, a marvel? You must cherish one another. You must work—we all must work—to make this world worthy of its children."

Is it really possible to live as if every moment is a stunning miracle? If so, how?

The desire for conformity with peers seems to be nearly universal among children. In that case, how do we teach our kids their uniqueness?

13. In Appalachian culture, there are two adages that speak to the same issue. One says, "Live like a bird on a dry twig, ready to fly away when it snaps." The other says, "Dig in one place."

Which is it?

17

Dance the Salsa

SOUL ARTISTS KNOW HOW TO HAVE A GOOD TIME.

God's time is dance time. Even in the midst of a cultural free-for-all and free-fall, disciples dance.

When I was seventeen, I deconverted from Christianity. Some people can give the date and time of their conversion. I can give the place (Saratoga Springs, New York), date (Pine Grove summer camp meeting), and time (Sunday morning's "Big Preaching" service during the altar-call hymn "Softly and Tenderly") of my deconversion. It was my most defining adolescent spiritual experience.

While playing the organ at the Pine Grove Free Methodist Camp Meeting, with my date (the district superintendent's daughter) sitting in the front row, I said of the Christian religion: been there, done that, out of here. Let's try the life of a pagan.

Some people sow wild oats. I planted a prairie.

During those years, I joined the roll call of the impious. I discovered that life's meaning and purpose can be found in lots of ways. There are untold pleasures in "stuff," "things," and "pleasure" itself. Let's not delude ourselves. Hedonism offers quite a meaningful belief system. But as the Bible says, the pleasures of sin are enjoyable . . . for a season (Hebrews 11:25). They don't keep pumping out their pleasures. The pleasures switch to pain. And the pain of those "pleasures of sin," no matter how short their season, lasts a lifetime.

What ignited my deconversion was the church's funereal spirit, its fussy buttoned-upness. Christians' stay-at-home-and-pickle-in-their-own-juices personalities, their vinegary countenances drained me emotionally, incapacitated me intellectually, and shut me down spiritually. The best I could say was this: by and large, Christians were kind people in a bad mood.

Bishop Ernest Fitzgerald tells the story of a prominent Atlanta millionaire who lamented the fact that his pastor never visited him. Then one day, he related to the bishop, he looked up the dictionary definition of *visitation* and discovered that a visitation was "a plague that is imposed on a person or persons because of their sins." He then wondered whether it shouldn't be counted a blessing that he wasn't "visited."

Many of us feel the same way about being visited by God. It's hardly "party time" in our minds.

"Party time" doesn't mean drunken hothouse affairs with lots of hanky-panky going on. "Party time" doesn't mean those prompt, promiscuous emotionalisms, that weak-head/soft-heart syndrome of spirituality that scrambles the screen of so many religious communications. "Party times" are those intelligent celebrations in life when one wholly enjoys existence, when one fully plays in the theological universe. *Play* and *pray* do more than rhyme.

The Joy of the Lord

Why is it that time stops for play and speeds up for work? Because when we play we are in ecstasy, and ecstasy is being "outside oneself," outside this dimension of time and inside divine dimensions of existence.

You can stop time, literally. Don't believe me? Try this little exercise, first proposed by science writer Itzhak Bentov, whereby you can halt time's passage by keeping your eye on the clock.

Lie down next to a clock or watch with a large second hand. Relax your muscles, calm your mind, and stretch out your spirit on that couch. Close your eyes and imagine yourself dancing the salsa or lying on a hammock in Hawaii. Hear the music? Feel the gentle swaying of the hammock in the breeze? At a point of deep relaxation, scarcely open your eyes. Make sure the first thing you see is the second hand.

Is it moving? Don't the hands appear stuck, or at least labored in their rotation? Your startled puzzlement actually starts the hands again on their normal rounds.

Of course, on one level time continued to pass. But on your level of repose and relaxation, time had stopped until you were startled back into another relative reality of time. Was your level of reality any less real than the level of reality kept by your watch's gears or computer chip? This is more than a demonstration of the relativity of time, or the power of the observer on the observed; it is an exercise in the power of play and party to stop time.

Church folk have lots of problems with this party talk. That's one reason they call their parties "socials." In the churched culture in which I grew up, I heard my share of sermons denouncing the "party pleasures of life." But with admonitions from the Bible like "Go, eat your bread

So dance for our God and blow all the trumpets,
So dance for our God and blow all the trumpets,
So dance for our God and blow all the trumpets,
And sing to our God, and sing to our God.

—BRAZILIAN FOLK SONG

with joy, and drink your wine lustily.... Let your clothes be fresh and clean and your head oiled" (see Ecclesiastes 9:7–8), Christians should be the ones who know how to party and be showing others how to party.

Yet we are more comfortable touting Jesus for being a man of sorrows, acquainted with grief, than we are with Jesus being a man of joy, acquainted with jubilation and celebration. One of the most memorable characters in the novels of John Steinbeck is Liza Hamilton from *East of Eden*. Steinbeck describes her as "a tight hard little woman humorless as a chicken." He goes on to say, "She had ... a code of morals that pinned down and beat the brains out of nearly everything that was pleasant to do.... She was suspicious of fun whether it involved dancing or singing or even laughter. She felt that people having a good time were wide open to the devil."

If "the joy of the LORD is your strength" (Nehemiah 8:10 NRSV), a lot of us are a lot weaker than we need to be. There is something harder on hearts than time. It's called gravity. The gravity that makes life gravid, joyless, and grave—the graveness that leads to the grave. At least two-thirds of all doctor visits are to deal with the results of mind-body interactions. Humorlessness is a malignant tumor on the soul.

Interpreters think Sarah laughed because she was old and pregnant. I suspect Sarah was old and pregnant because she laughed. She had a sense of humanity and humor that would make a chicken laugh.

Disney brags that no one has ever died while visiting Disneyland or Disney World. Whether it's because paramedics keep heart attack and stroke victims alive until they're off the grounds or whether it's because the spirit of the place is not conducive to mortality (as Disney would like us to believe), a merry heart is good medicine.

You need at least thirty deep laughs a day to keep healthy. Primary health ingredients in a "total wellness program" include love, faith, trust, hope ... and laughter. It's time to prescribe these medicines just like erythromycin, pavil, zentac, lasix, etc.

If I could, I'd write every disciple and every church a prescription for laughter. There are new Christians minted every year who think piety is seriousness, and seriousness, piety, and who forbid laughter to intrude in their spiritual activities.

The forty-four muscles, nerves, and blood vessels on your face can devise five thousand expressions. Each one of the nineteen versions of the smile uses a large proportion of these muscles, which helps explain why smiles can be seen across a football field. Moebius syndrome is an illness that makes it impossible for sufferers to move these facial muscles. When I go into some churches, it's as if I were attending a Moebius syndrome convention.

The moment one definitely commits oneself, then Providence moves too.
—JOHAN WOLFGANG VON GOETHE

Where's the joy? Why aren't more of us "trembling with joy" (see Psalm 2:11)? Why aren't more believers experiencing what the Bible calls the "joy and peace in believing" (Romans 15:13 KJV)? Jim McGuiggan wonders why so many Christians would rather be on the "whining side" than on the "winning side." "Every time they open their mouths, it's a bleating confession. You'd think the Bible had said, 'Blessed are the moaners.'" How can disciples of Jesus live life as a laugh-free zone?

As much as I love Victorian culture and Victorian antiques, I would not have made a good Victorian. No Victorian could even *imagine* that Jesus ever laughed. My favorite picture of Jesus is the smiling Jesus. But for many present-day Victorian Christians, a smiling Jesus is a Jesus they don't want to smile on them. Some people, after a tragedy or tribulation, get out of the habit of laughing and never find it again for the rest of their lives. They are convinced a smiling Jesus no longer smiles on them.

Jesus laughed and continues to laugh. Has it ever bothered you that in Michelangelo's Sistine chapel portrayal of heaven no one is smiling? To be sure, putting on the mind of Christ means more than putting on a happy face. There is nothing that makes me sicker than a "happy face" faith. Some church music is so sweet that just listening to it makes your teeth hurt. Joy has deeper dimensions than happiness or hilarity. I have blubbered into more handkerchiefs and tissue paper than an Italian tenor.

Joy drives away all despair but not all depression. We *will* get depressed. Perhaps not as depressed as Madame de Staël, who wrote that "the only good which we can find in life is something which produces an oblivion of existence." Perhaps not as depressed as Maeterlinck, who lamented that "the majority of humankind only enjoy life by forgetting that they are alive." But depressed we will get. Are any humorists *not* depressives?

Faith enables the dreary soul to become dreamy again through the power of these four words: "it came to pass." It took God three days to turn the worst for Jesus into the best. Should I expect better from God for myself?

Wait three days. Give God time to work on your behalf. Life is filled with nail-biting finishes, downcast days, and Titian-toned darkness. But joy always comes in the morning.

In India laughter is made into a form of medical therapy through "laughing clubs." Called the "laughing cure," organized giggling once a week reduces stress, boosts the immune system, and generally improves health. The first laughing club opened in 1995, with hundreds more

SoulSalsa

started since then. At these clubs one can practice certain laughs: the Lion Laugh, the Argument Laugh, the Bombay Laugh, and on and on.

A mayor of Bogotá, Colombia, in the 1990s was beset by an epidemic of road rage. Some drivers even took out their anger in ways that proved fatal to themselves and others. Rather than clamp down tighter, the mayor dressed the traffic police officers in clown costumes, both to diminish road rage and to deflect attacks from the police themselves. Much to everyone's astonishment, the experiment worked.

Postmodern disciples can find themselves in the funnies, and laugh as loud as Sarah when they do. Postmodern disciples create their own "funnies." That's why I liked the phenomenon of "positive partying" so much. You've heard of a born storyteller? The Reverend Ed Stivender claimed to be a "born-again storyteller." He said, "I've been born again so many times I've got stretch marks on my soul." A popular speaker on college campuses in the 1980s and early 1990s, "Rev. Ed of the Church of Partyology" taught that the kingdom of heaven is a party.

To those of us who imagine that our reception at the Pearly Gates is going to be St. Peter running the instant replay and our throwing up our hands and saying, "No contest!" Rev. Ed argues that there is only going to be one question asked at the Pearly Gates. It's the "inasmuch" question. The question has two parts. First: "Did you have a good time?" Second: "Did you help others to have a good time?"

That's it. Rev. Ed says Jesus is the Way, the Truth, and the Life . . . of the Party. Are *we* ready to party? For that's what the kingdom of heaven is like.

Shall We Dance?

A party is only as good as its guests. Are we ready to dance?

The German philosopher Friedrich Nietzsche (the one who wondered why John Calvin's followers didn't look more redeemed) said he could only believe in a God who could dance. Exactly. Jesus came to make all of life a dance. A Gnostic hymn of Jesus picked up this theme in graphic terms:

But as for Me, if thou wouldst know what I was:
In a word I am the Word who did dance
All things, and was not shamed at all.
'Twas I who leapt and danced.

The Bible may be filled with dancing, but modernist Christianity emptied its institutions of dancing, driving dancing into the secular

God is a party-giver.
—J. ELLSWORTH KALAS

domain in the name of transcendence and rationality. The word *carol* originally meant "dance," especially a ring dance accompanied by singing ("Here we go 'round the mulberry bush").

A triangle has been the usual symbol of the Trinity. But there is an early tradition of the church that styles the Trinity as a circle in which the three are dancing and caroling in their celebrations of life. One of the best of the English "carols" describes the eve of the Lord's marriage to the church:

To-morrow shall be my dancing day:
I would my true love so did chance
To see the legend of my play,
To call my true love to my dance.
In a manger laid and wrapped I was,
So very poor, this was my chance,
Between an ox and a silly poor ass,
To call my true love to my dance.

Various "reform" movements have driven dancing carols out of the church, or at least split off the acceptable carols from the unacceptable bodily accompaniments. Yet the haunting words of Jesus judge our prejudices against singing and swaying to the rhythms of the universe: "I piped for you, and you did not dance" (see Matthew 11:17). Or in the street-smart words of a 1990s hit song: "No parking, baby, no parking on the dance floor."

Church is a prep school in singing and dancing: learning the various dance steps, improving one's techniques, improvising on them and integrating them into one's own unique style. The party mode is when the dance begins—when individuals experience dance in life, when institutions live the dance of life. The party mode is when we dance with the Godhead in the love of creation.

Russell Freedman is one of the most respected and prize-winning children's book authors in the world today. He was awarded the Newbery Medal for *Lincoln: A Photobiography* and a 1992 *Hungry Mind Review* Children's Book of Distinction award for *The Wright Brothers*. Before he begins any new book, he retells himself a story his father used to tell about himself.

He was a small child when his family moved to a rock-bound farm near Windsor, Connecticut. One afternoon, as my father would tell it, he ran across a field to meet *his* father, who would soon be coming down the road with his horse and wagon. As my father waited and dawdled, he noticed a big stone on the other side of the field. He ran over, picked up the stone, which was almost too big for him to hold, and started carrying it back

Muster hither musicks
joyes,
lute, and lyre, and tabretts
noise:
lett noe instrument be wanting,
chasing grief, and pleasure planting.
—*Mary Sidney Herbert, poetic commentary on Psalm 81*

toward the road, stopping here and there to put the stone down and catch his breath, then picking it up again and carrying it a bit farther. When he reached the side of the road, he put the stone down for good.

When his father—my grandfather—came rolling down that dirt road and climbed out of his wagon, my father said: "Do you see that big stone? I picked it up and carried it all the way across the field."

"Why did you do that?" his father asked.

And my father replied: "God put that stone down over there, and *I* moved it over here!"

A cardboard sign found in a 1900 Gillette, Wyoming, saloon bore this message:

Preaching at 7:30 P.M.
Dance at 9:00 P.M.
After Dance, Big Poker Game

For Jesus, sitting out the dance is not an option. Indeed, Jesus makes the dancer and the dance one.

In the religions of the world, there are seated gods (Chinese Buddha) and dancing gods (Indian Hindu). The God of the Bible is both. Life is a perpetual dance, a balance of static and dynamic, inward-directed preparing and outward-directed partying, a rhythm of fasting and feasting, a blend of the kingdom of God at a distance and the kingdom of God at hand.

Like walking, life is a combination of steps. Like dancing, life is a combination of speeded-up steps: the static and the dynamic, finding one's center of gravity and venturing out of it by leaning forward and, just before falling, leaning back and returning to the center where the step begins all over again. All inward motion (preparation) and no outward expression (party) is a good way to burn out. One can easily discipline oneself out of existence. All preparation and no practice is an equally good way to burn out. One can just as easily party structures out of existence. Certain dance steps call us to be editing our selves and our structures; other dance steps call us to be enjoying our selves and our structures. The language of preparation is philosophy. The language of partying is poetry. The philosopher prepares the way—it is called criticism. The poet parties—it is called celebration.

Dance, my friends, dance.

Do more than "Say Amer, Somebody." Indeed, "Get up and Dance, Everybody."

We must try dancing. For the Universe is a dance and the rhythm of the dance determines the shape and pattern of Creation.

—THE SEER IN PETER BARNES'S TRILOGY THE SPIRIT OF MAN

SoulSalsa

1. James V. Schall, professor of government at Georgetown University, interprets a comment by G. K. Chesterton this way:

> Chesterton's profound remark, that the one thing that the Son of God did not show us while He was on earth was His "mirth," did not presume that the Lord did not know mirth. Indeed, it was Chesterton's view that the sort of joy for which we are made is so much more delightful than anything we can know, even by analogy to our actual laughter, that it would only depress us if we were to see it before we were really prepared for it. The real crisis of our being, if we would only reflect on it, is that we are given too much, not too little. We are made for a joy that, were it shown to us in advance, we would reject because we could not imagine it.

Do you see any evidence in the Gospels that Jesus was mirthful?

What do you think of the idea that understanding the magnitude of the joy in heaven would only make us depressed in this life because we aren't ready for it yet?

2. Babies learn from their mothers to smile when happy. Mothers reward babies for smiling when they are pleased. But all this begs the question of how mothers know when babies are happy. How do you think parents know when their children are happy?

3. Tex Sample's The Spectacle of Worship has a section on "Dance in the Church" in which he introduces readers to seven suggestions from theologically trained dancer Marcia McFee. Her final instruction insists that "people must be given permission to move" in church because "the worship of the future will involve congregational dance."

To learn about sacred dance, use as your starting point the "Dancing Reverend's" links to dance-related sites (http://www.geocities.com/Broadway/Stage/1254/link.html/). To find a church in your area that has a dance ministry, go to the Web site called Christian Sacred Dance (http://www.inet-port.com/~ruthann/sdchurch.htm/).

4. Celebration loves company. In his Celebration of Discipline (the book in which he states, "Far and away the most important benefit of celebration is that it saves us from taking ourselves too seriously") Richard Foster lists five ways to celebrate corporately:

- Through singing, dancing, and shouting
- Through laughing
- By accenting the creative gifts of fantasy and imagination
- By making family events into times of celebration and thanksgiving
- By taking advantage of the festivals of our culture

Are you taking advantage of all these opportunities to celebrate with others?

5. For a good laugh, visit one of the following Web sites:

- http://www.cybercheeze.com/
- http://www.newsjoke.com/
- http://www.jokes.com/

Or get a whole list of joke sites by going to this URL:

- http://dir.yahoo.com/Entertainment/Humor/Jokes/

6. Get our your Day-Timer and pick the soonest convenient day to throw a party. Invite a mix of Jesus followers and others, and let it be a time just for having fun and getting to know each other better.

7. Brennan Manning, in his book Abba's Child, identifies the greatest miracle:

> The central miracle of the gospel is not the raising of Lazarus or the multiplication of the loaves or all the dramatic healing stories taken together. The miracle of the gospel is Christ, risen and glorified, who this very moment tracks us, pursues us, abides in us, and offers Himself to us as companion for the journey! God pazzo d'amore and ebro d'amore ("crazed with love" and "drunk with love"—Catherine of Siena) is embodied in Jesus dwelling within us.

Close your eyes and imagine God pazzo d'amore and ebro d'amore about you. Pray to him whatever you feel.

If even dying is to be made a social function, then, please, grant me the favor of sneaking out on tiptoe without disturbing the party.
—DAG HAMMARSKJÖLD

Acknowledgments

As a youth, Dostoevsky promised his readers that his own "ugly mug" would be nowhere visible in what he wrote. That I was finally dragged into writing such a nakedly confessional and self-mugging book can be blamed on a friend and new neighbor: *Lex Rivers*.

Conversations with *Carol Mostad* (she's the one who counted twenty-three layers of cloth around the neck), *Bryan Borger* (the best theological bibliographer/religious bookstore manager around), *Mike Riddell* (New Zealand theologian/novelist/alternative worship architect/fellow foe of faculty-club culture), and *Gloria Gaither* (an artist's artist in moment making) helped shape this book's spine. *Anna Claire Mauerhan* was the inspiration for more than one chapter. *Martha Talton*, who helps me be my best self, daily wrapped this book in prayer.

Two research assistants, *Steve Kriss* and *Regina Snyder*, did their best to excise from the text Boomer phrases and biases (e.g., "sneakers spirituality" became "sandals spirituality"). They also offered me points of emotional entry into their native world, which otherwise would have been beyond my immigrant grasp. West Virginia pastor *Kathryn McIntyre* helped me locate Web sites that were off the scale, over the top, on the money. She protects me from missing the telling footprints of change on the Web.

Composer Sergey Prokofiev was said to have mastered a "wrong note" style. Sometimes I think I have a "wrong note" writing style: wanting to joke when I sound serious, wanting to be serious when I sound jokey. *Eric Stanford* gagged a lot of my "wrong notes." His purgings, parings down, and appendages made this a much better book. *Lyn Cryderman*'s role as the "reader's advocate" has taught me that the author is not the final authority in textual analysis.

There are some good things tucked away deep in the pleats and folds of this book that would not have been there without the reinforcing research of *Betty O'Brien*. My books get away from me too quickly—that's why I hate book interviews. Betty not only remembers whether or not I have said something before, but she keeps under control my schoolboy enthusiasms.

In appreciation of his thirty years of loyal service, the members of a Baptist congregation gave their pastor an all-expenses-paid trip to Paris. When he returned, they asked him about the trip. He replied,

"The only thing I can say is that I wish I had gone to Paris *before* I was born again."

Landrum Leavell III is a perturber and a disturber. He and *Suzanne* continue to teach me (helped by annual reinforcements from *Barry and Ginny Foster*) the Christian fact that when you let the Holy Spirit take charge of your life, you don't give up the fun of Paris. You discover the fun of Paris. You discover the true pleasures of Paris. Now when I sense that life's adventure and party is happening elsewhere, I know that something is wrong with my spirit. Landrum's fortnightly care packages of clippings (all photocopied on recycled paper) have become mental manna. But more than that, as Dante through the mouth of the Christian poet Statius put it in Canto 22 of the *Purgatorio:* "Through you was I a poet, through you a Christian."

Three guardian angels have been the marrow in the bones of SpiritVenture Ministries during the writing of this postmodern trilogy. *Phillip Connolly* believed in my ministry enough to offer a three-year grant that facilitated my research. Both as an attorney and friend, *Lyn Caterson* came to my aid and kept the blessed blip of hope on my life-screen when it threatened to fade out. The support and counsel of *Aana Lisa Whatley* and her colleague *Estelle Brendle* made possible more than once the convergence of "could be" and "did."

In one fell swoop two scientists made me a twice-over ancestor during the writing of this book. It is *Leonard Sweet Jr.'s* impossible assignment to keep me from becoming post-interesting while at the same time *Kathryn Sweet* prevents me from engaging in postmodern high jinks and low jokes.

Robert Duncan Jr. is one of God's spies (like Caleb and Joshua) who continually goes into the future and returns with good news of all that God can do there if only I/we will not be afraid. His friendship is one of life's treasures.

My assistant, *Lyn Stuntebeck,* doesn't wear her faith on her sleeve; she wears it on her feet. Her ferocity of dedication to the mission of SpiritVenture Ministries has taught me the art of dead-on-my-feet dancing. Our relationship nerves me to wage war with the obvious.

My non-dance-floor dance partner, *Elizabeth Rennie,* still hasn't gotten it through her head that "soulsalsa" is about a dance, not a condiment. But her spoken love and unspoken understanding are the real forcing and forging houses of a hot faith that makes me live up to the name of "Christian"—whether I'm in the Dantean depths or Sistine heights. Without her surprise birthing of an "impossible dream" that at the age of four has now become an "impossible reality," this book would have had a very different dedication.

SoulSalsa

Sources

Introduction

10. *"Orthodoxy is common life before it is common doctrine"*—Rowan Williams, *Ray of Darkness: Sermons and Reflections* (Cambridge, Mass.: Cowley, 1995), 231.

10. *"These are not people who are anti-religion...."*—For more on the unchurched, contact Barna Research Group, Ltd., 5528 Everglades St., Ventura, CA 93003. Telephone: 805-658-8885. Fax: 805-658-7298. Or check out *http://207.198.84.9/cgi-bin/Home.asp/*.

11. *My favorite book title of the 1990s...*—See Don Everts, *Jesus with Dirty Feet: A Down-to-Earth Look at Christianity for the Curious and Skeptical* (Downers Grove, Ill.: InterVarsity Press, 1999).

12. *Specialization is for insects*—Mark Frauenfelder, "Cure for Cluelessness," *Wired* (August 1998): 147.

12. *"I do believe, I really do believe, that we can be better than we are, ..."*—With thanks to Rick Diamond for this quote from James Baldwin.

13. The Doubter's Companion *(1994) defines "ethics" ironically as* ...—John Ralston Saul, *The Doubter's Companion: A Dictionary of Aggressive Common Sense* (New York: Free, 1994), 122.

13. *William Wordsworth wrote some of the greatest poetry ever penned, ...*—See "When Bad Things Happen to Good Poets," in *Very Bad Poetry*, ed. Kathryn and Ross Petras (New York: Vintage, 1998), 96–97.

13. *my "heart [can] dance at the sound of His Name!"*—Quoted in Crichton Mitchell, *Charles Wesley: Man with the Dancing Heart* (Kansas City, Mo.: Beacon Hill Press of Kansas City, 1994), 150.

14. *Plato said that humans should spend their lives "singing, sacrificing, dancing."*—Plato, *Laws*, trans. R. G. Bury, Loeb Classical Library (New York: Putnam, 1926), 55.

14. *In fact, the Aramaic word for "rejoice" is the same as the word for "dance," ...*—Cynthia Serjak, *Music and the Cosmic Dance* (Washington: Pastoral, 1987), 117. So far as I know, the first person who brought together theological education and dance is Charles S. McCoy, "Theological Seminary: School of the Dance" (paper presented at the American Academy of Religion, Chicago, Illinois, 19 October 1967).

15. *"How can we defend our poor privacy ..."*—Maria Teresa Porcile, "Solitude and Solidarity," *Ecumenical Review* 38 (January 1986): 36.

15. *"To them [postmoderns], the contemporary Christian church is a relic of a bygone era; ..."* and following quotes—Michael Riddell,

Threshold of the Future: Reforming the Church in the Post-Christian West (London: SPCK, 1998), 10–11.

16. *"I wasn't a human being. I was a human* doing."—Quoted in Chuck Salter, "Enough Is Enough," *Fast Company,* July–August 1999, 124.

1. Mezuzah Your Universe

18. *By the commandment on the mezuzah, . . .*—Quoted in *The First Jewish Catalog: A Do-It-Yourself Kit,* comp. and ed., Richard Siegel, Michael Strassfeld, and Sharon Strassfeld (Philadelphia: Jewish Publication Society of America, 1973), 13.

18. *Postmodern disciples read the signs of the divine . . .*—I have been most influenced here by the thinking of a British sociologist and an Anglican bishop: David Martin, *Divinity in a Grain of Bread* (London: Lutterworth, 1989); and Bishop Rowan Williams, "The Nature of a Sacrament," in *Signs of Faith, Hope, and Love: The Christian Sacrament Today,* ed. John Greenhalgh and Elizabeth Russell (San Francisco: Collins Liturgical, 1987), 32–44.

18. *In 1967 the sociologist Peter Berger defined secularization . . .*—Peter Berger, *Sacred Canopy* (New York: Anchor, 1967).

18. *In historian Christian Smith's recent look at American religion, . . .*—Christian Smith et al., *American Evangelicalism* (Berkeley: University of California Press, 1998), 106.

18. *we temple in our homes; we tabernacle in our meeting place.*—Thanks to Chicago Lutheran pastor Bruce Cole for this distinction.

19. *Psychologist James Hillman answers, . . .*—Quoted in Jonathan White, *Talking on the Water: Conversations about Nature and Creativity* (San Francisco: Sierra Club Books, 1994), 123.

19. *"So many houses, so big with so little soul."*—Sarah Susanka and Kira Obolensky, *The Not So Big House: A Blueprint for the Way We Really Live* (Newtown, Conn.: Taunton, 1998), 7.

20. *Glaze and shimmer, / luster and gleam, . . .*—See Mark Doty, "Concerning Some Recent Criticism of His Work," in his *Sweet Machine: Poems* (New York: HarperFlamingo, 1998), 36.

21. Milan Kundera, *The Book of Laughter and Forgetting,* trans. Michael Henry Heim (New York: HarperPerennial, 1994).

21. *I was glad to learn that, over the last fifty years, . . .*—"America in the '90s," *Funny Business* (5 February 1999), 2.

22. *"Those who go beneath the surface do so at their own peril."*—Oscar Wilde, preface to *The Picture of Dorian Gray* (New York: Book League of America, 1931), 8.

22. G.K. Chesterton, as quoted in Dudley Barker, G.K. Chesterton: A Biography (New York: Stein and Day, 1973), 65.

23. *Pay for someone's meal without them ever figuring out who the benefactor was.*—With thanks to Jim Futral, "The Discipline of Secrecy," *Baptist Record,* July 15, 1999.

24. *They even established endowments . . .*—Kathryn Argetsinger, "Birthday Rituals: Friends and Patrons in Roman Poetry and Cult," *Classical Antiquity* 11 (October 1992): 179.

24. *birthday cards alone are a $1.5 billion industry.*—Women send an average of seventeen birthday cards a year; men send an average of ten birthday cards a year. See Camala Brown, "Cakes, Cards, and Candles," *American Demographics* (March 1995), 22.

24. *Some argue that birthdays . . . are holy days for children.*—Cele Otnes and Mary Ann McGrath, "Ritual Socialization and the Children's Birthday Party: The Early Emergence of Gender Differences," *Journal of Ritual Studies* 8 (Winter 1994): 74.

24. *"My own birthday gave me life, . . ."*—Quoted in Argetsinger, "Birthday Rituals," 178.

25. *"Amazing grace, how sweet the sound, / Your name fills us with glee! . . ."*—Diane Loomans with Julia Loomans, *Full Esteem Ahead: 100 Ways to Build Self-Esteem in Children and Adults* (Tiburon, Calif.: Kramer, 1994), 49.

26. *If you could learn from any teacher in the world, . . .*—Ibid., 157.

27. *"In all our travels and movements, in all our coming in and going out, . . ."*—Quoted in *The Catholic Encyclopedia*, s.v. "The Sign of the Cross."

28. *"celebrating a birthday is exalting life and being glad for it."*—Henri J. M. Nouwen, *Here and Now: Living in the Spirit* (New York: Crossroad, 1994).

28. *"Birthdays need to be celebrated."*—Ibid., 18–19.

28. *Nouwen also told the story of his friend . . .*—Ibid.

29. *What is the probability that at least two members of a Sunday school class . . .*—Sergio Fantini and Jeffrey C. Grossman, "How Likely Is It That Two Classmates Have the Same Birthday?" *The Physics Teacher* 35 (January 1997): 42.

2. Make a Moment

31. *"All happenings, great and small, are parables whereby God speaks."*—Quoted in Ken Gire, "Faithful Companions and Guides: Art and Nature as God's Chosen Vocabulary," *Mars Hill Review* 6 (Fall 1996): 8–20.

31. *First, "What is the quality of their bread?"*—Quoted in Max DePree, *Leadership Jazz* (New York: Dell, 1992), 118.

32. *"He was an original and no man's copy."*—William Penn, "The Testimony of William Penn concerning That Faithful Servant George Fox," in *The Journal of George Fox*, ed. Rufus M. Jones (New York: Capricorn, 1963), 45.

33. *"The truth is out there, but how do you download it?"*—For more on Urban Mosaic, see Michael Luo, "A Creative Approach to Worship," *Los Angeles Times* (16 March 1999), B2. Or visit Mosaic's Web site at *http://mosaic.org/*.

33. *"Despair is but hope blinded by its tears."*—Edward Thomas, "Last Poem [The Sorrow of True Love]," in *The Collected Poems of*

Edward Thomas, ed. R. George Thomas (Oxford: Clarendon, 1978), 277.

33. *A team of researchers at St. Olaf College...*—St. Olaf College, "Student Research Project Demonstrates That Sharing Family Tales Improves Physical Well-Being—for Both the Teller and the Listener," *http://www.stolaf.edu/inside/981123/feature.html/.*

34. *The Enlightenment world deodorized smell...*—Constance Classen, David Howes, and Anthony Synnoff, "Following the Scent: From the Middle Ages to Modernity," in their *Aroma: The Cultural History of Smell* (New York: Routledge, 1994), 50–92.

34. *Fragrances are one way I keep my sanity,...*—For more on the role of smell in biblical theology, see "The Fragrance of Integrity" in Leonard Sweet, *A Cup of Coffee at the SoulCafe* (Nashville: Broadman & Holman, 1998), 114–26.

34. *One church in Venice, Italy,...*—Richard Monastersky, "Against the Tide: Venice's Long War with Rising Water," *Science News* 156 (24 July 1999): 63.

36. *"Sometime I'd like to hear someone say, 'Pray for me,'"...*—Dean Elliott Wolfe, "Just One Thing before I Go" (last sermon before leaving Trinity Church, Boston, Massachusetts, to become vice rector at Saint Michael and All Angels Church in Dallas, Texas, 30 August 1998).

36. *prayer walks,...*—For more on "prayer walking," see my "Prayer Walking" in *Homiletics* 6, no. 4 (October–December 1994): 23–26.

36. *concerts of prayer,...*—For an example of a concert of prayer, see my "Concert of Prayer," *Homiletics* 8, no. 1 (January–March 1996): 11–14.

38. *"The Trinity is limitless and we mortals want limits,..."*—Madeleine L'Engle, *Penguins and Golden Calves: Icons and Idols* (Wheaton, Ill.: Harold Shaw, 1996), 158–59.

38. *"To live an ordinary day...."*—Dow Edgerton, "Left-Handed Prayer," in *Theology and the Human Spirit: Essays in Honor of Perry D. LeFevre,* ed. Theodore W. Jennings and Susan Brooks Thistlethwaite (Chicago: Exploration, 1994), 48.

39. *"One ought, every day at least, to hear a little song,..."*—Johann Wolfgang von Goethe, Escati Quote of the Day Archive, *http://www.escati.com/quote_archive.htm/.*

39. *Journalist/novelist Daniel Defoe...*—Quoted in Classen, Howes, and Synnoff, *Aroma,* 62.

39. *"We draw straight lines...."*—Karen Neudorf, "Life and Belief in One Dimension," *Beyond Magazine,* 12 (1999), 12.

3. Think Methusaleh

40. *"If we must suffer, it is better to create the world in which we suffer,..."*—Richard Ellmann, "Yeats without Analogue" (1964), in his *Along the Riverrun: Selected Essays* (New York: Knopf, 1988), 32.

40. *"riding on a limited express."*—Carl Sandburg, "Limited," in *Modern American Poetry: A Critical Anthology*, ed. Louis Untermeyer, 5th ed. (New York: Harcourt, Brace, 1936), 240.

41. *Ninety-year-old management guru Peter Drucker . . .*—By the middle of 2000, the number of USAmericans at over one hundred years of age will have reached eight hundred thousand. According to Theodore Roszak in *America the Wise: The Longevity Revolution and the True Wealth of Nations* (Boston: Houghton Mifflin, 1998), 33, 69, by the year 2020, one in four people on the planet will be over sixty, and more than a quarter of that group will be over eighty. Already over seventy countries are below population replacement levels due to increasing longevity and decreasing fertility. See also Nicholas Rankin, "The Greying of America," *Times Literary Supplement* (19 February 1999), 9; and Peter Drucker, "The Future That Has Already Happened," *The Futurist* (November 1998), 16.

41. *They are not twenty-first-century kids but twenty-second-century kids*—"Back in 1900 there was only a 7% chance that a 60-year-old would have a living parent, according to a University of North Carolina study. By the year 2000 that number is projected to hit 44%. It's no longer out of the question to find parents and children living together in the same nursing home." For more, see Carter Henderson, "Today's Affluent Oldsters: Marketers See Gold in Gray," *The Futurist* 32 (November 1998), 20.

42. *"For age is opportunity no less / Than youth itself, . . ."*—The last lines of Henry Wadsworth Longfellow, "Morituri Salutamus," in *The Poetical Works of Henry Wadsworth Longfellow* (Boston: Houghton Mifflin, 1886), 3:196.

42. *"Then God called me unto sacred art, . . ."*—Frederica Mathewes-Green, "Confounder of the Wise," *World* (27 April–4 May 1998), 14. Finster has multiple accounts of his dive into the art world. In another one, while he was repairing a bike, a smudge of white paint on his finger turned into a face and spoke to him: "Paint sacred art." See also Edward Knippers, "Howard Finster: Dancing through the Culture Wars," *Image: A Journal of the Arts and Religion* 19 (Spring 1998): 32.

42. *"God give me work / Till my life shall end . . ."*—Quoted in D. J. Enright, *Interplay: A Kind of Commonplace Book* (New York: Oxford University Press, 1995), 235.

43. *"Youth is something to be endured . . ."*—Quoted in Cheryl Russell, "The New Consumer Paradigm," *American Demographics* (April 1999).

43. *As with all the lifeware design components, . . .*—In my *SoulTsunami* I say this about the double-ring phenomenon: "One of the characteristic features of postmodern culture is that opposite things happen at the same time without being contradictory. Anyone who doesn't feel pulled in conflicting directions doesn't understand Heisenberg's uncertainty principle, Pauli's exclusion principle, and Schrödinger's wave equation. Where the modern age was predominantly either-or, the postmodern world is and/also. Or phrased more memorably, 'the postmodernist always

rings twice.'" Leonard Sweet, *SoulTsunami* (Grand Rapids: Zondervan, 1999), 27.

43. *Where "old" used to be defined as over sixty, . . .*—May 1998 online research poll by Cyberdialogue, cited in "Are Your Normal?" *American Demographics* (September 1998), 46.

44. *"Time corrupts all. What has it not made worse?"*—Horace, *The Odes of Horace, with the Latin Text*, trans. James Michie (New York: Orion, 1963), 192–93.

44. *Elizabeth Somer calls pursuing physical wellness "age-proofing" your body.*—Elizabeth Somer, *Age-Proof Your Body: Your Complete Guide to Lifelong Vitality* (New York: Morrow, 1998).

44. *The National Institute on Aging says that 80 percent . . .*—For additional information, contact the National Institute on Aging, Public Information Office, Building 31, Room 5C27, 31 Center Drive, MSC 2292, Bethesda, MD 20892. Or phone the NIA at 301-496-1752. Or check out its Web site at *http://www.nih.gov/nia/*.

45. *Boomers are not looking to retiree-rich counties in which to retire . . .*—Quoted in Glenn Thrush, "When I'm 64," *American Demographics* (January 1999), 68.

45. *This is why college towns are sprouting "age in place" retirement communities . . .*—Some leading-edge "retirement" college towns include the intellectually and culturally stimulating environments of Cornell, Dartmouth, Florida, Iowa State, and Penn State.

45. *"I believe the overwhelming message is the grace and the love and the mercy of God, . . ."*—Billy Graham, "Just As I Am," interview by Dan Wooding, *The Plain Truth* (March–April 1997), 8.

46. *"I do messages, for the spiritual people that believes in my messages, . . ."*—Mathewes-Green, "Confounder," 14.

46. *"If you have ever seen a person die, . . ."*—Thomas à Kempis, *The Imitation of Christ: A New Reading of the 1441 Latin Autograph Manuscript*, trans. William C. Creasy (Macon, Ga.: Mercer University Press, 1989), 26–27.

47. *Paradoxically, contemplation of the bitters . . .*—Friedrich Nietzsche's aphorism, first published in 1880, would beg to differ: "Death—The certain prospect of death could introduce into every life a precious, sweet-smelling drop of levity *[Leichtsinn]*— and yet you marvelous apothecary souls have made it an ill-tasting drop of poison through which all life is made repulsive!" Friedrich Nietzche, *Human, All Too Human*, trans. R. J. Hollindale (Cambridge: Cambridge University Press, 1996), 390.

47. *It is Manguel's contention that the burst in book reading . . .*— Quoted in Stephen Henighan, "Putting Trust in the Words on the Page," *Times Literary Supplement* (16 April 1999), 27. See the final essay in Alberto Manguel, *Into the Looking-Glass Wood* (London: Bloomsbury, 1999).

48. *"Your tears come easy, when you're young, . . ."*—Wilkie Collins, *The Moonstone* (Garden City: Garden City, 1874), 179.

48. *One of my favorite meditations . . .*—Stephen Strauss, *The Sizesaurus* (New York: Kodansha, 1995), 175.

49. *"You can't turn back the clock...."*—Quoted in TPCN: "Great Quotations to Inspire and Motivate You—Time and Time Management," *http://www.cybernation.com/victory/quotations/subjects/quotes_timeandtimemanagement.html/*.

50. *"There are no final missions."*—Jonathan Alter, "Eject Button on Cynicism," *Newsweek* (9 November 1998), 28.

50. *"I meant to write about death, ..."*—Virginia Woolf, "Friday 17 February [1922]," in *The Diary of Virginia Woolf*, ed. Anne Oliver and Andrew McNeillie (New York: Harcourt Brace Jovanovich, 1978), 2:167.

50. *"The true wealth of nations,"* Theodore Roszak insists, ...—Quoted in Rankin, "Greying of America," 9.

50. *Thirty-seven percent of USAmericans say age is unrelated to chronology ...*—Cited in Bernice Kanner, "You're Getting Better, Not Older," *American Demographics* (September 1998), 46.

50. *Twenty-three percent of USAmericans dread getting older, ...*—Cyberdialogue, "Are You Normal?" 46.

51. *For an example of a sixteenth-century antiaging publication, ...*—This influential work was, over the course of centuries, translated into several languages with numerous title variations. One English translation, published in London as early as 1704, appeared as *Sure and Certain Methods of Attaining a Long and Healthy Life*, 1st American ed. (Philadelphia: Reprinted for the Rev. M. L. Weems by Parry Hall, 1743).

4. Bounce Your Last Check

52. *"This, then, is held to be the duty of the man of wealth: ..."*—Andrew Carnegie, *Gospel of Wealth and Other Timely Essays* (New York: Century, 1900), 15.

53. *In fact, the two New Testament Greek words translated most often as "stewards" ...*—For a fuller treatment of these issues, see "From a Theology of Giving to a Theology of Receiving" in my *SoulTsunami: Sink or Swim in New Millennium Culture* (Grand Rapids: Zondervan, 1999), 270–76.

53. *"The BMW of the next decade will be the personal charitable trust fund."*—Quoted in Kevin Kelly, "The Roaring Zeros," *Wired* (September 1999), 154.

54. *"You do not consider, money never stays with me: ..."*—John Wesley, "To Mrs. Hall, Kingswood, October 6, 1768," in *The Letters of the Rev. John Wesley*, ed. John Telford (London: Epworth, 1931), 5:108–9.

56. *By this they mean that it is internally consistent, ...*—Even two of America's best-known mathematicians, Philip Davis and Reuben Hersh, have been forced to concede that mathematics in the strictest sense belongs in the humanities along with art, music, and

literature. See Philip J. Davis and Reuben Hersh, *The Mathematical Experience* (Boston: Birkhauser, 1981), 410.

56. *"Pennyless at the Wishing Well"*—This is the title of a song written and sung by Michael Heard.

57. *Living well is not the same thing as being well off.*—Kennon M. Sheldon, "Pursuing Personal Goals: Skills Enable Progress, but Not All Progress Is Beneficial," *Personality and Social Psychology Bulletin* (24 December 1998), 1319.

58. *"How many interesting ideas and experiences are enough?"*—Quoted in Anna Muoio, "The Philosopher Tom Morris," *Fast Company*(July–August 1999), 144.

58. *"Heav'n above is softer blue / Earth around is sweeter green; . . ."*—George Wade Robinson, "I Am His, and He Is Mine," 2d stanza, in *Hymns of Glorious Praise* (Springfield, Mass.: Gospel, 1969), 289.

58. *Up until the late nineteenth century, . . .*—See Dianne Apostolis-Cappadona, *The Spirit and the Vision: The Influence of Christian Romanticism on the Development of Nineteenth-Century American Art* (Atlanta: Scholars, 1995).

59. *According to his calculations, if this one group donated just one percent of their income for microloans, . . .*—Ronald Sider, "What Do We Do with Poor, Hungry People?" *Charisma* (24 December 1998), 56–60.

60. *"enough money so that they would feel they could do anything, . . ."*—Quoted in Richard I. Kirkland Jr., "Should You Leave It All to the Children?" *Fortune* (29 September 1986), 18.

60. *Sing the doxology "We Give Thee but Thine Own."*—William W. How, "We Give Thee but Thine Own," *The Methodist Hymnal: Official Hymnal of the Methodist Church* (Nashville: Methodist Publishing House, 1939), 456.

60. *"Gain all you can, without hurting either yourself or your neighbour, . . ."*—John Wesley, "The Use of Money" (1760), in his *Sermons*, ed. Albert C. Outler, *The Works of John Wesley* (Nashville: Abingdon, 1985), 2:278–79.

60. *"In my late teens I had gained an insight . . ."*—David A. Cooper, *Entering the Sacred Mountain: A Mystical Odyssey* (New York: Bell Tower, 1994), 30.

61. *"It's silly to pretend that you can be talented and rich and not messed up. . . ."*—Quoted in Melina Gerosa, "I'm Cher," *Ladies' Home Journal* (November 1996), 256.

61. *Can you guess what place money occupies among the most common sources of marital strife in the U.S. today?*—It's number one, at 29 percent. (TV follows close behind at 28 percent.) See Shannon Dorch, "Money and Marital Discord," *American Demographics* (October 1994), 11. Interestingly, 33 percent of husbands say they usually win the arguments, and 33 percent say their wife usually does. Of the wives, 30 percent say they win, while 32 percent say their spouses do.

SoulSalsa

63. *Self-directed learning is also knowing one's natural mode of learning . . .*—David Kolb divides the four discrete learning modes into concrete experiences (CE), reflective observation (RO), abstract conceptualization (AC), and active experimentation (AE). He calls these learning modalities divergers, assimilators, convergers, and accommodators. For more, see David Kolb, *Experiential Learning: Experience as the Source of Learning and Development* (Englewood Cliffs, N.J.: Prentice-Hall, 1983).

63. *"The writer who postpones the recording of his thoughts . . ."*—Henry David Thoreau, 10 February 1852, in his *Journal*, ed. Bradford Torrey (Boston: Houghton Mifflin, 1906), 3:293. The entire quote is, "Write while the heat is in you. When the farmer burns a hole in his yoke, he carries the hot iron quickly from the fire to the wood, for every moment it is less effectual to penetrate (pierce) it. It must be used instantly, or it is useless. The writer who postpones the recording of his thoughts uses an iron which has cooled to burn a hole with. He cannot inflame the minds of his audience."

63. *"Every natural object is a conductor of divinity."*—Quoted by Steven M. Rosman, *Spiritual Parenting: A Sourcebook for Parents and Teachers* (Wheaton, Ill.: Theosophical, 1994), 66.

64. *"The entire object of true education . . ."*—John Ruskin, "One World: A Source for International and Intercultural Education: Quotes on Education," *http://www.fiu.edu/~escotet/web/quotes.html/.*

64. *This is what it used to mean to "read" a text . . .*—See Mary Carruthers, *The Book of Memory: A Study of Memory in Medieval Culture* (New York: Cambridge University Press, 1990), 44, 167.

65. *Less than twenty-five years after the first test-tube baby . . .*—For how all these are possible (frozen embryos, ovary transplant from aborted fetus, etc.), see Gilbert Meilaender, "Biotech Babies," *Christianity Today* (7 December 1998), 55–58.

65. *"the world's fund of information is doubling every two to two-and-a-half years."*—Graham T. T. Molitor, "Trends and Forecasts for the New Millennium," *The Futurist* (August–September 1998), 59.

65. *The new law is "the Law of the Photon," . . .*—Besides, photonics materials have such sonorous names: Pyralin 2611D, aluminum gallium indium phosphide, zirconium tetrafluoride.

65. *fewer than one in three say they are suffering from information overload, . . .*—G. Evans Will, "Out of Touch in the Media: Journalism's Credibility Slides Even Further," *American Demographics* (June 1999), 26.

65. *"Progress is impossible without change; . . ."*—CHA's "Quotations by Topics," *http://www.cha4mot.com/q_cha.html/.*

66. *"By the time I would have finished my review, . . ."*—F. A. Hayek, *Hayek on Hayek: An Autobiographical Dialogue*, ed. Stephen

Kresge and Leif Wenar (Chicago: University of Chicago Press, 1994), 12.

66. *Here are some of the job titles of the future,...*—Rolf Jensen, *The Dream Society: How the Coming Shift from Information to Imagination Will Transform Your Business* (New York: McGraw-Hill, 1999), 147.

67. *"A single word even may be the spark..."*—Percy Bysshe Shelley, *A Defense of Poetry*, ed. Albert S. Cook (Boston: Ginn, 1891), 11.

68. *Leaders "Must Be Readers, Perceivers, Sensers,..."*—George Cladis, *Leading the Team-Based Church: How Pastors and Church Staffs Can Grow Together into a Powerful Fellowship of Leaders* (San Francisco: Jossey-Bass, 1999), 141.

69. *"We would rather be ruined than changed."*—W. H. Auden, quoted in "Focused Performance: Unconstrained Quotes," *http://www.focusedperformance.com/goodies/quotes.html/*.

69. *"Life-long learning is far more a mindset than a regimen."*—Leith Anderson, *Leadership That Works* (Minneapolis: Bethany House, 1999), 168–69.

69. *There is even a company now that will design a learning vacation for you,...*—Write to EduVacations at 1431 21st St. NW, Suite 302, Washington, DC 20036. Or call 202–857–8384. Or go to *http://www.eduvacations.com/*.

70. *The mark of his creative genius...*—Quoted in John Shand, "Short Cuts to Great Minds," *Times Literary Supplement* (31 July 1998), 14.

70. *"Originality is nothing but judicious imitation."*—"Thought-Provoking Quotes," *http://www.geocities.org/CollegePark/2639/quotes.html/*.

71. *In January 1913 Cawein published...*—Robert Ian Scott, "The *Waste Land* Eliot Didn't Write," *Times Literary Supplement* (8 December 1995), 14.

71. *"Of course I wrote Dr. Holmes and told him..."*—Quoted in *Funny Business* (December 1996), 4.

71. *"He who receives an idea from me,...."*—"Creative Quotations from Thomas Jefferson," *http://www.bemorecreative.com/one/39.htm/*.

72. *"to guard against becoming superficial..."*—Denis Brian, *Einstein: A Life* (New York: Wiley, 1996), 389.

72. *"I cannot live without books."*—Thomas Jefferson to John Adams, 10 June 1815, in *The Adams-Jefferson Letters: The Complete Correspondence between Thomas Jefferson and Abigail and John Adams*, ed. Lester J. Cappon (Chapel Hill: University of North Carolina Press, 1959), 2:443.

72. *"I wish to have one Copy of every Book in the World!!!!"*—Phillipps wrote this in a letter to Robert Curzon, 28 April 1869. See "Sir Thomas Phillipps" in William Baker and Kenneth Womack, ed., *Nineteenth-Century British Book-Collectors and Bibliographers*, Dictionary of Literary Biography, 184 (Detroit: Gale, 1997), 349.

72. *Nineteenth-century British prime minister William Gladstone*
    ...—Janet Ing Freeman, "The Lustre of the Library," *Times Literary Supplement* (31 July 1998), 28.
72. *At his death in 1833, Richard Heber ...*—See "Richard Heber" in Baker and Womack, *Book-Collectors and Bibliographers*, 223.
73. *"Everything has been said before, ..."*—Quoted in Laura S. Moncur, "The Death of Andre Gide, February 19, 1951," *Quotes of the Week* (15 February 1998), *http://www.starlingtech.com/quotes/w980215.html/*.

6. Do Dirt and Do the Dishes

74. *When we separate ourselves from whence we came ...*—Minna Morse, "Get Down and Dirty: Our Squeaky Clean Culture Is Making Us Sick," *Utne Reader* (January–February 1999), 14–15.
74. *The "hygiene hypothesis" ...*—For more on the "hygiene hypothesis," see Siri Carpenter, "Modern Hygiene's Dirty Tricks," *Science News* 156 (14 August 1999): 108–10.
75. *"Dirt is only matter out of place."*—John Chipman Gray, in the preface to his *Restraints on the Alienation of Property*, 2d ed. (1895; reprint, Littleton, Colo.: Rothman, 1997).
76. *never watched the program watched by one-fifth of the people in the world ...*—Poet/essayist Katha Pollitt as quoted by Karen Springen, "Eyes of the Beholders," *Newsweek* (3 June 1996), 68.
77. *"Look in the mirror before you look out the window."*—Steve Rabey, "Pastor X," *Christianity Today* (11 November 1996), 40.
78. *And God said, "Life? What life?"*—Steve Smith, "A 'Too Clean' Life Is No Life at All," *Baptist Standard* (30 June 1999), 5.
78. One of the first things the SPG managers did ...—For the story of the Codrington estates, see H. P. Thompson, *Into All Lands: The History of the Society for the Propagation of the Gospel in Foreign Parts 1701–1950* (London: SPCK, 1951), 158–60; for the story of the treatment of the slaves, see 162–65. See also Lawrence James's *The Rise and Fall of the British Empire* (New York: St. Martin's, 1994), 22–23.
81. Barbara Moses, *Career Intelligence* (Berrett-Roehler, 1998).

7. Cycle to Church

82. *those who go to church are healthier than those who don't.*—Marilyn Elias, "Attending Church Found Factor in Longer Life," *USA Today* (9 August 1999), 1a.
82. *Weekly churchgoers have healthier immune systems ...*—Reported in the *International Journal of Psychiatry in Medicine*,

October 1997. See also H. G. Koenig et al., "Does Religious Attendance Prolong Survival?" *Journal of Gerontology* 54 (July 1999): M370–76.

82. *The curative and causative role of faith in healing . . .*—What seemed to break open the formerly taboo subject of spirituality and health was Claudia Wallis, "Faith and Healing," *Time* (24 June 1996), 59–62.

83. *Georgetown University physician Dale Matthews, . . .*—Dale A. Matthews, *The Faith Factor: Proof of the Healing Power of Prayer* (New York: Viking, 1998).

83. *Drinking four cups of coffee a day . . .*—Edward Giovannucci, "Meta-analysis of Coffee Consumption and Risk of Colorectal Cancer," *American Journal of Epidemiology* 147 (1998): 1043–52.

83. *Simply smelling the aroma of coffee . . .*—See the study conducted by a research team at the University of California at Davis led by Takayuki Shibamoto as reported in Thomas Ropp, "They Say It Isn't So, Joe!" *The Arizona Republic* (19 August 1999), HL1, HL3.

83. *"Man eats too much. . . ."*—Quoted in Arthur Wallis, *God's Chosen Fast* (Fort Washington, Pa.: Christian Literature Crusade, 1971), 81.

84. *. . . if you live in the Spirit, you will be able to drink deadly poison . . .*—In fact, at the Mayo Clinic they provide intravenous caffeine (two hundred milligrams) for patients required to keep stomachs empty for twelve hours before surgery. As mentioned in Scott McCormack, "Take a Double Espresso and Call Me in the Morning," *Forbes* (27 July 1998), 41.

85. *Then one stuck one's fork in the potato, . . .*—Sidney W. Mintz, *Tasting Food, Tasting Freedom: Excursions into Eating, Culture, and the Past* (Boston: Beacon, 1996), xvi.

85. *. . . it is "proof of a lack of vitality in religion."*—Referenced in Eric Zencey, *Virgin Forest* (Athens, Ga.: University of Georgia Press, 1998), 152.

85. *It's not just Willard Scott who worships in "the church of Krispy Kreme."*—The North Carolina company even has a "Minister of Culture" who produces commercials and industrial films for the doughnut company. See "Job Titles of the Future," *Fast Company* (September 1998), 64.

85. *. . . the number who are clinically overweight . . .*—Cited by Graham T. T. Molitor, "Trends and Forecasts for the New Millennium," *The Futurist* (August–September 1998), 55.

85. *. . . the more religious the person, the more rotund the bodyscape. . . .*—See the study by sociologist Kenneth Ferraro at Purdue University as reported by Stacey Fuemmeler, "Purdue Study Finds Faith and Flab Often Go Together," *http://courierpress.evansville.net/cee/articles/stories/199804/04/purdue_news.html/*.

85. *"I fit the mold. I don't think God gives a flip either way."*—Quoted in Terry Beahm, "No Kidding: Quick News Items That You Need to Know," *The Arizona Republic* (12 July 1998), E2.

86. *. . . cleanse your mind and body, especially through "moodling" . . .*—For more on "moodling," see my *Jesus Prescription for a*

Healthy Life (Nashville: Abingdon, 1996), 187–98. "If you gotta ask what 'moodling' is, you ain't got it.... Perhaps it is better described than defined: lying in the shade under a tree by a lake, watching the clouds roll by; sitting in a hot tub, letting your thoughts flow; sleeping in a hammock under a harvest moon; riding horseback through a field; lollygagging on your walk home; marveling in a garden" (187).

86. *The more sedentary one's lifestyle,...*—For the ways in which exercise can reduce the incidence and prevalence of Alzheimer's disease, see *Neurology Reviews for the Primary Care Physician* 6 (July 1998): 15. See also Linda Teri et al., "Exercise and Activity Level in Alzheimer's Disease a Potential Treatment Focus," *Journal of Rehabilitation Research and Development* 35 (1998): 411–19. Exercise has also been shown to reduce heart disease and cancer. See K. S. Courneya and C. M. Friedenreich, "Physical Exercise and Quality of Life Following Cancer Diagnosis: A Literature Review," *Annals of Behavioral Medicine* 21 (Spring 1999): 171–79.

86. *The rise in psychiatric services in the U.S. has been spectacular.*—Paul Crichton, "A Prescription for Happiness?" *Times Literary Supplement* (2 July 1999), 14.

86. *Novelist William Styron,...*—Quoted in Liam Hudson, "What's Getting You Down," review of *Malignant Sadness: The Anatomy of Depression,* by Lewis Wolpert, *Times Literary Supplement* (25 June 1999), 35.

87. *"The church is inhuman in the dual sense..."*—Michael Riddell, *Threshold of the Future: Reforming the Church in the Post-Christian West* (London: SPCK, 1998), 123.

88. *Princeton sociologist Robert Wuthnow believes that the church ...*—Robert Wuthnow, *Christianity in the 21st Century* (New York: Oxford University Press, 1993), 32.

88. *M. Scott Peck, in his book* A World Waiting to Be Born *(1993),...*—M. Scott Peck, *A World Waiting to Be Born: Civility Rediscovered* (New York: Bantam, 1993), 274–75.

88. *The flow of living waters cuts a new channel, leaving the old riverbed...*—With thanks to my Arkansas friend John Dill for this analogy.

89. *A church like Steve Ayers's aquachurch, Hillvue Heights,...*—For more on their de-evangelism, see my *AquaChurch* (Loveland, Colo.: Group, 1999), 265.

90. *Eucharist is sacred, sacramental, holy consumption:...*—Vincent Rossi, "Consumerism and the Christian," *Green Cross* (Fall 1995), 8.

90. *Tim Dearborn has suggested that the role of Christians is "as 'appetizers' for the world...."*—Tim Dearborn, *Taste & See: Awakening Our Spiritual Senses* (Downers Grove, Ill.: InterVarsity Press, 1996), 81.

90. *"Early in the '50s," she said, "after one taste of French food—that unforgettable lunch—I was hooked...."*—This is one of many differing accounts of Julia Child's lunch in Rouen. See Noël Riley

Fitch, *Appetite for Life: The Biography of Julia Child* (New York: Doubleday, 1999), 155–56.

91. *"There is more silence, yet more of worth gets said. It is like music. . . ."*—Peck, *World Waiting to Be Born*, 274–75.

8. Brush Your Tongue

93. *A microbiologist at the University of Arizona in Tucson . . .*— Cited in Hugh Garvey, "Hi, Anxiety! Be Afraid. Be Slightly Afraid: A Paranoid's Guide to Things You Never Knew You Should Be Worried About," *Details* (October 1998), 98.

95. *"cancer mortality rates have remained essentially flat . . ."*—See the argument of John Horgan in "Nothing Left to Learn," *Times Literary Supplement* (29 January 1999), 31.

95. *. . . what John Betjeman called derisively "foot and note disease". . .*—Quoted in John Byrne, "Curzon St. Customers," *Times Literary Supplement* (22 May 1998), 34.

96. *It came to refer to any friend or acquaintance of the parents of the baptized child . . .*—See, for example, Walter W. Skeat, *Etymological Dictionary of the English Language*, rev. ed. (Oxford: Clarendon, 1910), 246; and Eric Partridge, *Origins: A Short Etymological Dictionary of Modern English* (New York: Macmillan, 1966), 259. (Under "gossip" it says: "see God, para. 8.")

96. *It all depends on whether these grapevines produce wine or vinegar, . . .*—By "drawing employees together through shared interests and beliefs," the rumor mill "produces teamwork, builds company loyalty, and can motivate employees to perform their best," writes Donald B. Simmons, "The Nature of the Organizational Grapevine," *Supervisory Management* 30 (November 1985): 41.

97. *Vicious, malicious gossip is the postmodern equivalent of the persecution of witches.*—So argues John Carroll in *Guilt: The Grey Eminence behind Character, History, and Culture* (Boston: Routledge and Kegan Paul, 1985), 26.

97. *Gossip is dictionary-defined as "idle chatter."*—See "gossip" in *The New Shorter Oxford English Dictionary on Historical Principles*, ed. Lesley Brown (Oxford: Clarendon, 1993); or *Oxford English Dictionary*, ed. J. A. Simpson and E. S. C. Weaver (Oxford: Clarendon, 1989), 6:699–701.

97. *"Gossip is a beast of prey . . ."*—George Meredith, *Diana of the Crossways* (London: Virago, 1980), 314.

98. *"I have learned that prayer is not asking for what you think you want . . ."*—Quoted in Dick Duerksen, "Living the Vision, Time for Change," *http://www.cuc.edu/cu/visitor/vol102/may_15_1998/a2.html/*.

98. *"Now we are to talk of no absent persons, . . ."*—John Wesley, "To Philothea Briggs, Whitby, Saturday, June 10, 1722," in *The*

Letters of the Rev. John Wesley, ed. John Telford (London: Epworth, 1931), 324.

100. *"I have seen flowers come in stony places;..."*—John Masefield, "The Meditation of Highworth Ridden," in his *Poems* (New York: Macmillan, 1951), 2:454.

100. *"What had begun as an execution turned into a ceremony of knighting,..."*—Milenko Matanovic, *Meandering Rivers and Square Tomatoes* (Issaquah, Wash.: Morningtown, 1988), 32.

101. *"Gossip is a sort of smoke..."*—George Eliot, *Daniel Deronda,* ed. Graham Handley (Oxford: Clarendon, 1984), 1:125.

101. *Why can't we receive more? Our hands are so small. "We don't open [our] mouths wide enough,"...*—Jonathan Edwards, *Religious Affections*, ed. John E. Smith (New Haven, Conn.: Yale University Press, 1959), 382–83. The full quote is "If men ben't satisfied here, in degree of happiness, the cause is within themselves; 'tis because they don't open their mouths wide enough."

102. *Max Gluckman, in a 1963 study,...*—Max Gluckman, "Gossip and Scandal," *Current Anthropology* 4 (1963): 307–15.

102. *Studies have shown that where gossip is repressed or outlawed,...*—See, for example, Kathleen Kinkade, *A Walden Two Experiment: The First Five Years of Twin Oaks Community* (New York: Morrow, 1973), 150–51.

102. *"Gossip feels good, I am saying:..."*—Patricia Meyer Spacks, "Gossip: How It Works," *Yale Review* 72 (Summer 1983): 562–80. The quote is on page 580.

102. *"Real honesty is speaking the right truth to the right person at the right time..."*—Donald McCullough, "White Lies, Hard Truths," *Christian Century* (9–16 September 1998), 820–21.

103. *"Would that the Lord would grant us grace, / And with clear shining let his face..."*—Martin Luther, "Would That the Lord Would Grant Us Grace," in *Liturgy and Hymns*, ed. Ulrich S. Leupold, vol. 53 of *Luther's Works*, ed. Helmut T. Lehmann (Philadelphia: Fortress, 1965), 234.

9. Cheer Rivals from the Bench

104. *"What do you see when the sun rises?..."*—William Blake, "A Vision of the Last Judgment," in *The Complete Poetry and Prose of William Blake*, ed. David V. Erdman (Berkeley: University of California Press, 1982), 566.

105. *Not everything Bataille says is wrong,...*—Roger Shattuck, *Forbidden Knowledge: From Prometheus to Pornography* (New York: St. Martin's, 1996), 241–44.

105. *Ford Madox Ford, "the one man who is really happy when someone else writes a good book."*—Quoted in Tony Tanner, "Hueffer Is All Right," *Times Literary Supplement* (16 February 1996), 3.

106. "*I have a number of enemies whose very faces I have never seen, . . .*"—Quoted in Grevel Lindop, "Things Not All the World Knows," *Times Literary Supplement* (27 April–3 May 1990), 441.

106. *Anton Chekhov sneered: "Success? Write about my success? . . ."*—Quoted in Dannie Abse, *Intermittent Journals* (Bridgend, Wales: Seren, 1994), 253.

106. "*People are shocked to hear that I think of* The Godfather *series with sadness. . . .*"—Quoted in Harriet Rubin, "In Praise of Excess," *Fast Company* (October 1998), 136.

106. "*Now I had for some years a bitter prejudice against three scorn-full men . . .*"—Quoted in Gerald R. McDermott, *Seeing God: Twelve Reliable Signs of True Spirituality* (Downers Grove, Ill.: InterVarsity Press, 1995), 97.

107. "*The ultimate goal of science is to remove all mystery.*"—Quoted in Chris Floyd, "A Trick of the Light: Richard Dawkins on Science and Religion," *Science & Spirit* (July–August 1999), 26.

107. *. . . the mystery of a "love, so amazing, so divine, . . ."*—Isaac Watts, "When I Survey the Wondrous Cross," hymn 7 of *Hymns and Spiritual Songs*, Book 3, as found in *The Psalms, Hymns, and Spiritual Songs of the Rev. Isaac Watts*, ed. Samuel M. Worcester (Boston: Crocker & Brewster, 1855), 478.

108. "*Nobody sees a flower—really—it is so small . . .*"—Lloyd Goodrich and Doris Bry, *Georgia O'Keeffe* (New York: Praeger, 1970), 17.

108. "*A saying of Chrysostom's has always pleased me very much, . . .*"—John Calvin, *Institutes of the Christian Religion*, ed. John T. McNeill, trans. Ford Lewis Battles, Library of Christian Classics 20 (Philadelphia: Westminster, 1955), 1:268–69.

109. "*If you have any good qualities, believe that other people have better ones.*"—Thomas à Kempis, *The Imitation of Christ: A New Reading of the 1441 Latin Autograph Manuscript*, trans. William C. Creasy (Macon, Ga.: Mercer University Press, 1989), 9.

109. "*Attack me, I do this myself, but attack me rather than the path I follow . . .*"—Cited in *The Lion and the Honeycomb: The Religious Writings of Leo Tolstoy*, ed. A. N. Wilson, trans. Robert Chandler (London: Collins, 1987), 147. Thanks to James Emery White, *A Search for the Spiritual* (Grand Rapids: Baker, 1998), 112, for this reference.

109. "*Early one morning another man and I had gone out to snipe at the Fascists . . .*"—George Orwell, "Looking Back at the Spanish War," in his *Collected Essays* (London: Secker & Warburg, 1961), 207–8.

111. *As the priest would wave these three fingers over the congregation, . . .*—These three fingers were deemed the holiest part of the body, so much so that at the end of the ninth century, when the decaying corpse of Pope Formosus was dug up, but before it was put on trial, the three fingers of his right hand he had used for blessing and signing papal decrees were cut off and

preserved. As related in Margaret Hebblethwaite, "Don't Be Surprised," *Times Literary Supplement* (5 September 1997), 31.

112. *Get a copy of the essay by Søren Kierkegaard called "Ultimatum: . . ."*—Søren Kierkegaard, "Ultimatum: The Upbuilding That Lies in the Thought That in Relation to God We Are Always in the Wrong," in his *Either/Or*, trans. Howard V. Hong and Edna H. Hong (Princeton: Princeton University Press, 1987), 2:339–54.

112. *What might poet Emily Dickinson have meant . . .*—Emily Dickinson, *The Letters of Emily Dickinson* (Cambridge, Mass.: Belknap, 1986).

10. Give History a Shove

113. *For Christianity to have reached the size it did in the time it did, . . .*—Rodney Stark, *The Rise of Christianity: A Sociologist Reconsiders History* (Princeton: Princeton University Press, 1996), 6.

113. *In A.D. 165 an epidemic (perhaps smallpox) spread like wildfire throughout the Roman Empire. . . .*—Ibid., 76–77.

113. *"Most of our brother Christians showed unbounded love and loyalty, . . ."*—Ibid., 82.

114. *"At the first onset of the disease, . . ."*—Ibid., 83.

114. *As a Christian himself and a church leader, Dionysus . . .*—Ibid., 83–84.

114. *"To cities filled with the homeless and impoverished, . . ."*—Ibid., 161.

115. *"Receive this kingly Sword, brought now from the Altar of God, . . ."*—Found at *http://www.oremus.org/liturgy/coronation/cor1953b.html/*.

116. *The Beatitudes, then, are not "a throwaway list of bedtime benedictions," . . .*—Christopher Levan, *Living in the Maybe: A Steward Confronts the Spirit of Fundamentalism* (Grand Rapids,: Eerdmans, 1998), 118–19.

117. *. . . as the world's population soars past 6 billion . . .*—World population reached 6 billion in October of 1999. It took all of human history for the human race to achieve a population of 1 billion in 1804; it took only twelve years to leap from 5 billion to 6 billion.

118. *"The structure of the universe is sympathetic to the ideas of many spiritual traditions, . . ."*—Kevin Sharpe and Jon Walgate, "Patterns of the Real: Quantum Nonlocality," *Science & Spirit* (April–May 1999), 10–12.

118. *Just as the figure skater spins faster the smaller he or she becomes, . . .*—With thanks to Walter Wink for this image of the figure skater. See his "Power of the Small," *The Other Side* (July–August 1993), 36–41, 38.

120. *"On one occasion, I was visiting a young man who was dying of AIDS...."*—J. Martin, ed., "How Can I Find God?" *America* (30 September 1995), 19–20.

120. *"We have succeeded in separating Christ from people,..."*—Michael Riddell, *Threshold of the Future: Reforming the Church in the Post-Christian West* (London: SPCK, 1998), 123.

121. *"If Washington is the most powerful city in the nation, D.C. is the most powerless..."*—Jim Wallis, "Life's Unlimited Value and Our Limited Resources" in *Life as Liberty, Life as Trust,* ed. J. Robert Nelson (Grand Rapids: Eerdmans, 1992), 18.

122. *"For sheer primitive rage, commend me to a thorough-going humanitarian..."*—Quoted in Eugene Weber, "The Last Days of Los Angeles," *Times Literary Supplement* (9 July 1999), 6.

11. Kill Two Birds with One Stone

123. *Some people see the "stacking" phenomenon...*—For more on stacking, see my *Eleven Genetic Gateways to Spiritual Awakening* (Nashville: Abingdon, 1998), 69–82. There I tell the story of my West Virginia Gramma Boggs, who first taught me the principle that not only can you do many things at once, but you can never do only one thing (70). And earlier, my *Quantum Spirituality: A Postmodern Apologetic* (Dayton, Ohio: Whaleprints, 1991), 268–71.

123. *... "vaunting such skill makes good corporate advertising sense; ..."*—Sidney W. Mintz, *Tasting Food, Tasting Freedom: Excursions into Eating, Culture, and the Past* (Boston: Beacon, 1996), 120.

124. *"The Christian historian will regard history at once as a mystery and as a tragedy..."*—Georges Florovsky, "The Predicament of the Christian Historian" in his *Christianity and Culture*, vol. 2 of *The Collected Works of Georges Florovsky* (Belmont, Mass.: Nordland, 1974), 65.

125. *"Eating multiple pieces within a short time period..."*—Kids become warheads and warlords. One kid who ate five in one hour admitted, "After that your tongue gets all these sores on it." Mark Frauenfelder, "Gross National Product: Xtreme Candy Gets Real," *Wired* (June 1999), 212.

125. *Reading the Bible is an exercise in seeing double.*—For more on the "double ring," see the first two volumes in this trilogy, *SoulTsunami: Sink or Swim in New Millennium Culture* (Grand Rapids: Zondervan, 1999) and *AquaChurch* (Loveland, Colo.: Group, 1999).

126. *"What is going to kill reading in our time is writing."*—Quoted in Ian Sansom, "Who Is Eating the Omelet?" *Times Literary Supplement* (19 June 1998), 28.

126. *Mix family vacations with business trips.*—According to the *Travel Market Report,* 7.4 million business trips included a child

in 1987, with 24.4 million including a child in 1997. That's a 230-percent increase. See Tom Maguire, "A Pleasure Doing Business," *American Demographics* (January 1999), 18.

127. *I have taken David Gelernter's advice...*—For David H. Gelernter's case for more beauty in computing, see *The Aesthetics of Computing* (London: Weidenfeld and Nicholson, 1998). Gelernter was one of the Unabomber's targets.

127. *"e-vangelism"*—The phrase is that of Andrew Careaga in *E-vangelism: Sharing the Gospel in Cyberspace* (Lafayette, La.: Vital Issues, 1999).

130. *Didymus of Alexandria said that "Paul was full of Christ."*—Brennan Manning, *Abba's Child: The Cry of the Heart for Intimate Belonging* (Colorado Springs, Colo.: NavPress, 1994), 112.

130. *"Decide, Are You More of a Specialist or a Generalist?"*—Barbara Moses, *Career Intelligence: The 12 New Rules for Work and Life Success* (San Francisco: Berrett-Koehler, 1998), 194–96.

12. Build a Compost Heap

131. *I consume most of my own body weight in basic materials each day.*—Alan Durning, "Asking How Much Is Enough," *State of the World: 1991* (New York: Norton, 1991), 161. USAmericans are generating 700 million pounds of garbage a day, 3 billion tons of solid waste every year. We produce, each one of us, three pounds of garbage per day. Each year USAmericans discard 16 million disposable diapers, 1.6 billion pens, 2 billion razors and blades, 220 million tires, and enough aluminum to replace every commercial airplane in the country every three months (6000 DC–10 airplanes annually).

131. *I discard six pounds of trash a day.*—According to a 1993 EPA study, USAmericans discard 4.3 pounds of trash per day for every man, woman, and child. When you take into account waste from sewage treatment plants and construction projects, the figure climbs to six pounds per day.

131. *In my throwaway world 70 percent of all the metal I use...*—A total of 133 million tons of aerial garbage is dumped into the atmosphere of the U.S. each year—more than the weight of our entire steel production.

132. *"My whole life had been spent waiting for an epiphany,..."*—Bette Midler, "Out of Rot, All Good Things Cometh," in *Heaven Is under Our Feet*, ed. Don Henley and Dave Marsh (Stamford, Conn: Longmeadow, 1991), 54–55.

132. *It is not just this "Waste Land"...*—T. S. Eliot, *Waste Land* (New York: Boni and Liveright, 1922). See also Vance Packard, *The Waste Makers* (New York: McKay, 1960).

132. *Bloated dumps, overflowing landfills, overcrowded prisons, homeless dopesters,...*—Our households are filled with toxic substances—paints, thinners, furniture oils, degreasers, disinfec-

tants, polishes, glues. One fifteen-year study of Oregon housewives found that women who stayed home all day had a 54 percent higher rate of cancer than women who worked at jobs away from the home.

134. *"Defensively in the Waste Culture, our redemptive activities, . . . "*—Kingsley Widmer, "In Praise of Waste: Some Reflections on Contemporary Culture," *Partisan Review* 46 (1979): 544.

134. *"Dung Coffee."*—See *http://www.ai.mit.edu/~shivers/luwak.html/*.

134. *God can turn any Sheol into a Shiloh.*—I obtained this image from Geoffrey Hill's *Canaan* (Boston: Houghton Mifflin, 1997), which includes the three-poem "Dark-land," an elegy for the poet's home, Cambridge in the U.K. The third poem tells how "very late he saw it / at Dedham: the English / church as it must be / charred in its own standing," a site which is "Sheol if not Shiloh" (54).

134. *"fount of every blessing."*—From the first line of Robert Robertson's "Come, Thou Fount of Every Blessing," written in 1758.

134. *Take the story of how rugby began.*—I initially had this rugby story all wrong. Mac Buttram, pastor of St. Andrew's United Methodist Church in Cullman, Alabama, helped set me straight. As did Frank Barker, a native New Zealander who now ministers in Seattle.

134. *Someone who saw Ellis's "mistake" let it spark his imagination . . .*—Ellis went on to Oxford University and became a priest. He served in London and Essex parishes until he died and was buried at Menton in France in 1872. He obtained legendary status when, in 1880, Matthew Bloxam identified him as the originator of the distinctive feature of the rugby football game. It was not until the early 1840s that carrying the ball was fully integrated into the official school rules.

137. *" 'Paper or plastic?' is a moral choice, . . . "*—Eric Zencey, *Virgin Forest: Meditations on History, Ecology, and Culture* (Athens, Ga.: University of Georgia Press, 1998), 148.

137. *The teacher then made Thelma sit down in that puddle . . .*—This story is from a firsthand account in Shirley McClaine's *Don't Fall off the Mountain* (New York: Norton, 1970), 141.

138. *"We have seen / The moon in lonely alleys make . . ."*—Hart Crane, "Chaplinesque," in *The Poems of Hart Crane*, ed. Marc Simon (New York: Liveright, 1986), 11.

140. *"proselytizing, activist belief systems"*—Zencey, *Virgin Forest*, 151.

140. *"If I alone among two hundred and fifty million Americans recycle, . . ."*—Ibid., 150.

140. *"recycling has become the primary ritual activity . . ."*—Ibid., 148.

141. *"Many of the insights of the saint . . ."*—Cited in Martin Marty's *Context* 26, (15 December 1994): 5.

13. Declare a Sabbatical

143. *... originally chanted by Jewish congregants ...*—Quoted in Arthur Green, *Keter: The Crown of God in Early Jewish Mysticism* (Princeton: Princeton University Press, 1997), 12.

143. *"Tell me, what is it you plan to do with your one wild and precious life?"*—Quoted in "Heart Quotes," *http://www.heartlink.com/quote1.htm/*.

144. *In early synagogue worship the* qedushah *was a daily enthronement of God ...*—In Jewish liturgy "this act has to do both with the role of Israel, those who accept and proclaim God's kingship in this world, and that of the angels, officiants in what is claimed to be the 'original' coronation rite on the heavenly plane." See ibid., 19.

144. *I now say,* "Create *a good day."*—I learned this from a Continental flight attendant, who said, "Create a good day," as I was leaving the plane.

144. *In a culture where the less time you have to yourself, ...*—For more on this phenomenon, see James Gleick, *Faster: The Acceleration of Just about Everything* (New York: Pantheon, 1999).

144. *"Think how severely we should be judged ..."*—James V. Schall, *Unexpected Meditations Late in the Twentieth Century* (Chicago: Franciscan Herald Press, 1985), 131.

145. *Sabbath was a "sanctuary in time," ...*—Joseph Heschel Abraham, *The Sabbath: Its Meaning for Modern Man* (New York: Farrar, Strous, and Giroux), 29.

145. *I still try to "stack" ...*—For the "stacking" component to post-modern living, see my *Eleven Genetic Gateways to Spiritual Awakening* (Nashville: Abingdon, 1998), 69–82.

147. *The scientific evidence is overwhelming.*—Robert E. Thayer, *The Origin of Everyday Moods* (Oxford: Oxford University Press, 1999).

147. *Take a ten-minute walk.*—Ibid., 186.

148. *"Beloved Companion* [Yedid Nefesh], *merciful father, ..."*—Quoted in Daniel Gordis, *God Was Not in the Fire: The Search for a Spiritual Judaism* (New York: Scribner, 1995), 54. This is the *Yedid Nefesh* prayer that begins the Friday evening Shabbat service. As the sun is setting, these words of poetry are spoken.

148. *The club motto is "Not so Fast."*—Lead Pencil Club, "Surf Your Brain, Not the Net," *http://www.rit.edu/~cyberwww/8.htm/*.

148. *"Be glad your being is unnecessary."*—W. H. Auden, "Epistle to a Godson," in his *Epistle to a Godson and Other Poems* (New York: Random House, 1972), 6.

149. *"No one can be a Christian alone."*—Gordis, *God Was Not in the Fire*, 105.

149. *"We are travelers on a journey / Fellow pilgrims on the road; ..."*—Paraphrase of John Wesley, "To Frances Godfrey," 2 August 1789, in *The Letters of the Rev. John Wesley,* ed. John Telford (London: Epworth, 1931), 8:158. The actual quote is "It

is a blessed thing to have fellow travelers to the New Jerusalem
. . . none can travel that road alone."

150. *The Hebrew term for the verb "to pray"* . . .—Hans-Georg
Gadamer, *The Enigma of Health: The Art of Healing in a Scientific Age* (Stanford, Calif.: Stanford University Press, 1996), 167.

150. *"thinking is the dialogue of the soul with itself,"*—Richard
Gillard, "The Servant Song," in *Scripture in Song* (Nashville:
Maranatha, 1977).

151. *"A true artist always puts something of his time in his art, . . ."*—
Quoted in Albert E. Elsen, *The Gates of Hell by Auguste Rodin*
(Stanford, Calif.: Stanford University Press, 1985), 223.

151. *"moodling,"*—For more on "moodling," see my *Jesus
Prescription for a Healthy Life* (Nashville: Abingdon, 1996),
187–98.

152. *"living room records,"* . . .—Dwight Ozard, "Music Notes,"
Prism 4 (March–April 1997): 32.

153. *Theodore Zeldin, renowned French scholar and author* . . .—
Theodore Zeldin, *An Intimate History of Humanity* (New York:
HarperCollins, 1994), 355.

154. *"I know, it was useless, of course, her dancing . . ."*—Andrew
Motion, "The Dancing Hippo," in his *Selected Poems* (London:
Faber and Faber, 1998), 52.

154. *Management guru Tom Peters talks about "The Big R," . . .*—
Thomas J. Peters, *The Pursuit of Wow! Every Person's Guide to
Topsy-Turvy Times* (New York: Vintage, 1994), 306–8.

14. Play at Life

155. *. . . there is now more wordplay than at any previous period of
history.*—David Crystal, *Language Play* (London: Penguin,
1998), 1.

155. *. . . Sir Karl Popper's most famous lectures.*—Sir Karl R. Popper,
"Of Clouds and Clocks: An Approach to the Problem of Rationality and the Freedom of Man," in his *Objective Knowledge:
An Evolutionary Approach* (Oxford: Clarendon, 1972), 206–55.

156. *"If you follow only one recommendation from this book, . . ."*—
Larry Downes and Chunka Mui, *Unleashing the Killer App:
Digital Strategies for Market Dominance* (Boston: Harvard
Business School Press, 1998), 217.

156. *It was the Newtonian view of the clockwork universe . . .*—Ibid.,
207–8.

156. *"only clouds exist, though clouds of very different cloudiness."*—
Ibid., 213.

156. *"It was some time ago when I wrote to the secretary of Yale University. . ."*—Quoted in ibid., 229–30.

158. *Studies have shown that "active listening"* . . .—John Gottman et
al., "Predicting Marital Happiness and Stability from Newlywed
Interactions," *Journal of Marriage and the Family* 60 (February

1998): 5–22.

158. *Some have argued that the recent emergence of intimacy-based marriages . . .*—John Welwood, *Love and Awakening: Discovering the Sacred Path of Intimate Relationship* (New York: HarperCollins, 1996).

159. *The greater the relationship, the fewer the rules.*—Dick Wills, *Waking to God's Dream: Spiritual Leadership and Church Renewal* (Nashville: Abingdon, 1999), 59.

160. *Let your motto be "If you do it, they will let you."*—Thanks to my Montana colleague Jim Marshall for this motto.

162. *Those who go to church regularly are 2.5 times less likely to have been divorced . . .*—Cited in *Current Thoughts and Trends* (September 1998), 11.

15. Make Love Like Tobias and Sarah

163. *"dead from the waist down."*—Conor Cruise O'Brien, "Maria Cross," in his *Maria Cross: Imaginative Patterns in a Group of Modern Catholic Writers* (London: Burns and Oates, 1963), 239.

163. *"God loves you, and He's gonna send you to hell; . . ."*—Quoted in *Current Thoughts and Trends* (July 1998), 12.

163. *. . . sex is one of the most important of the fifteen universal fundamental motives that drive human behavior.*—The others are family, order, curiosity, physical exercise, social contact, social prestige, aversive sensations, rejection, food, honor, citizenship, power, independence, vengeance. See Kevin Sharpe and Rebecca Bryant, "God's Purpose: A Contradiction in Terms?" *Science & Spirit* 10 (July–August 1999): 10–11.

163. *It was not Kant's best moment when he defined marriage . . .*—Kant's definition of marriage was this: "a *jus mutuum perpetuum ad commercium sexuale* (an enduring mutual right to sexual intercourse), i.e., for a continuing enjoyment of the *membra sexualia et facultates* (sexual organs and functions)." Immanuel Kant, *Lectures on Ethics*, ed. Peter Heath and J. B. Schneewind, trans. Peter Heath (Cambridge: Cambridge University Press, 1997), 378. See also Kant's definition of the mutual commitment and right to the whole person (158).

164. *"When people put faith, scholarship, and science in front of their sexual creativity . . ."*—Susie Bright, "Fully Charged," *Utne Reader* (September–October 1999).

164. *In Jewish households it held much the same position, . . .*—James Stevenson, *The Catacombs: Rediscovered Monuments of Early Christianity* (London: Thames and Hudson, 1978), 81.

164. *First, it's the only book of the Bible that says nice things about a dog.*—The dog reference is omitted from the Aramaic and Hebrew versions of Tobit.

164. *. . . enough for Verrocchio's most gifted pupil, Leonardo da Vinci, to paint the dog . . .*—So argues David Alan Brown, *Leonardo da*

Vinci: Origins of a Genius (New Haven: Yale University Press, 1999), 51. This painting has sat undocumented in the National Gallery in London since it was acquired in 1867.

164. *What has been called "one of the dullest books in the Bible"*— The designation is that of Clifton Fadiman in his preface to Stella Benson, *Far-Away Bride* (1941). Quoted in David McCracken, "Narration and Comedy in the Book of Tobit," *Journal of Biblical Literature* 114, no. 3 (1995): 403.

165. *... a third of newlyweds admit to not having sex on their wedding night ...*—The actual percentage is 32. See Ron Geraci, "Facts of Life," *Men's Health* (November 1998), 54.

165. *"Nothing is free but love."*—Nadya Aisenberg, "The Home Museum," in her *Before We Were Strangers: Poems* (Boston: Forest, 1989), 13.

165. *Those men who had the most sex had a 50 percent lower mortality risk ...*—George Davey Smith, Stephen Frankel, and J. Farnell, "Sex and Death: Are They Related?" *British Medical Journal* 315 (1997): 20–27.

166. *... married Christian women enjoy a vibrant and vigorous sex life ...*—Archibald D. Hart, Catherine Hart Weber, and Debra Taylor, *Secrets of Eve: Understanding the Mystery of Female Sexuality* (Nashville: Word, 1998).

167. *"How do we design a culture in which love is possible?"*—This is a paraphrase of the question asked by David Orr, "Love It or Lose It," in his *Earth in Mind: On Education, Environment and the Human Prospect* (Washington, D.C.: Island, 1994), 131–53, where he states: "If we are to preserve a world in which biophilia can be expressed and can flourish, we will have to decide to make such a world" (132).

167. *"white ecstasy of frictional satisfaction"*—"Uganda" was once a euphemism for sexual intercourse. So too was "firkytoodling."

167. *USAmericans pray more often than they have sex.*—Cited in Jeremiah Creedon, "God with a Million Faces," *Utne Reader* (July–August 1998), 45.

16. Don't Fall Out of the Family Bed

170. *"It used to be that music was here today and gone tomorrow. Now it's here today and gone today."*—Quoted in Michael J. Wolf, *The Entertainment Economy: How Mega-Media Forces Are Transforming Our Lives* (New York: Times, 1999), 73.

171. *"Neither here nor there, and therefore home."*—Bernard O'Donoghue, "Westering Home," in his *Here Nor There* (London: Chatto and Windus, 1999), 51.

171. *But if the Lexus runs over the olive tree, the dangers of globalization are real: ...*—Thomas L. Friedman, *The Lexus and the Olive Tree: Understanding Globalization* (New York: Farrar, Stroux, and Giroux, 1999), 221, 248.

171. *But for every telecommuter who is returning to a premodern home/work life, . . .*—Elizabeth M. Hoekstra, *Keeping Your Family Close When Frequent Travel Pulls You Apart* (Wheaton, Ill.: Crossway, 1998).

171. *Two-paycheck families are increasingly problematic, . . .*—Leith Anderson, "Clocking Out," *Christianity Today* (12 September 1994), 30–32.

173. *"Jesse, I was your son's coach."*—With thanks to Judge Caldwell for permission to tell this story.

173. *. . . the basic social unit for the disciples, as taught by Jesus, was not the family but the community of believers.*—See Rodney Clapp, *Families at the Crossroads: Beyond Traditional and Modern Options* (Downers Grove, Ill: InterVarsity Press, 1993).

174. *Adam Kuper's* The Chosen Primate *demonstrates that . . .*—Adam Kuper, *The Chosen Primate: Human Nature and Cultural Diversity* (Cambridge: Harvard University Press, 1994), 170–78.

174. *. . . explains the marked increase in the incidence of divorce.*—Ibid., 174. Kuper summarizes his survey of the significance of the nuclear family in these words: "In short, the family may be universal but it is a flexible institution, its internal arrangements adapted to the structure of the broader society, its breeding policies responsive to economic signals" (178).

174. *If the mission of the true first family was to embody in their relationship the triune image of God, . . .*—For more, see Michael D. Warner, "A Response to Marriage and the Family," in *Applying the Scriptures,* ed. Kenneth Kantzer (Grand Rapids: Academie, 1987), 211–12.

174. *"I can't abide children, have never taught them Scripture, and shouldn't like to try."*—Quoted in A. N. Wilson, "The Dear Dante! Years," *Times Literary Supplement* (2 April 1999), 36, in response to a letter from Felix Rose. See Barbara Reynolds, ed., *The Letters of Dorothy L. Sayers: Volume Three: 1944–1950: A Noble Daring* (New York: St. Martin's, forthcoming).

174. *"God instituted prayer to communicate to his creatures the dignity of causality."*—Blaise Pascal, *Pascal's Pensées,* no. 513, ed. T. S. Eliot (New York: Dutton, 1958), 140.

175. *So I read resources like the book . . .*—Clint Kelly, *How to Win Grins and Influence Little People* (Tulsa: Honor, 1996).

176. *"I'd rather have a little of Bill than a lot of any other man."*—William Martin, *A Prophet with Honor: The Billy Graham Story* (New York: Morrow, 1991), 92.

176. *"Our family will work, play, pray, and study God's Word together . . ."*—For some examples of mission statements, see Victor Lee and Jerry Pipes, *Family to Family* (Alpharetta, Ga.: NAMB, 1999), 35–36.

177. *"You will act like a Christian, or I will slap the snot out of you."*—Quoted in Molly Ivins, "It's a Jumble Out There," *Time* (12 July 1999), 86.

178. *The cohousing movement originated in Denmark in the late 1960s . . .*—Kathryn McCamant and Charles Durrett, *Cohousing: A Contemporary Approach to Housing Ourselves* (Berkeley,

Calif.: Ten Speed, 1994); Chris Hanson, *The Cohousing Handbook: Building a Place for Community* (Vancouver, B.C.: Hartley and Marks, 1996); and Naomi Davis, "CoHousing and Other Cooperative Housing," *http://www.doubleclickd.com/Articles/cohousing.html/*.

180. *What one generation passes on to the next is understood biblically* . . . —This is why sometimes I sign off letters with my initials preceded by the opening words of the Gloria Patri: "*Sicut Erat* . . . , LIS" ("As it was in the beginning, is now and ever shall be . . .").

182. *Best-selling author John Bradshaw estimates that 96 percent of all USAmericans are products of dysfunctional homes.*—John Bradshaw, *Bradshaw on the Family: A New Way of Creating Solid Self-Esteem,* rev. ed. (Deerfield Beach, Fla.: Health, 1996).

182. *. . . every state in the nation except Idaho has distressed neighborhoods, . . .*—William O'Hare, "Distressed Neighborhoods Are Everywhere," *American Demographics* (November 1994), 19.

182. *. . . 4 million American kids who are growing up in danger . . .*—This list is based on a 1996 ranking of ten categories used to define distressed neighborhoods. See the *Kids Count Data Book: State Profiles of Child Well-being* (Baltimore: Casey Foundation, 1999), 145.

182. *In the mid to late 1980s, only two family films came out of Hollywood. . . .*—Cited in Ted Baehr, "*Movieguide* Analysis of All 1998 Theatrically Released Movies," *Movieguide* (March 1999), 18–19.

183. *"the whole catastrophe,"*—With thanks to Bruce Jenneker of Trinity Church, Boston, for reminding me of this incident.

183. *"Each second we live is a new and unique moment of the universe, . . ."*—Jewish Reconstructionist Federation, *Prayerbook for the Days of Awe* (Elkins Park, Pa.: Reconstructionist, 1999).

17. Dance the Salsa

186. *Was your level of reality any less real than the level of reality kept by your watch's gears or computer chip?*—This is described more fully in Paul Pearsall, *Ten Laws of Lasting Love* (New York: Simon and Schuster, 1993), 182–83. Pearsall notes that this phenomenon was first discovered by biofeedback pioneers. "Patients who learn through biofeedback to put themselves in a deeply meditative state (producing theta brain waves) and watch the second hand of a clock discover that the second hand will come to a complete stop under their gaze! As remarkable as this phenomenon may seem, it has been repeatedly documented" (182).

This phenomenon is documented as well in Keith Floyd, "Of Time and Mind: From Paradox to Paradigm," in *Frontiers of Consciousness: The Meeting Ground between Inner and Outer*

Reality, ed. John White (New York: Julian, 1974), 258–75, especially 261–64; and Arthur J. Deikman, "Experimental Meditation" (204), and Walter N. Pahnke and William A. Richards, "Implications of LSD and Experimental Meditation" (403), both in Charles T. Tart, *Altered States of Consciousness: A Book of Readings* (New York: Wiley, 1969).

187. *"She had . . . a code of morals that pinned down and beat the brains out of nearly everything that was pleasant to do. . . ."*—John Steinbeck, *East of Eden* (New York: Bantam, 1955), 6, 8.

188. *"A cheerful intelligent face is the end of culture, . . ."*—Ralph Waldo Emerson, *The Conduct of Life*, rev. ed. (Boston: Houghton Mifflin, 1885), 153.

188. *Jim McGuiggan wonders why so many Christians would rather be on the "whining side" than on the "winning side."*—Jim McGuiggan, *Jesus: Hero of Thy Soul: Impressions Left by the Savior's Touch* (West Monroe, La.: Howard, 1998), 55.

188. *. . ." the majority of humankind only enjoy life by forgetting that they are alive."*—Madame de Staël and Maeterlinck quoted in Richard Davenport-Hines, "Getting Out of It," *Times Literary Supplement* (31 July 1998), 32.

189. *"God is a party-giver."*—J. Ellsworth Kalas, "God Called a Party, but Nobody Came" in *Parables from the Back Side: Bible Stories with a Twist* (Nashville: Abingdon, 1992), 19.

189. *Much to everyone's astonishment, the experiment worked.*—Cited in Marina Warner, *No Go the Bogeyman: Scaring, Lulling and Making Mock* (New York: Farrar, Straus, and Giroux, 1998), 329.

189. *"But as for Me, if thou wouldst know what I was: . . ."*—As quoted by Wilfrid Mellers, *Bach and the Dance of God* (New York: Oxford University Press, 1981), 18.

189. *The Bible may be filled with dancing, . . .*—The dance metaphor has been adopted by the business world in such titles as Rosabeth Moss Kanter's *When Giants Learn to Dance: Mastering the Challenge of Strategy, Management, and Careers in the 1990s* (New York: Simon and Schuster, 1989).

190. *"Muster hither musicks joyes, lute, / and lyre, . . ."*—Mary Sidney Herbert, *The Psalmes of David*, ed. Margaret P. Hanney, Noel J. Kinnamon, and Michael G. Brennan, vol. 2 of *The Collected Works of Mary Sidney Herbert, Countess of Pembroke* (Oxford: Clarendon, 1998), 117.

190. *But there is an early tradition of the church that styles the Trinity as a circle . . .*—For more on Trinity symbolism, see Leonardo Boff, "The Trinity in Theological Imagery," in his *Trinity and Society* (Maryknoll, N.Y.: Orbis, 1988), 100–110.

190. *"To-morrow shall be my dancing day: / I would my true love so did chance . . ."*—See T. G. Crippen, *Christmas and Christmas Lore* (1923; reprint, Detroit: Gale, 1971), 59.

190. *"He was a small child when his family moved to a rock-bound farm near Windsor, Connecticut. . . ."*—Cited in *Hungry Mind Review* (Summer 1992), C–12.

191. *"... After Dance, Big Poker Game"*—Quoted in Ferenc Morton Szasz, *The Protestant Clergy in the Great Plains and Mountain West, 1865–1915* (Albuquerque: University of New Mexico Press, 1988), 101.

192. *"We must try dancing...."*—Peter Barnes, "The Night of the Sinhat Torah," in *The Spirit of Man and More Barnes' People: Seven Monologues* (London: Methuen Drama, 1990), 45.

192. *"Chesterton's profound remark,..."*—James V. Schall, S.J., "Philosophy: Why What Is Useless Is the Best Thing about Us," *Vital Speeches of the Day* 65 (1 August 1999): 628–32.

192. *Tex Sample's* The Spectacle of Worship *has a section on "Dance in the Church"*...—Tex Sample, *The Spectacle of Worship in a Wired World: Electronic Culture and the Gathered People of God* (Nashville: Abingdon, 1998), 74.

193. *"If even dying is to be made a social function,..."*—Thanks to Eskil H. Frederickson of the Metropolitan United Methodist Church, Detroit, for reminding me of this Hammarskjöld quote.

193. *Richard Foster lists five ways to celebrate corporately:...*—Richard J. Foster, *Celebration of Discipline: The Path to Spiritual Growth*, rev. ed. (San Francisco: Harper and Row, 1988), 190–201.

193. *"The central miracle of the gospel is not the raising of Lazarus..."*—Brennan Manning, *Abba's Child: The Cry of the Heart for Intimate Belonging* (Colorado Springs, Colo.: NavPress, 1994), 111.

We want to hear from you. Please send your comments about this book to us in care of the address below. Thank you.

ZondervanPublishingHouse
Grand Rapids, Michigan 49530
http://www.zondervan.com

SoulSalsa